The Beast in Me
AND OTHER ANIMALS

*Other Books
by James Thurber*

MY WORLD—AND WELCOME TO IT
MEN, WOMEN AND DOGS
THE WHITE DEER

for Children

MANY MOONS
THE GREAT QUILLOW

JAMES THURBER

○ ○ ○ ○ ○ ○

The Beast in Me and Other Animals

A COLLECTION OF PIECES AND DRAWINGS ABOUT HUMAN BEINGS AND LESS ALARMING CREATURES

A Harvest/HBJ Book
Harcourt Brace Jovanovich, Publishers
San Diego   New York   London

Library of Congress Cataloging in Publication Data
Thurber, James, 1894–1961.
  The beast in me and other animals.
  (A Harvest book, HB 261)
  I. Title.
PS3539.H94B4 1973   818'.5'207   73-5563
  ISBN 0-15-111249-5
  ISBN 0-15-610850-x *(Harvest/HBJ : pbk.)*

For Ronnie and Janey Williams
In memory of the serene hours at Felicity Hall

Contents

vii

Foreword

A WRITER verging on his middle fifties, when he should be engaged on some work dignified by length and of a solemnity suitable to our darkening age, is a little surprised to find himself coming out with still another collection of short pieces and small drawings. He toys for a while with the idea of a prefatory note pointing out that all this is a necessary and natural rehearsal for the larger project that awaits the increase of his patience and the lengthening of his view. Then, in re-examining his material for evidence to sustain this brave theory, he finds little to support his argument and a great deal to contradict it. Take the imaginary animals in this book, for example. No labor of ingenuity could fit them into a continuable pattern. They emerged from the shameless breeding ground of the idle mind and they are obviously not going anywhere in particular. Faced with this fact, the author tries the desperate expedient of pulling the bestiary out of his pages only to discover to his dismay that it serves as the legendary thread that stubbornly unravels the whole. In the end, abandoning justification or apology, he wisely decides to confine his foreword to small explanations on behalf of clarity and credits.

Most of the things in this collection were originally published in *The New Yorker*, but "Extinct Animals of Bermuda" appeared in *The Bermudian*, "Prehistoric Animals of the Middle West" in *Mademoiselle*, "How to Name a Dog" in *Good Housekeeping*, "Look Homeward, Jeannie" and "The Lady on the Bookcase" in the New York Sunday *Times*. "The Beast in the Dingle" was written for Cyril Connolly's *Horizon*.

The series of drawings called "The Patient" was published in the London magazine *Night and Day*, and some of the other drawings appear here for the first time, including "A Gallery of Real Creatures," which was inspired by my cherished volumes of Lydekker's "New Natural History," brought out in England toward the close of the last century. The Lydekker animals were checked against other sources, and my Gallery is a composite and, I trust, accurate enough representation of the inhabitants of this corner of the jungle. Nature is ever more fanciful than the artist, and I envy her the invention of Bosman's Potto. Bosman was an actual Dutchman who came upon an actual potto one day many years ago. It was the first time a human being had ever seen a potto, and the first time a potto had ever seen a human being. The shock must have been mutual and equal.

"Soapland" is the record of a year's sojourn in the strange and fascinating country of daytime radio serials. This country is so vast and complicated that the lone explorer could not possibly hope to do it full justice, and I offer my apologies to the courteous people I encountered everywhere I turned in Soapland for whatever errors I may have made of omission, fact, and interpretation. The list of persons who generously aided and abetted these researches would fill a long page, and the weary traveler might leave out one or two by unhappy accident. For their kindness, patience, and invaluable help, from April to April, I especially want to thank Frank and Anne Hummert, Robert D. Andrews, William A. Ramsey and Robert J. Landry, who must have answered all together at least a thousand questions.

"Time Exposures" is a selection of "visit pieces" written for the *New Yorker's* Talk of the Town over a period of years a long time ago. These fragments of the New York scene were the result of random wanderings around the city from 1928 to 1936, and they are reprinted here for whatever nostalgic value they may have for the collector of such things.

JT

West Cornwall, Connecticut

"There is the tiger that lurks in motor cars, crouches in sealed envelopes and prowls between the doorbell and the phone, ready to pounce upon the dreamer by day, the reveler by night, or any man at any hour; but I am concerned with the beast inside, the beast that haunts the moonlit marges of the mind, never clearly seen, never wholly lost to view, never leaving, in its wanderings, pawprints sharp enough to follow, or strange and promising enough, it well may be, to lure the wary hunter from the surer spoor of bigger game."

—From *The Tenant of the Room* by Douglas Bryce

I

MAINLY MEN AND WOMEN

My Friend Domesticus

*If, to Man, the cricket seems to hear with its legs, it is possible
that to the cricket Man seems to walk on his ears.*

—*Anon., 19th Century.*

IT HAS BEEN established beyond doubt that the auditory
organs of the Gryllidae (crickets) are situated in their
front legs, but it will be the purpose of this article to suggest that, in the case of a certain group of crickets, this
morphological oddity may also serve as the sensitive apparatus of a much more remarkable function.

In the country it is possible to be oblivious of a million
crickets and conscious suddenly of one. This soloist, whose
violin rises so compellingly out of the full orchestra, is
Gryllus domesticus, the house cricket. He is the cricket on
the hearth, but his appearances there are fleeting, for he
spends most of the time, when he is audibly in residence,
deep in the wall of the fireplace chimney. He is also, as we
shall see, the cricket behind the grandfather's clock and
the cricket in your lady's blue satin mule. It is useless to
pick him up and put him out on the lawn "where he belongs," because he doesn't belong there at all and he will
come in again as soon as your back is turned. He is not to
be confused with *Gryllus campestris*, the field cricket, who
has a burrow under the grass and is only casually interested
in houses constructed by man. The cricket in the grass is
bigger, blacker and shinier than its cousin of the hearth and
looks more like a wrecked Buick. If you do put *domesticus*
out, it is well to take him up in a handkerchief, because he
may bite. The house cricket is companionable, but he resents

3

the taking of liberties. The house is big enough for both of you; he will keep his place if you will keep yours.

Early in September, two years ago, a *domesticus* began to chirp from somewhere inside the chimney of the dining-room fireplace in my house in the country. He took part in conversations at table and joined lustily in concertos for violin, cricket, and orchestra when they were played on the victrola. He appeared to enjoy the special quality the human voice has when it is reading aloud, but it is probably my imagination that *domesticus* offered, in occasional long silences, an adverse criticism of certain noisy half-hour radio programs. If he was spoken to loudly and sharply by a voice very close to his winter quarters, he would abruptly cease chirping. It was easy to entertain a friendly feeling for *Gryllus domesticus* even though we caught sight of him only on rare occasions, when, it may be, he was starting off to forage for crumbs in the kitchen. There were never any signs to bear out the common suspicion that the house cricket, like the field cricket, eats carpets, shawls, dinner jackets, and the seats of bathing suits.

The cricket left the chimney in late March or early April, or at least I thought he'd left. All I actually knew was that he stopped chirping. There was silence in the fireplace for five months, but when September came round again the fiddling in the wall was resumed abruptly one night just after the dinner candles were lit. It was like a familiar knock at the front door. We had the feeling that the season had begun, as it used to begin in Saratoga with the advent of E. Berry Wall. The winter passed, and again in late March or early April the chirping in the fireplace stopped.

If my interest in house crickets up to this point had been casual, it has been sharpened into curiosity by the unusual events of the month that has just gone by. The chirping in our fireplace wall this year began several weeks ahead of time, at the very height of the mid-August heat wave. Furthermore, the dining-room cricket did not come alone.

4

He was accompanied by a string quartet of *Grylli domestici*, who scattered gleefully about the house like a detachment of billeted soldiers. One began to tune up in back of the grandfather's clock in the hall, another made for the kitchen, a third hopped upstairs and got under a chest of drawers in the master bedroom, and the fourth began to saw away at prophecy behind a set of F. Marion Crawford on a bookshelf in the living room. They brought with them at least one female. (The sex of the cricket can be determined by the fact that the female has no stridulating apparatus and thus is invested with "inviolable mutism," to steal a phrase from the late William Bolitho.) In the days that followed she took to hopping up and down the stairs leading to the second floor. There was a wild abandon in her descents which led me to believe she was having as much fun as a skier.

I have used the word "prophecy" in connection with the song of the cricket advisedly, because I have been won over to the natural philosophy of old Mrs. Selby, a profound student of portent in our neighborhood with whom I discussed the cricket situation one day over a glass of elderberry wine and a slice of saffron cake. Her own empirical study occasionally gives way to intuition or superstition, as when she holds that mirrors attract lightning and bees will not inhabit an unhappy house, but I think her analysis of natural phenomena is, on the whole, sound. She told me that various signs indicate a chill and early autumn. The goldenrod bloomed several weeks ahead of time, the tree spider began to twirl lower toward the earth than is his custom in August, and the house cricket began to play his bright arrangement of foreboding nearly a month ahead of schedule. Mrs. Selby contends that the house cricket differs from the field cricket in that he is more concerned with foretelling the weather than serenading his mate. She says that the cricket who comes late to the hearth means an Indian summer, the cricket who comes before September sings of early frost.

There are indeterminate or undetermined factors and phases in the morphology and behavior of many animals, but I have no intention of basing on this misty region of knowledge a body of purely romantic speculation and conclusion. In a word, I have turned to science as well as to Mrs. Selby in my investigation of *Gryllus domesticus*. I first consulted the Encyclopaedia Britannica, which I found to be not a little haphazard and uncertain in its treatment of the salutary Orthoptera. Under the heading "cricket" it moons along loosely, as if it were repeating information casually picked up at a rather noisy dinner party. Its report is not only incomplete; it is also occasionally in error, as when it assumes that the house cricket chirps only at night. It affirms cautiously that house crickets "frequent" houses, particularly those in rural districts, but to "frequent" means to "drop in," and there is no explanation of the whereabouts of my house crickets in their silent months or of what they are up to. There is a brief quotation from a treatise by a man referred to only as "Bates," but when I tracked him down in another volume of the encyclopaedia, there was nothing about crickets under "Bates, Henry Walter (1825-1892), English naturalist." The Britannica notes that house crickets like warm places, especially the vicinity of fireplaces and ovens, but it does not explain why my crickets put in their appearance this summer when it was ten degrees cooler in the house than outdoors because we had shut all doors and windows to keep out the mid-August heat. There is a somewhat sentimental description of the love life of the field cricket but nothing about the love life of the house cricket.

It is under, of all headings, "Hearing, Sense of," that the Britannica offers its most extended examination of the Gryllidae, but here again *domesticus* is largely overlooked. This treatise is chiefly concerned with the experiments of

6

one Regen, an Austrian naturalist, who discovered that field crickets, like roosters, call in rotation rather than in concert, each male trying to outdo in volume every other male within earshot. These experiments were conducted partly to determine the auditory responses of crickets, and Regen and his disciples went pretty far. A male cricket, which was most certainly a field cricket, although this is not stated, was set to chirping into the transmitter of a telephone while his mate listened near the receiver of a telephone in another house. She instantly made for the sound and this clearly established that crickets can hear and that the female is attracted by the stridulation of the male. I arrived independently at the same conclusion, but in a far less impressive and diverting way, by observing a female house cricket making for the exact part of a wall in which an unseen male was chirping. For indoor experiments, involving telephones and the like, the house cricket is patently the perfect subject, and I can only conclude that naturalists feel more at ease in the fields than they do crawling about a house on their hands and knees, listening at walls, removing bricks from fireplaces, peering under bureaus, and shoving grandfather's clocks and bookcases around. The notable tendency of the human female to disapprove of, or even put a stop to, experiments of this nature has, no doubt, operated more strongly than any factor in diverting the attention of the naturalist from *Gryllus domesticus* to *Gryllus campestris*.

After setting down the foregoing, it occurred to me that my treatise, based on the scanty references of the Britannica and my own meagre observation, scarcely did justice to the orthopterist, the cricket, myself, or even perhaps the human female (or common housewife). Two considerations, however, militate against a long and thorough investigation of the subject. First, my interest in the house cricket may conceivably deteriorate, and second, circumstances of a meteorological nature, obviously beyond my control, set a time limit on the validity of prophecy, and prophecy is the point and essence of the conclusions I have arrived at in this fascinating field of research. The range of this prophecy has been immeasurably extended by certain scientific data which have come to hand during the writing of this article. I had originally intended only to advance the theory that the appearance of warmth-loving *Gryllus domesticus* in a house perceptibly cooler than the outdoors, during a period of extraordinarily high summer temperature, indicated an awareness in the creature of the premature approach of cold weather. The cricket's prescience, I figured, grew out of the functioning of some highly sensitized apparatus, perhaps the curious tympanic membrane on the cricket's front legs, hitherto believed by naturalists to be the auditory organs of the creature and nothing else. If I am right, this apparatus may record something more than the sexual plaint of the male. If I am right, the male may be crying, on occasion, not "Sweet! Sweet!" but *"Vite! Vite!"* or, freely, "Look out, here it comes!" It is absurd to assume that any animal would sing all night and much of the day exclusively of love.

The scientific data I have mentioned, which have abruptly enlarged the scope of the cricket prophecy for me, were contained in a recent article in the *Herald Tribune* by John J. O'Neill. It begins as follows:

Hidden behind the prolonged dry torrid heat which smashed temperature records through the Middle Plains states, through the Ohio Valley and up to New England during this summer may be the transition to a new type of climate for the whole Northern Hemisphere and perhaps the entire earth. Weather-bureau officials, limited to day-by-day reports and short-range forecasts of the weather, have nothing to say about this larger aspect of the weather change, but the weather maps reveal a change which may be of tremendous importance, insofar as it may be an indication that the North Pole ice cap is in process of moving to some other part of the earth.

This momentous climatic change is predicated on a shift in the world's high- and low-pressure areas, and Mr. O'Neill foresees the possibility of an ice-capped Sahara and a riotously verdant North Pole. Moreover, there is a note of ominous urgency in his forecast of a world turned wrong side to. The shift of the great ice cap may not be so very far off, he suggests. *"Vite! Vite!"* Is it too fantastic to suppose that a greater agitation than I had at first suspected is exciting the tympanum of the house cricket and sent him scurrying, perhaps earlier than ever, into a sanctuary dubious enough, God knows, in the light of what may come?

It would be fair for my readers to cry *"Rien ne va plus!"* if I postponed this article until even human beings could sniff November in the late September air and sense the cold that never was, descending from the North. But even at the risk of overstepping the deadline for prophecy, I have taken the time at the last moment to supplement what little the Britannica and I know about house crickets by consulting in a roundabout way a volume called "Blatchley's Orthoptera." I say "roundabout" because Blatchley on *Gryllus domesticus* was read to me over the telephone by a charming and gracious lady at the Museum of Natural History. Blatchley begins where Regen left off, and unless the ice cap is too fast for me, I intend to explore his book more carefully. Perhaps I shall find in it what I failed to get over the telephone: where the house cricket goes in the summer, if he goes anywhere. Blatchley would have us believe (if I heard aright) that the house cricket may not exist in the summer. I myself have a strong conviction, growing, it may be, out of wishful thinking, that *domesticus* has a much longer life expectancy. But let us have the courage to examine the gloomier theory. Perhaps his adulthood is short-lived and is never attained in the period between April and August. Perhaps *domesticus* dies in the spring, leaving children who are not old enough to show themselves in the house and stridulate until late summer. If so, my fireplace *domesticus* may be the grandson of *domesticus* 1946, born, however, like his ancestors, with a gift of song and a sense

9

of foreboding. I shall at any rate believe in his feeling for the future until I find out I am wrong.

One of the most interesting and colorful items of cricket news supplied by Blatchley concerns the house cricket's avidity for fluids. He will leap into a pan or bowl of almost any liquid if it is placed on the floor. Blatchley set down a basin of beer one night and in the morning it was full of lifeless crickets who had died of submersion and acute alcoholism. In my own living room there is a small bar and on the top of it drops of Scotch and rye must occasionally accumulate. You surely see what I am getting at. I am convinced that most of the time the lady cricket who uses the living-room stairs for a toboggan is as high as a kite.

Perhaps a new simile, "as drunk as a cricket," may be my only lasting contribution to the literature and science of the Orthoptera. Meanwhile, we must all wait as calmly and patiently as possible until it can be ascertained whether the end of summer and the end of the world are actually just around the corner.

The Glass of Fashion

IN THE PRESENT Era of Suspicion, it is a wise citizen who disproves any dark rumors and reports of his secret thoughts and activities before they can be twisted into charges of disloyalty by the alert and skillful minds now dedicated to that high-minded and patriotic practice. In my own case, unfortunately for me, certain rumors and reports had reached the stage of published revelations before I could defend myself. Indeed, an article called "Lester Gaba Looks at Display," in *Women's Wear*, had been circulated for several weeks before it was brought to my attention. I shall reprint here, before asserting my defense, the portion of Mr. Gaba's article that reveals my hitherto undisclosed association with—if not, indeed, my hold upon—the profitable world of fashion and merchandising.

Mr. Gaba wrote as follows:

It's not generally known that restaurants have display directors, but window trimming is an absolute MUST for headwaiters, captains and *maîtres d'hôtel* in New York's smart eating places. The dining-rooms present the most glamorous displays in town. François or Steve at the Ritz, and David Cowles at the Penguin seat their guests with the same care that Sidney Ring or John Luke lavish on their mannequins. At Le Pavillon, for instance, it was no accident the other night that Frank Sinatra was placed importantly at the bar, Leonora Corbette [*sic*] received a front table, and Judith Anderson was set slightly to her right. It made a beautiful display as you came in. At the Algonquin, John, captain in the "big room," takes great pains to get the most display value out of the big names in the fashion and merchandising world who regularly lunch there. Tobe occupies star position, with Fanny Arms of Halle Bros., Louise

11

Sloane, house furnishings expert, Bill Riordan, president of Stern's, Alice Hughes, James Thurber and Adelia Byrd Ellis forming a dramatic grouping. At the Colony, Gene works with a display-man's skill to make an interesting picture of tables occupied by Elizabeth Arden, Beth Leary, Kay Inglis-Jones, Kate Cross, James Farley, Carrie Munn and Eleanor Lambert. At "21," the important display is in the front room upstairs where Lana Turner, Mrs. Byron Foy, Henry Dreyfus, Jean Dalyrmple [*sic*], Sam Slotkin, George Kaufman and the Frank Bucks are shown off—while the back room is used very much as a displayman uses his "side-street windows"— for unglamorous but necessary merchandise.

It will have been readily deduced by suspicious minds that I am hand in glove (and a fetching arrangement it makes, too) with some of the most important figures in the fashion and merchandising industries, and nobody will believe that I serve as a decoration for nothing, like a wax banana, or a striped gourd, or a sprig of pussy willow. Some investigator must already have begun to suspect the existence of handsome profits from my styling activities, unreported year after year in my income-tax returns. Mr. Gaba, of course, doesn't say that I have received moneys, to use a Congressional term, for my work as a live dummy, but then he doesn't say that I haven't, either. It is well known that I drive a hard bargain in a business deal, and I would not be likely to allow the use of my graceful, well-groomed body as an appointment for a restaurant or bar free of charge.

The truth of the matter is, however, that if I have ever been used as a decoration in a public display, it was without my knowledge or consent. Since a well-dressed friend once asked me if my clothes were made by the American Can Company, I seriously doubt if I could be effectively arranged in the Rose Room of the Algonquin, even by Constance Spry or Irene Hayes, to make a perfectly stunning pattern with Eric Johnston on my left and Bercovici on my right. I don't know Mr. Slotkin—maybe he stays where he is put and can preserve for a whole evening the charming design he figures in—but I do know George Kaufman, and, like me, he is much too restless to serve as a satisfactory unit in a living tableau. He has none of the immobility of a Dresden shepherdess or a jar of bittersweet, and neither have I.

I am forced to admit that since Kaufman and I are of pretty much the same height and built, and are both capable of a worried expression, we might make a striking pair of bookends in Brentano's window—for a large display, say, of books about the precarious nature of the world situation —but then, again, I doubt if we could stand still long enough to take anybody's breath away. Furthermore, if Kaufman, Slotkin, and I were to go into the business of living ornaments professionally, our services would come high.

I have pondered over the Gaba document, or Black Paper, ever since I read it, and I have concluded that a Congressional investigation into whatever became of my profits from the stylish world of fashion might reveal some facts that would look funny, in the uncomical sense of that word. Although I have never been placed in an arrangement with the particular persons Gaba mentions as forming gorgeous designs with me in the Rose Room, I do know Fanny Arms, and I once got a fifteen-dollar tie—or cravat, I guess it was—from the Countess Mara as part of a promotion project for that lady's smart Park Avenue shop. I believe my name had been put on the list of giftees, as we merchandisers call them, at the suggestion of Kay Halle, who had probably got my name from Miss Arms. It was a distinguished tie of high visibility, bearing, as I remember it, a design of cockles and periwinkles, and I am glad I never wore it to the Algonquin or "21," for it would have dimmed the splendor of Clifton Webb, or even James Kevin McGuinness, and upset the patterns of the maîtres d'hôtel.

Investigators will search in vain for any other gift I ever received from a merchandiser, unless you could count a ten-pound box of animal crackers presented to me by the National Biscuit Company in 1927. I could explain that, but I am not going to—call it contempt if you will. I have given my memory a good going over, but I have not come up with anything less tenuous and innocent than the matter of the tie and the animal crackers. Once, it is true, I went into Best & Co.'s store and bought a hostess gown all by myself, but the exploit was rather more daring than devious, and some years ago I wrote an article for a Best & Co. publication, but this scarcely suggests a conspiratorial tie-up. Best & Co. and I are just friends, and I have never thrown anything their way, nor have they ever kicked back anything to me.

Outside of a business deal with B. H. Wragge, under the terms of which I got a print dress but no money, there is little else to report. In 1940, I did some drawings for the show windows of Bergdorf Goodman (the main ones, on Fifth Avenue, naturally). These were, I must admit, in connection with "The Male Animal," a subversive play of the period, but I have promised to submit any plays I may write in the future to either Congressman Thomas or Mrs. Lela Rogers, the eminent authorities on the Drama, and I don't think my old transgressions will weigh heavily against me when I am subpoenaed. After all, I was only forty-six at the time.

At any rate, I haven't got the courage to write a play now. I spend all my time slumped in a chair, brooding over the gags I must endure from my friends from now on. "You were framed," a lady with laughing eyes will say, "and I know just where to hang you—on the other side of the fireplace, opposite . . ." The men will grin and say, "Nellie and I saw you displayed at the Cort last night. She thought you should have been a little farther down and just a teensy-weensy bit to the left, but *I* thought you were as cute as a little woolly lamb."

It's not my fault if diners entering a restaurant gasp "Ah!" or "Oh!" or "Lookit, Myrtle!" when they see what the maître d'hôtel has done with me. I go into restaurants to eat, and into bars to drink, and I sit where I am put. I guess I just happen to drape becomingly. Can I help that?

Am Not I Your Rosalind?

" 'A RARE FIND is an able wife,' " George Thorne recited.
"There are cigarettes in that box, Fred."

"I got some right here." Fred Stanton pulled a pack from
his pocket.

Thorne walked over, snapped his lighter, and held the
flame for his guest. " 'A rare find is an able wife,' " he
began again. "She rises early and pays off the servants, and
so on, but she invariably mucks up the cocktail hour. I'll
stir up some more Martinis for us." He went over to the
bar. "They'll be up there a good half hour. Let 'em catch
up."

Stanton watched his host's ritual with bottles, ice, and
shaker. "Lydia always shows her friends over the house,
too," he said, "even if they've seen everything a hundred
times."

"Pride of possession." Thorne stirred his mixture
thoughtfully. "These are my jewels, and so on. I gave Ann
an old lace fan when we were in Rome before the war. Too
fragile to handle, so she's just had it shadow-boxed. That'll
take up a good fifteen minutes. Then, there's the Landeck
dry point in the hall up there."

"Thanks." Stanton studied the cocktail pouring into his
glass.

Thorne filled his own glass, set it and the shaker down,
and went out into the hall and frowned up the stairs.

"I wouldn't yell at 'em," Stanton said. "Women don't
like to be yelled at."

"Ann!" Thorne called. There was no answer, no sound from upstairs. Thorne came back into the room and picked up his glass. "To the ladies!" he declaimed. "We can drink with 'em or without 'em."

"Women like to do things in the house their own way," Stanton brought out after some thought. "That's a good cocktail."

Thorne walked over and filled his guest's glass again. "O.K.?"

"Perfect."

Thorne refilled his own glass. "You're oversimplifying a pretty profound difference, Fred. Did you ever see directors at a board meeting exclaiming over a perfectly darling new water cooler or a desk calendar just too cunning for words?"

Stanton stirred uneasily and recrossed his legs. "How do you shadow-box a fan?" he asked after an obvious search for something to turn the conversation.

"You set it in a deep frame against a rose-colored background," Thorne explained. "Effective and expensive." He glanced at his wristwatch and went out again to the bottom of the stairs. "Hey! Girls!" he yelled. "Ann! It's seven-thirty, for heaven's sake!"

A faint "Shut up" drifted down from somewhere above. Stanton was sitting on the edge of his chair looking unhappy when his host came back, saying, "A woman should be yelled at regularly, like an umpire—to paraphrase Noel Coward. Clears the air. Here."

"Thanks," said Stanton.

"Ann snaps back—I'll mix some more—but what the hell. Are they dry enough for you? She's got temperament—you know that—but I like it." He went to the bar after swallowing his drink.

"Lydia's got temperament, too," Stanton said defensively.

"Seems awful calm and levelheaded." Thorne poured the last measure of gin into the shaker.

"Lydia's got a lot—a lot of variety," Stanton said, sitting up straighter.

"Oh, sure, sure," Thorne said, stirring. "Lydia's a swell gal."

"Lydia, you know, Lydia"—Stanton's left hand seemed to be trying to pull out of the air an instance of his wife's variety—"Lydia played Rosalind in her senior-class play when she was in high school," he said loudly. And, apparently surprised at his outburst, and embarrassed, he lit a cigarette with unnecessary care. "Oh, that was twenty, twenty-one years ago, in Binghamton. Played only one performance, of course. Every class—"

"For God's sake, this is wonderful!" Thorne cut in. "This is really wonderful! Ann was Rosalind, too, in *her* senior-class play, in a high school in Nebraska. For God's sake! Hold out your glass."

"Thanks," said Stanton. He had the expression of a man who has unwarily touched something old and precious, like an heirloom, and seen it suddenly fall apart.

"Both the girls were born in 1909, so they must have been ranting and posturing at practically the same time," Thorne cried.

"I don't know that we better mention it," Stanton said. "You know how women are."

Thorne laughed gleefully. "What I want to find out is how women *were*, and I got just exactly the right thing. Do you know what a sound mirror is?"

"Have you got one of those wire recorders?" Stanton asked apprehensively. "You could never get Lydia to talk into it. She'd never do that."

"Look, you get a hambo high, any hambo, and he'll act." Thorne chortled.

"After all, this was years ago," Stanton said.

18

"Here they come. Leave it to me." Thorne winked at him.

"If I were you—" Stanton began.

The two women came down the stairs and into the room laughing and talking.

"You don't know what you got coming to you," Thorne said.

"Fred, you simply *must* see the perfectly lovely fan George got Ann in Rome!" Lydia cried.

"What's the matter—are the drinks that bad?" Ann asked her husband.

"The drinks are excellent," Stanton said. "Excellent."

Thorne went to the bar, chuckling.

"Has he rigged up a booby trap, or is he just merry and gay?" Ann said to Stanton.

"What's the matter with *you*, Fred?" his wife demanded. "You look worried. Did Ewell Blackwell die, or something?"

"George has been showing off, probably," Ann said.

Thorne gave each of the women a glass and filled it up.

"No more for me," Stanton said, raising his hand.

"Come on, we're going to have toasts, old boy. Here."

"Thanks." Stanton sighed.

"I was doing that big scene of mine from 'A Night at an Inn,' " Thorne told his wife.

"George was all over the stage in college," Ann said. "He was picked as the man most likely to flop out of town." The two women laughed, Thorne grinned, and Stanton shifted in his chair.

"We are poor little hams that have lost our way," Thorne said, bowing to the women. "Raise glasses." Lydia and Ann looked at him. Stanton stared at the floor.

"What are you mumbling about?" Ann said.

"To the two fairest Rosalinds who ever strutted their little hour!"

"George!" Ann made a gavel rap of the name.

19

Then, suddenly, the two women looked at each other. There was a swift, almost reflex interchange of appraisal. It was as if each had clicked on and off the searching beam of a flashlight.

"Did you play Rosalind, too?" Ann cried.

"I'm afraid I did." Lydia laughed. They laughed together.

"I think Rosalind is really horribly boring," Lydia said. She looked at her husband, but he wouldn't meet her eyes.

"It's terribly hard to make her *appealing*," Ann said. "She's like Diana of the Crossways in a way. Didn't you *hate* Diana of the Crossways?"

Thorne went around draining the shaker, and moved tentatively to the bar. He could tell that it was all right to mix another round when Ann didn't say anything.

"Ewell Blackwell has his ins and outs, but he'll live to pitch another twenty years." Stanton came up, a little heavily, with this pronouncement.

"Rosalind is one of the first ten aggressive ladies in literature." Thorne had no intention of letting Diana or Blackwell sidetrack the topic of conversation. "That's what makes her a hell of a challenge to an actress. Being aggressive, she's also gabby, and that makes it a fat part."

"George's descriptions are always so charming," Ann said.

"Any child in her teens could enchant the Parent-Teacher Association by being cute as a little red wagon," Thorne said.

"Oh, for God's sake, George!" Ann spanked out a cigarette she had just lighted.

"Anybody can be precocious," Thorne went on. "The real test comes in the years of maturity."

"I know what you're up to, but it isn't going to work." Ann turned to Lydia. "He has one of those damn recorders, and he thinks he'll get us a little tight and make us perform."

"You talk into it, turn a gadget, and—zip!—your voice comes out clear and perfect as a bell," George explained.

"Really?" Lydia said.

"They used 'em in the Air Corps," Stanton put in. "Combat reports. Invented for that purpose."

"George'll do Jeeter Lester for you at the drop of a hat," Ann said. "And that big going-to-pieces scene from 'What Price Glory?'"

Lydia, holding out her glass, laughed in a higher key than before. "Goodness," she said, "I haven't done a thing since college."

"College?" Ann gave her the appraising glance again.

"I don't know why Fred didn't bring it *all* out, in his cups." Lydia gave a little disparaging laugh. "Yes, I did Nora in 'A Doll's House,' and Candida."

"Well!" Ann made a polite quaver of the exclamation. She held out her glass.

A white-coated colored man appeared at the dining-room door.

"Herbert, would you ask Florence if she'll give us fifteen minutes more?" Ann said. He nodded and went away.

"There are several makes, all of them hard to get," Stanton said, and coughed.

"I simply didn't have the time for it in college." Ann waved it all away lightly with her left hand. "So many *other* outside activities."

Lydia brushed from her skirt a thread that was not there. "Of course," she said quietly.

Thorne stood grinning at his wife.

"We'll have time for another quick round," she said. She looked coolly at Lydia. "The wine can stand a bit more chilling."

The two women smiled at each other, brightly. Thorne, mixing the Martinis, began to hum, "I can do anything better than you. Anything you can do, I can do better . . ."

Over the soup, Stanton wrenched the talk away from

21

acting by launching into a vehement attack on Rube Marquard's record of nineteen straight victories on the mound, attributing the old pitcher's success to the dead baseball of his period. This led into an argument with Thorne as to the exact date of the Oeschger-Cadore twenty-six-inning pitching duel, during which the ladies discovered that they saw precisely eye to eye in the case of an enormous mutual friend who had let herself go with shocking results not only in girth but in intelligence. They were both reminded, in the same instant, of their common incredulity upon encountering a certain blonde whose youth and beauty had been utterly destroyed in less than a year of marriage. The talk joined when the women attacked and the men defended the blonde's husband—a heel, a swell guy, a lush, a drinker of incomparable moderation. It was all amiable enough. Thorne repeated a witticism about marriage that Ann had heard a dozen times, but she laughed merrily with the others.

Over the coffee and brandy in the living room, the men revealed their secret knowledge of what was going on in the mind of Stalin, and pointed out how any child could have avoided the blunders of Attlee and Bevin. The women, meanwhile, were exchanging candid praises of each other's subtlety of taste in arrangement, working in a fleeting counterpoint of small self-deprecations.

Thorne gave one ear to Stanton's fluent attack on Roosevelt. With the other ear, he sounded the temper of the women, the strength of whose mutual esteem he decided to test with further applications of brandy. The women did not protest when Thorne refilled their glasses. They were now shrewdly exploring the possibility that the enormous woman's vapid stare and slow mental activity might be the result, in part, of persistent overdoses of barbiturates.

"My dear," Thorne said mockingly, grinning at each one in turn, "if *I* were married to *that* man, I should *certainly* take—"

22

"Shut up," said Ann.

Although the conversation took a dozen different turns, Thorne was careful not to let the mouse of Rosalind get too far away from the cat of his stubborn intention. He filled four or five lulls in the talk with interested questions. How many lines of the play, if any, could they remember? Had there been reviews? Had they saved the programs? How large were their audiences? Why had neither of the girls gone in seriously for a stage career when so many inconsiderable talents had achieved undeserved success? Ann and Lydia waved it all away with little laughs and "Oh, for heaven's sake!" and "I haven't the faintest idea," but Thorne thought he saw the embers of pride glow again in the ashes of old dreams.

Between eleven o'clock and midnight, Stanton made several abortive moves to go, but he finally gave up. One o'clock found him sitting uncomfortably in his chair with the strained expression of a man who has resigned himself to a sleepless night in a hotel taken over by a convention of surgeons. Furthermore, his attempts to rise and his repeated "Lydia, dear" had had the disturbing effect of bringing out, one after another, George Thorne's imitations of W. C. Fields, Ed Wynn, Al Jolson, Peter Lorre, and Henry Hull as Jeeter Lester.

During these sporadic performances, the smooth surface of Ann Thorne's dutiful attention had developed cracks obvious to her husband's trained eye, which had also discerned Lydia Stanton's polite amusement changing to brave tolerance and deteriorating at last into the restlessness of posture and precise dreaminess of eye that Thorne had been so energetically working to produce. During it all, Thorne had managed to keep the highball glasses constantly refreshed, and the success of this phase of his strategy showed in a glowing relaxation of manner, except in the case of Stanton, and a tendency in the women to use each other's name in every sentence.

"What do you say we run off my Chevalier recording?" Thorne said suddenly.

"He really does do a very good invitation of Chevalier, Lydia," Ann said.

"We had about six of us here one night after a big party broke up," Thorne explained. "Everybody read or recited something into the recorder mike. I remember Tom Sessions read an editorial from the Phi Psi *Shield*—I had one lying around. Well, everybody shot off his mouth except Dot Gardner and Julia Reid. Oh, no—no, indeed—not for them! You wouldn't catch *them* making a fool of themselves. Of course, at three o'clock they elbowed the other hambos aside and took over the mike."

Stanton cleared his throat. "Lydia, dear," he said.

"It was really too wonderful, Lydia," Ann said, laughing.

"Dot read that Cornford poem—uh—'Autumn Morning in Cambridge,'" Thorne said. "I had a first edition lying around."

"And what was it Julia did, George?" Ann giggled.

"Lizette Woodworth Reese's, as God is my judge, 'Tears.'"

"Oh, no!" Lydia shouted. "That tiny voice, Ann, coming out of that enormous hulk!"

"It was rich," Thorne said. "What the hell, it *is* rich! The goddam thing is preserved for lucky people of the future, digging around in the atomic rubble. Let's play it. My Chevalier imitation, a perfect gem, is thrown in for good measure."

"Lydia," Stanton said.

"It's in the library, the recorder is in the library," Thorne said.

"Come on, Fred." Lydia took his arm, smiled, and whispered savagely, "For God's sake, keep your eyes open!"

"Bring your drink, Fred," Thorne said. "Let me put some more ice in it."

"No, thanks," said Stanton. "It's fine." He saw, first, the small microphone on the table in the library, and his reluctant eyes followed the cord attached to it as if it were a lighted fuse glittering toward the ominous box at the other end.

"I think you better get Herbert to do it, George," Ann said. "Or maybe Fred could—"

Her husband scowled. "For God's sake, Ann, I've worked this thing a hundred times."

"I know," she said, with the look of a woman riding in a car driven by a little boy.

"It's a perfectly wonderful-looking thing," Lydia said. "Was it terribly expensive?"

"Around two hundred and fifty bucks," Thorne said. "We're in luck. That spool's on here now."

Stanton was gazing with tidy disapproval at the reproduction of Dufy's "Marne" over the fireplace.

"Are you sure you can make it go without breaking it?" Ann asked.

Thorne did not look at her. "Here we go!" he yelled.

The machine began to hum, low and menacingly. There was a loud electric whine, a sudden roar, and George's recorded voice bawled from the machine, "O.K., Herbert? Is it O.K.?"

"Yes, sir, you can go ahead, sir," the butler's voice bellowed.

"Turn down the volume! For the love of heaven, turn it down!" Ann screamed.

Thorne succeeded at last in finding the knob that controlled the volume. They listened while the solemn voice of Tom Sessions turgidly read an editorial from the Phi Psi *Shield* entitled "The Meaning of Fraternity in Wartime." Lydia began to squirm in her chair. She turned on a frosty smile when the voice of her host began a burlesque of Chevalier explaining in English the meaning of "Auprès de Ma Blonde." During this performance, Thorne modestly

25

left the room, carrying the four highball glasses. He spiked the women's drinks, shooting in only two squirts of soda. He came back in time to hear the voice of Dorothy Gardner reciting, in a curiously uneven mixture of eloquence and uncertainty, the Cornford lyric.

"Sounds like a crippled halfback running through a broken field," Thorne said.

"Sh-h," said Lydia. She put her tongue out at the first taste of the powerful highball.

"Go get that seltzer bottle," Ann commanded.

Thorne grinned and went out to the bar.

"Don't miss this coming now!" Ann cried.

The voice of Julia Reid, exalted, abnormally low, got by "A rose choked in the grass . . ." and then died. There was a long pause. "What the hell comes next?" the diseuse demanded. A dim voice that had spoken far from the microphone prompted her. The voice of the unseen, elated lady then went on to finish Miss Reese's sonnet in a tone of almost sepulchral dignity.

"I really think, Lydia—" Stanton said.

Ann took the seltzer bottle from Thorne and diluted Lydia's drink and her own. "Turn it off," she said. The reel was still unwinding, but no voices came from it.

"Wait a second," Thorne said. "Don't you want to hear Mark and Ken sing 'I Had a Dream, Dear'?" Two male voices began a ragged rendition of the old song in a key too low for them. Ann went over and shut off the machine.

"Well, sir, that was very fine," Stanton proclaimed loudly. He stood up.

"I'm going to put on a new spool for the gals," Thorne said. "Sit down, Fred."

Ann and Lydia protested quickly, but not, Thorne's ear told him, with sharpness or finality. There was a hint of excitement, an unmistakable eagerness in their chimed "Oh, no, you're not!"

26

"I can put on a new one faster than you can say Sarah Bernhardt," he said.

"I've never heard my own voice," Lydia said. "They say you never recognize your own voice."

"It's because you hear the sound internally, inside your mouth," Ann explained. "It's really fascinating."

" 'As You Like It' is right there on the second shelf, Volume Two, the collected comedies," Thorne said.

"Oh, for heaven's sake," Ann squealed. "I haven't looked at that damn play for twenty years!"

Lydia quietly finished her drink.

"There we are," Thorne said, stepping back and scowling at the sound mirror. "All ready to shoot. Here, I'll get the book."

Stanton, eyes closed, hands gripping his chair arms, seemed to be awaiting the impact of a dentist's drill. The women made little arrangements of their hair and skirts. Thorne flipped through the pages of the Shakespeare volume. "May the best Rosalind win!" He grinned. "How about this?"

Stanton tightened his grip on the chair. Ann examined her wedding ring. Lydia studied the floor.

" 'A lean cheek, which you have not, a blue eye and sunken, which you have not, an unquestionable spirit, which you have not—' "

"For heaven's sake, George, read it straight," Ann broke in. "Don't act it."

" 'A beard neglected, which you have not; but I pardon you for that, for simply your having in beard is a younger brother's revenue: then your hose should be ungartered, your bonnet unbanded, your sleeve unbuttoned, your shoe untied and everything about you demonstrating a careless desolation; but you are no such man; you are rather point-device in your accoutrements as loving yourself than seeming the lover of any other.' "

"That *awful* speech," Ann said. "I hated it."

"You don't happen to have a copy of 'Candida'?" Lydia asked.

"No fair," Thorne said. "Ann never did Candida. How about this passage? 'Yes, one, and in this manner. He was to imagine me his love, his mistress; and I set him every day to woo me: at which time would I, being but a moonish youth, grieve, be effeminate, changeable, longing and liking, proud, fantastical, apish, shallow, inconstant, full of tears, full of smiles, for every passion something and for no passion truly anything, as boys and women are for the most part cattle of this color; would now like him, now loathe him; then entertain him, then forswear him; now weep for him, then spit at him; that I drave my suitor from his mad humour of love to a living humour of madness; which was, to forswear the full stream of the world and to live in a nook merely monastic. And thus I cured him; and this way will I take upon me to wash your liver as clean as a sound sheep's heart, that there shall not be one spot of love in't.' "

"Wouldn't you just *know* a man wrote that?" Ann lifted her hands hopelessly.

"It has to be thrown away, you know—parts of that speech." Lydia sighed, as if it were impossible to explain how to attack this particular passage.

"Oh, let's do it and get it over with, Lydia," Ann said. "Do you want to go first?"

"You go ahead, darling." Lydia waved at Thorne, and he handed his wife the book, pointing at the selected speech. Ann's eyebrows went up when she looked at the page. "The type is funny," she announced.

"Read it over a couple of times while I fix a nightcap." Thorne gathered up all the glasses.

"Just one sip," Ann said when, a few minutes later, he brought in the fresh highballs.

"Ready?" asked Thorne.

"Roll 'em," she said.

28

The machine began to hum. Ann leaned toward the microphone on the edge of the table. Then she leaned back with a shy little run of laughter. "Heavens, I can't do it in front of people!" Her girlish ripple coagulated when she caught the professional glint of amusement in Lydia's eye. "All right, George," Ann said. "Start the damn thing."

She seemed to her watchful husband to lunge suddenly, like an unwary boxer. She gave the speech at the very beginning a brisk blow from which it never recovered. The swiftness of her attack was too much for the old lines, and although she slowed down halfway through, the passage could not regain its balance. It faded, brightened unexpectedly, faded again, and collapsed with a dignified whisper at the end. Thorne repressed a wild impulse to jump over and raise his wife's right hand.

Stanton applauded loudly, and all three of her audience called out "Fine!" and "Wonderful!"

Ann showed charming dismay. "Mercy! I was *horrible!*" she wailed. "You'll murder me, Lydia."

"You were perfectly fine," Lydia said.

"Here we go, Lydia!" Thorne shouted. "Your time has come."

"Oh, dear, I hate to follow Ann," Lydia almost whispered. She made an elaborate rite of lifting her highball glass and taking a final sip, and then began to read.

Fred Stanton turned a slow, wondering head toward the source of a voice he had never heard before. It was low, resonant, and strange.

Closing his eyes and pursuing his image of the prize ring, Thorne saw Lydia circle cautiously about the lines, waiting for an opening. She did not find one. Her slow, monotonous tactics went on to the end. It reminded Thorne of the first few rounds of the second Louis-Conn fight.

Thorne led the loud applause this time, Ann shrieked with delight, Stanton said, "Well, well, well!", and Lydia sat back, covered her eyes with her hand, and shook her head despondently, like a frustrated prima donna whose trunks have gone astray in a small town.

"Well, well, well," Stanton said again. He got to his feet.

"Sit down, Fred," Thorne said. "We got to play it back." Worrying the machine as if it were a tangled fishing line, he finally made the necessary shifts and adjustments. "Quiet! Here we go!" he yelled. The volume was stepped up as high as it would go. "I set him every day to woo me!" Ann howled from the machine. Thorne made a wild leap and cut the volume down.

"Goddam it!" Ann said, glaring at him. Then, "Oh, no," she whispered, her startled stare disowning the unfamiliar voice that mocked her from the sound mirror. Stanton started to applaud at the end, but Thorne cut him off with "Sh-h, here comes Lydia!" and moved quickly to the recorder and, as if in an innocent effort to ensure perfection of reproduction, shot up the volume on Lydia's opening line, so that she also bawled it. He turned it down instantly. "Well," Lydia said. Then, "That's not me!" "Perfect," Stanton said. Everybody stared fixedly at the machine.

When it was over, Stanton broke through the chatter with a determined "Very fine, very fine! We must go, Lydia." "Can't I sell a nightcap, one nightcap?" Thorne kept saying. But the others moved out of the library, Stanton firmly leading the way. Five minutes later, a high tide of gaiety flooded the front hallway and bore out into the night a bright flotsam of pledge and promise, praise and disclaimer, regrets at parting, and wonder at the swiftness of time.

The Stantons drove in silence until they were a good three hundred yards from the house.

"Well." Lydia sighed with tired satisfaction, ran up the window, and settled back comfortably. "I've heard some strange performances in my life, but I never heard anything like that. I sat there biting my lip." She made a Jane Cowl gesture.

"Yeah," Stanton said.

"That silly little singsong voice," she went on. "Why, she can barely *read*. And the way she kept batting her eyes, trying to look cute and appealing."

"She doesn't drink very well," Stanton said. "She had an awful lot to drink."

Lydia laughed harshly. " 'Invitation of Chevalier!' I thought I would *scream*. I really thought I would *scream!*"

"What was that?" Stanton asked.

"Oh, you didn't get it, of course, sitting there with your eyes closed, a million miles away. You didn't say one word, one single, solitary word, from ten o'clock until we left that house, except 'Lydia, dear—Lydia, dear—Lydia, dear,' until I thought I would go *out* of my mind."

"Aw," Stanton said. He reached for the pack of cigarettes in his pocket.

"I'll light it for you. Keep your hands on the wheel."

"Light the match toward you," he said. "Don't strike it away from you. You always strike it away from you."

She wasted three matches striking them away from her. "Slow down," she said.

He stopped the car. "I'll light it," he told her. "That guy always gets me down. He won't sit still and he won't stop talking. Yammering all over the place."

"At least he stays awake, at least he knows what's going on."

"Anyway, you were wonderful," Stanton said quickly. "You made Ann look like an amateur. You were marvellous."

She sighed a hopeless little sigh. "Well, you either have talent, Fred, or you haven't. She must have been the only girl in that Wyoming school, or wherever it was. You went past that turn again."

31

Stanton stopped the car and began to back up. "What was that goddam fan like?" he asked.

"It was awful," she told him. "And if she said 'George got it for me in Rome' once, she said it fifty times. George obviously got it from some Italian street peddler for a few francs. Eighteenth century, my foot!"

They drove awhile in silence. "Lire," Stanton said.

Lydia sniffed. "I doubt it," she said.

Back in their living room, the Thornes were having a short nightcap. "I wish the hell you wouldn't always act as if I couldn't make anything work," Thorne said. "I can do more with my feet than that big dolt can do with his hands. 'Better let Fred do it, George. Better get Herbert to do it.' For God's sake, lay off, will you? I made the thing work. I always make it work."

"Shut up, George, and give me some more ice," Ann said. "The thing that really got me, though, was that horrible affectation. She sounded like a feeble-minded Lady Esther on the radio." She paused and put on a frown that her husband recognized. She wore it when she was hunting for a grievance. She found one. "If you can make it work so well, why did you turn it up so high people could hear me yelling for three blocks?"

"I cut it down right away, didn't I, and I made her yell even louder."

Ann laughed. "That was wonderful. That was really wonderful, George."

"At your service." Thorne bowed. "Come on, let's go with unlighted candle dark to bed. The light that breaks through yonder Eastern window is not the setting sun, my pet."

They got up and Thorne turned out the lights. "Does he know *anything?* Has he got a brain in his head?" she demanded.

"Fred? God, no!"

"If he'd only yawn and get it over with, instead of working his mouth that way."

Halfway up the stairs, Ann turned suddenly. Thorne stopped and looked up at her. "Do you know the most ghastly thing about her?" she asked.

"That moo-cow voice?"

"No. Heaven knows that's bad enough, but can you possibly imagine her in doublet and *hose?* Those *legs*, George, those *legs!*"

Thorne jumped a step, caught up with her, and they went the rest of the way to their bedroom arm in arm.

The Princess and the Tin Box

ONCE UPON a time, in a far country, there lived a king whose daughter was the prettiest princess in the world. Her eyes were like the cornflower, her hair was sweeter than the hyacinth, and her throat made the swan look dusty.

From the time she was a year old, the princess had been showered with presents. Her nursery looked like Cartier's window. Her toys were all made of gold or platinum or diamonds or emeralds. She was not permitted to have wooden blocks or china dolls or rubber dogs or linen books, because such materials were considered cheap for the daughter of a king.

When she was seven, she was allowed to attend the wedding of her brother and throw real pearls at the bride instead of rice. Only the nightingale, with his lyre of gold, was permitted to sing for the princess. The common blackbird, with his boxwood flute, was kept out of the palace grounds. She walked in silver-and-samite slippers to a sapphire-and-topaz bathroom and slept in an ivory bed inlaid with rubies.

On the day the princess was eighteen, the king sent a royal ambassador to the courts of five neighboring kingdoms to announce that he would give his daughter's hand in marriage to the prince who brought her the gift she liked the most.

The first prince to arrive at the palace rode a swift white stallion and laid at the feet of the princess an enormous apple made of solid gold which he had taken from a dragon

34

who had guarded it for a thousand years. It was placed on a long ebony table set up to hold the gifts of the princess's suitors. The second prince, who came on a gray charger, brought her a nightingale made of a thousand diamonds, and it was placed beside the golden apple. The third prince, riding on a black horse, carried a great jewel box made of platinum and sapphires, and it was placed next to the diamond nightingale. The fourth prince, astride a fiery yellow horse, gave the princess a gigantic heart made of rubies and pierced by an emerald arrow. It was placed next to the platinum-and-sapphire jewel box.

Now the fifth prince was the strongest and handsomest of all the five suitors, but he was the son of a poor king whose realm had been overrun by mice and locusts and wizards and mining engineers so that there was nothing much of value left in it. He came plodding up to the palace of the princess on a plow horse and he brought her a small tin box filled with mica and feldspar and hornblende which he had picked up on the way.

The other princes roared with disdainful laughter when they saw the tawdry gift the fifth prince had brought to the princess. But she examined it with great interest and squealed with delight, for all her life she had been glutted with precious stones and priceless metals, but she had never seen tin before or mica or feldspar or hornblende. The tin box was placed next to the ruby heart pierced with an emerald arrow.

"Now," the king said to his daughter, "you must select the gift you like best and marry the prince that brought it."

The princess smiled and walked up to the table and picked up the present she liked the most. It was the platinum-and-sapphire jewel box, the gift of the third prince.

"The way I figure it," she said, "is this. It is a very large and expensive box, and when I am married, I will meet many admirers who will give me precious gems with which to fill it to the top. Therefore, it is the most valuable of all the gifts my suitors have brought me and I like it the best."

The princess married the third prince that very day in the midst of great merriment and high revelry. More than a hundred thousand pearls were thrown at her and she loved it.

Moral: All those who thought the princess was going to select the tin box filled with worthless stones instead of one of the other gifts will kindly stay after class and write one hundred times on the blackboard "I would rather have a hunk of aluminum silicate than a diamond necklace."

How To Name a Dog

EVERY FEW MONTHS somebody writes me and asks if I will give him a name for his dog. Several of these correspondents in the past year have wanted to know if I would mind the use of my own name for their spaniels. Spaniel owners seem to have the notion that a person could sue for invasion of privacy or defamation of character if his name is applied to a cocker without written permission, and one gentleman even insisted that we conduct our correspondence in the matter through a notary public. I have a way of letting communications of this sort fall behind my roll-top desk, but it has recently occurred to me that this is an act of evasion, if not, indeed, of plain cowardice. I have therefore decided to come straight out with the simple truth that it is as hard for me to think up a name for a dog as it is for anybody else. The idea that I was an expert in the business is probably the outcome of a piece I wrote several years ago, incautiously revealing the fact that I have owned forty or more dogs in my life. This is true, but it is also deceptive. All but five or six of my dogs were disposed of when they were puppies, and I had not gone to the trouble of giving to these impermanent residents of my house any names at all except Hey, You! and Cut That Out! and Let Go!

Names of dogs end up in 176th place in the list of things that amaze and fascinate me. Canine cognomens should be designed to impinge on the ears of the dogs and not to amuse neighbors, tradespeople, and casual visitors. I remem-

37

ber a few dogs from the past with a faint but lingering pleasure: a farm hound named Rain, a roving Airedale named Marco Polo, a female bull terrier known as Stephanie Brody because she liked to jump from moving motor cars and second-story windows, and a Peke called Darien; but that's about all. The only animals whose naming demands concentration, hard work, and ingenuity are the seeing-eye dogs. They have to be given unusual names because passers-by like to call to seeing-eyers—"Here, Sport" or "Yuh, Rags" or "Don't take any wooden nickels, Rin Tin Tin." A blind man's dog with an ordinary name would continually be distracted from its work. A tyro at naming these dogs might make the mistake of picking Durocher or Teeftallow. The former is too much like Rover and the latter could easily sound like "Here, fellow" to a dog.

Speaking of puppies, as I was a while back, I feel that I should warn inexperienced dog owners who have discovered to their surprise and dismay a dozen puppies in a hall closet or under the floors of the barn, not to give them away. Sell them or keep them, but don't give them away. Sixty per cent of persons who are given a dog for nothing bring him back sooner or later and plump him into the reluctant and unprepared lap of his former owner. The people say that they are going to Florida and can't take the dog, or that he doesn't want to go; or they point out that he eats first editions or lace curtains or spinets, or that he doesn't see eye to eye with them in the matter of housebreaking, or that he makes disparaging remarks under his breath about their friends. Anyway, they bring him back and you are stuck with him—and maybe six others. But if you charge ten or even five dollars for pups, the new owners don't dare return them. They are afraid to ask for their money back because they believe you might think they are hard up and need the five or ten dollars. Furthermore, when a mischievous puppy is returned to its former owner it invariably behaves beautifully, and the person who brought it back is likely to be regarded as an imbecile or a dog hater or both.

Names of dogs, to get back to our subject, have a range almost as wide as that of the violin. They run from such plain and simple names as Spot, Sport, Rex, Brownie and Rover—all originated by small boys—to such effete and fancy appellations as Prince Rudolph Hertenberg Gratzheim of Darndorf-Putzelhorst, and Darling Mist o' Love III of Heather-Light-Holyrood—names originated by adults, all of whom in every other way, I am told, have made a normal adjustment to life. In addition to the plain and the fancy categories, there are the Cynical and the Coy. Cynical names are given by people who do not like dogs too much. The most popular cynical names during the war were Mussolini, Tojo, and Adolf. I never have been able to get very far in my exploration of the minds of people who call their dogs Mussolini, Tojo, and Adolf, and I suspect the reason is that I am unable to associate with them long enough to examine what goes on in their heads. I nod, and I tell them the time of day, if they ask, and that is all. I never vote for them or ask them to have a drink. The great Coy category is perhaps the largest. The Coy people call their pets Bubbles and Boggles and Sparkles and Twinkles and Doodles and Puffy and Lovums and Sweetums and Itsy-Bitsy and Betsy-Bye-Bye and Sugarkins. I pass these dog owners at a dog-trot, wearing a horrible fixed grin.

There is a special subdivision of the Coys that is not quite so awful, but awful enough. These people, whom we will call the Wits, own two dogs, which they name Pitter and Patter, Willy and Nilly, Helter and Skelter, Namby and Pamby, Hugger and Mugger, Hokery and Pokery, and even Wishy and Washy, Ups and Daisy, Fitz and Startz, Fetch and Carrie, and Pro and Connie. Then there is the Cryptic category. These people select names for some private reason or for no reason at all—except perhaps to arouse the visitor's curiosity, so that he will exclaim, "Why in the world do you call your dog *that?*" The Cryptics name their dogs October, Bennett's Aunt, Three Fifteen, Doc Knows, Tuesday, Home Fried, Opus 38, Ask Leslie, and Thanks for the Home Run, Emil. I make it a point simply to pat these unfortunate dogs on the head, ask no questions of their owners, and go about my business.

This article has degenerated into a piece that properly should be entitled "How Not To Name a Dog." I was afraid it would. It seems only fair to make up for this by confessing a few of the names I have given my own dogs, with the considerable help, if not, indeed, the insistence, of their mistress. Most of my dogs have been females, and they have answered, with apparent gladness, to such names as Jeannie, Tessa, Julie, and Sophie. Sophie is a black French poodle whose kennel name was Christabel, but she never answered to Christabel, which she considers as foolish a name for a dog as Pamela, Jennifer, Clarissa, Jacqueline, Guinevere and Shelmerdene. Sophie is opposed, and I am also, to Ida, Cora, Blanche and Myrtle.

About six years ago, when I was looking for a house to buy in Connecticut, I knocked on the front door of an attractive home whose owner, my real estate agent had told me, wanted to sell it and go back to Iowa to live. The lady agent who escorted me around had informed me that the owner of this place was a man named Strong, but a few minutes after arriving at the house, I was having a drink in the living room with Phil Stong, for it was he. We went out into the yard after a while and I saw Mr. Stong's spaniel. I called to the dog and snapped my fingers but he seemed curiously embarrassed, like his master. "What's his name?" I asked the latter. He was cornered and there was no way out of it. "Thurber," he said, in a small frightened voice. Thurber and I shook hands, and he didn't seem to me any more depressed than any other spaniel I have met. He had, however, the expression of a bachelor on his way to a party he has tried in vain to get out of, and I think it must have been this cast of countenance that had reminded Mr. Stong of the dog I draw. The dog I draw is, to be sure, much larger than a spaniel and not so shaggy, but I confess, though I am not a spaniel man, that there are certain basic resemblances between my dog and all other dogs with long ears and troubled eyes.

The late Hendrik Van Loon was privy to the secret that the dog of my drawings was originally intended to look more like a bloodhound than anything else, but that he turned up by accident with legs too short to be an authentic member of this breed. This flaw was brought about by the fact that the dog was first drawn on a telephone memo pad which was not large enough to accommodate him. Mr. Van Loon labored under the unfortunate delusion that an actual bloodhound would fit as unobtrusively into the Van Loon living room as the drawn dog does in the pictures. He learned his mistake in a few weeks. He discovered that an actual bloodhound regards a residence as a series of men's rooms and that it is interested only in tracing things. Once, when Mr. Van Loon had been wandering around his yard for an hour or more, he called to his bloodhound and was dismayed when, instead of coming directly to him, the dog proceeded to follow every crisscross of the maze its master had made in wandering about. "That dog didn't care a damn about where I was," Mr. Van Loon told me. "All he was interested in was how I got there."

Perhaps I should suggest at least one name for a dog, if only to justify the title of this piece. All right, then, what's the matter with Stong? It's a good name for a dog, short, firm and effective. I recommend it to all those who have written to me for suggestions and to all those who may be at this very moment turning over in their minds the idea of asking my advice in this difficult and perplexing field of nomenclature.

Thix

I WAS tiptoeing along the radio dial the other afternoon, trying to steal past Superman and reach a string quartet, when I bumped spang into Captain Midnight, trapped again, this time in the flaming elevator shaft of an ominous loft building on a godforsaken stretch of sinister waterfront. Stuck between floors in an elevator, with strong flames licking the floor of the car, you and I would have no more chance than so much Wheatena, but Captain Midnight is uncookable. The ablest villains of the air waves have tried in vain for years to sauté this agile hero. The scroll charged with his punishments and jeopardies is unrolled at teatime every afternoon except Saturday and Sunday. The menaces of Midnight trouble the dreams of millions of children, largely because the great man's every plight and peril is shared by two kiddies, a little boy and a little girl. I swear to God they were in the elevator with him that day. What their parents can be thinking of I don't know. I do know that when these children should be in bed or in school, they are usually at the point of a flame, or lying bound and gagged somewhere.

Captain Midnight is not the only monstrously patriotic guardian of the American commonwealth who works hand in mitten with moppets and nippers on the air. Out of the terror that stalks the living room these winter twilights, I have heard many tiny voices squealing, "Drop that, Bloody Dan, or I'll let you have it!" or "Rev up all ten engines and we'll catch Floyd Fiend before he can reach the White

House." Just as soapmakers sponsor the radio serials dealing with the dilemmas of paralyzed ladies of bright fortitude whose lovers have wandered away in amnesia, the wild adventures of the armed youngsters are paid for by various manufacturers of breakfast foods. I may be the only adult who listens in on all the juvenile gunfire and motor roar, except, of course, the studio engineers and announcers. Come to think of it, though, there is one announcer—on which particular crunchy hour I cannot remember—who probably no longer has his job. During a commercial one afternoon some months ago, he departed from the script and said, out of the depths of an abysmal boredom with the little sharpshooters, "Tell your mother to hightail it down to the grocery store and get you some Cracklies. Hear?"

I can picture, in Technicolor, the grimly florid ritual that must have taken place later in the outraged executive offices of the shocked broadcasting company. Let us run through the scene quickly and then break for lunch.

The guilty announcer stands before the pale and quivering figure of Mr. Bodney, vice-president in charge of taste and propriety. There are three other persons in the room—General Mills, in full uniform, who stands with head averted, and two secretaries, Hopkins and Bradshaw. "Marquis Van Bassingham," Bodney says harshly, "there are three cardinal ideals in Radio to the perpetuation of which all decent networks, their main stations, and affiliated outlets are forever dedicated in the interest of a healthier and happier America. These ideals are Motherhood, Blessed Regularity, and Personal Daintiness. They must be spoken of in awe and reverence and never spelled backward. This afternoon, at four-fifty-two, during our second most beloved program, 'Buster and Betty, Young Avengers,' you offended, you grossly insulted, you heinously affronted the mothers of the United States by advising them to—uh—name the phrase, Hopkins." Hopkins clears his throat. "To, and I quote, 'hightail it,' unquote." "Great God!" breathes

43

Bodney. "That was not Radio, Bassingham. It was ungentlemanly, un-American, and unnetwork. Have you anything to say?" "I shall shoot myself tonight, sir, tomorrow at the latest," Bassingham says, the quality of his famous diction still true. "Hopkins!" Bodney snaps. "Shatter the transcription! . . . Good. Bradshaw, unstrap his Bulova! General Mills, would you care to break it over your knee? No? Then give it to me, Bradshaw. . . ."

In defense of my occasional practice of tuning in on "Buster and Betty" and other programs of the sort, I want to protest that what I have had in mind is a comparative study of blood-and-thunder entertainment for the young. When I was between eight and fourteen years old, in the reign of Theodore Roosevelt, radio was not even a well-developed call for help at sea, much less the wondrous miracle that sends the voice of Red Skelton to the farthest corners of the earth. Looking back on those placid years, when the wildest adventure in aviation was the wobbly flight at Kittyhawk, and the most daring shot was fired on a New York roof garden by a gentleman in evening dress, I can find, in fact or fiction, little of the stuff that modern childish nightmares are built on.

In Columbus, Ohio, in the first decade of the century, the High Street Theatre housed such terror as came to town. The Hanlons' "Superba" must have disturbed my dreams for several nights, for I remember to this day the evil dark lady of the extravaganza, but something usually happened in the melodramas to blunt the horrid edge of fear. I recognized one of the Indians in "Custer's Last Fight" as a young man of the community at whom I had once successfully thrown snowballs, and in the awfullest scene of "The Flaming Arrow" a section of the beleaguered stockade toppled gently to the stage with a low, papier-mâché *whoosh*, considerably retarding the activity of my pulse. Advertisements for "The Round Up" at the Southern (with Maclyn Arbuckle), which must surely remain the noisiest play in his-

44

tory, announced the number of shots—three hundred and fifty, it may have been—which would be fired at each performance, and you found yourself counting, a preoccupation that has the definite effect of easing apprehension. As for the two offstage pistol shots in "The Great Divide," they were fired, at the matinée I attended, into what must have been a large iron can, the resulting explosions bringing instantly to mind the amusingly monumental vision of two men shooting at each other with cannon. I must admit that I sometimes turned to the familiar and reassuring program ads for Hatton's Drug Store and the Bancroft Jewelry Shop during moments too tense for me in the Civil War plays put on by the Empire Stock Company. I will always remember the dimming of the lights of the telegraph office in "Secret Service," and the figure of the wounded young Confederate soldier (Charles Waldron) crawling painfully upstairs to finish off the Northern hero in "Barbara Frietchie." The worst villain of the plays of my boyhood, I suppose, was Professor Moriarty in "Sherlock Holmes," but he did not inspire in me the excited concern aroused in the breasts of youngsters I know today by such fiends as Gentle John Hubbard, who seeks to fry Captain Midnight, and Destan, the ghoul from the planet Mercury (or is it Neptune?), whose ambition it is to conquer the earth once he has given Buck Rogers a good shot of methane.

In the tranquil period between McKinley and Taft, the closest approach to the adventure serial and its prototype, the adventure comic, was the nickel novel. ("The Perils of Pauline" and the other movie serials were still in the womb of Hollywood.) The first nickel novel I read was called "Jed, the Trapper." I bought it in 1905 at a little drugstore on the corner of Town and Sixth, run by a Mr. Collison, one of whose sons was destined to write "Getting Gertie's Garter." "Jed" was a mild tale of wintry treachery, but it gave me a taste for the genre, and in a year or so I had a formidable collection—frowned upon by Aunts Lou, Hat-

45

tie, and Melissa—of "The Liberty Boys of '76," "Young Wild West," "Fred Fearnot," and "Old King Brady." I recall vividly the garish cover of one of the "Old King Brady" stories. Clad in a sky-blue suit and a red derby, the venerable detective was shown leaping from a purple fire escape upon the shoulders of a young bank robber. Except for the marks of his age, it would have been difficult to tell the great sleuth from the culprits he pursued. The artist invariably depicted his contorted face wearing the nasty expression, to my eye, at least, of a defaulting bank president, elderly and cornered. The exacerbated countenance of King Brady gave me a bit of a turn, but the text that lay behind the lurid covers never failed to restore my faith in the old fellow's character. I had my doubts about Fred Fearnot, too. Missing, at the age of ten, the subtle compounding of his name, I pronounced it to rhyme with "dear no." It was not until 1907 that my hope of his being suddenly revealed as a French spy was discouraged and I was forced to classify him, along with the snarling Brady, as a hero of unimpeachable honor.

It is a reflection, perhaps, on the skill of the nickel-novel authors that the names and deeds of their actual villains do not come to mind now. They were a dim gallery of surly miscreants, each doomed to imprisonment or death at the end of his particular brief tale. They did not recur from story to story like the radio scoundrels of today or, for that matter, like Dan Baxter, the pallid threat to the Rover Boys' peace of mind, memorable only for his persistence.

I should say, in this mere outline of a proper thesis, that in the long look back on the heroes of my childhood, in the awful and magnificent light of the atomic era, some of the old boys' very frailties bring them nearer to my heart. They could not project themselves five centuries into the future, they could not change the course of mighty rivers with their bare hands or fly through the air with the speed of a rifle bullet, and they could not decompose the cellular structure of their enemies with fantastic squirt guns. They fought with both feet on the ground. They were not above using their fists or laying about them with a simple two-by-four or a homely brickbat in a free-for-all. (I shudder to think what Brady would say about radio's Green Hornet, who calls his high-powered racing car Black Beauty, descends upon lawbreakers with a loud buzzing sound, and defends himself with an asphyxiation pistol.) With the exception of Frank Merriwell, who pitched his way out of my life with his curve ball that broke in two directions, they were up to no magical funny business.

Best of all, bless their grown-up hearts, they never engaged in desperate battles hip to shoulder with twelve-year-old boys and girls. They left child characters to the funny papers, to the mischievous world of Foxy Grandpa, Buster Brown, and the Katzenjammer Kids. My mature friends, Captain Dick Slater and Lieutenant Bob Estabrook of the Liberty Boys of '76, would not have permitted some Buzzy and Sistie of those stalwart times to set a trap for Tarleton or harry the flanks of Cornwallis. King Brady had a son who helped mete out justice to criminals, but this chip off the old hickory block was a grown man in long trousers and a blue derby.

It is true that Young Wild West sometimes rode into action against the Indians in the company of a yellow-haired blonde in a filmy green dress, but it was always against his will. He spent several paragraphs in each novel of the series trying to persuade Arietta—I think that was her name—to go back to school in Kansas City. It was not the great plainsman's fault that she was forever riding out of forest fires with arrows in her hair, strapped to the back of a horse. Arietta suffered from the most dangerous hallucination I have ever encountered in fiction: she was convinced that she could outfox the Oglala Sioux. It must be said on behalf of the foolhardy lady, however, that it never

47

occurred to her to match the wits of her little brother against the cunning of Sitting Bull.

I think it was in 1908 that my older brother sent to Sears, Roebuck for a book about the Wild West. When it arrived, it turned out to be a bulky volume, cheaply bound and poorly printed. It was generously spotted with murky illustrations, which appeared to have been drawn with one of those charred carbon sticks that used to fall out of the street lamps of the era. But it was well worth the ninety-eight cents it cost. The hero who emerged most brightly for me from the muddy pages was Wild Bill Hickok. One illustration, held up to a strong light, showed him shooting down six desperadoes singlehanded in the back room of a cowboys' saloon. Since the most successful drawing of Buffalo Bill depicted him engaged in a kind of lugubrious wrestling match with an Indian named Yellow Hand, on horseback, Wild Bill seemed to me a far superior figure. I found not long ago that my admiration for the old gunfighter is still too high to brook any slurs from the radio on the great man's prowess with a six-shooter. In one of the "Lone Ranger" programs, that masked and impudent myth was described as encountering Hickok one time in the Western gloaming. They were friends, it seems, but in the waning light Wild Bill did not recognize his old pardner and mistook him for a cattle rustler. He drew first, but *the Lone Ranger shot his gun out of his hand*. The indignant italics are mine.

That gave me an idea for a radio serial based on famous episodes in American history. The first program deals with the capture of Major André, who, you may remember, was taken by three alert soldiers, Van Wart, Williams, and Paulding. Skipping the opening announcement, music, war whoops, shrieks, musketry, and commercial, let us jump directly to—

ANNOUNCER: In a white Colonial house, not far from the United States Military Academy, Major André, British

48

secret agent, is talking in low tones to the beautiful but paralyzed American patriotess, Priscilla Schuyler, whose father, General Schuyler, having received false orders from General Washington, delivered by the renegade Armand Dupré, disguised as Light Horse Harry Lee, has set out for Clifton's Crossing, guided by old Barthold, who is, in fact, Clement Hanty, Major André's nephew.

ANDRÉ: If I were only not suffering from amnesia, I should recall which one of General Washington's aides I am. Regimental physicians have advised me that I can recover my memory only by poring over plans of the fortifications of West Point while bound for England on a ship now lying off the New Jersey coast.

PRISCILLA: It so happens that I picked up a set of the plans you seek, for the restoration of your dear memory, at the Graduation Ball in 1773, little realizing their therapeutic value at the time. I give them to you on condition that my brother Timothy, seven, shall lead you to the ship off the Jersey shore.

ANDRÉ: Well, all right.

ANNOUNCER: The plans securely strapped to his body, Major André sets out for New Jersey in the darkness of a moonless night, unaware that in some bushes near Dobbs Ferry three American patriots lie in wait for him: Junior Van Wart, Janey Williams, and Mary Helen Paulding. We interrupt this program to bring you a special message. Mr. Thurber does not know how long he can keep this up. We repeat. Mr. Thurber does not know how long he can keep this up. We return you now to the program in progress. In the bushes near Dobbs Ferry, Junior is speaking.

JUNIOR: Now, remember—when I count three, jump out with pistols drawn. Hark! I think I hear footsteps.

JANEY: I do, too. Do you hear footsteps, Mary Helen?

MARY HELEN: Yeth. Footthepth.

JUNIOR: Sh-h. Here they come! (*The children stop talking; the crickets stop chirping.*)

TIMOTHY: This way, sir.

ANDRÉ: It seems crowded here, curiously enough.

JUNIOR: One—two—three! (*The music comes up loudly. Voice of Announcer rises over it.*)

ANNOUNCER: Will Major André have the courage to shoot it out with Junior and his little companions? Will love restore the use of Priscilla Schuyler's wasted limbs? Will General Schuyler realize in time that he is not at Clifton's Crossing but in West Hartford? In just a moment we will return to our story. Meanwhile—Mother, have you tried Champies, the three-way breakfast food that does everything except deodorize? Remember—Champies stay in tiny mouths all day, like chewing gum, freshening the breath and cleansing the teeth, while they nourish little bodies. Get Three-Way Champies today! Now, back to our story.

JUNIOR: One—two—three! Throw up your hands, Major André!

MARY HELEN: Did he thwallow hith hanth? (*She fires.*)

ANDRÉ: That tot shot my pistol right out of my hand!

JUNIOR: Good work, Mary Helen!

TIMOTHY: I led him straight to the bushes, as we planned. Mary Helen is my girl, Major André.

ANDRÉ: Why, that child can't be a day over five years old!

MARY HELEN: I'm thix.

Why doesn't somebody take this doddam thcript away from me?

The Waters of the Moon

I HAD BROKEN away from an undulant discussion of kinetic dimensionalism and was having a relaxed moment with a slender woman I had not seen before, who described herself as a chaoticist, when my hostess, an avid disturber of natural balances and angles of repose, dragged me off to meet the guest of honor, a Mr. Peifer, editor of a literary review. "Holds his liquor beautifully," my hostess said. "Burns it up, I guess. He's terribly intense." Peifer was pacing back and forth on a rug, haranguing a trapped etcher whose reluctant eyes kept following him as if he were a tennis rally.

"No, I'm not interested in the aging American *female* author," Peifer was saying. "That's a phenomenon that confounds analysis. The female writer's fertility of invention and glibness of style usually survive into senility, just as her artistic gestation frequently seems to be independent of the nourishment of thought."

Peifer made three turns of the rug in silence. He had the expression of a chemist absorbed in abstruse formulae. "I am interested in the male American writer who peters out in his fifties, who has the occupational span of a hockey player. The tempo of our American life may have something to do with it, but there must be a dozen other factors that dry up the flow of ideas and transform a competent prose style into the meagre iterations of a train announcer."

My hostess finally broke in, and Peifer stopped pacing to shake hands. The etcher seized the opportunity to disappear.

"Mr. Thurber is fifty-three," my hostess said. "He hasn't written anything since last April." Peifer looked at me as if I were the precipitate of a moderately successful test-tube experiment. My first name suddenly reminded him of a tangent of his theme. "Take Henry James," he said. "If he had lived in this country, he would probably have spent his middle years raising collies or throwing darts. It is preposterous to assume, however, that region or climate is the important factor. There must be something, though, in the American way of life and habit of thought. I want to get Wylie or De Voto or somebody to do a comprehensive treatise on the subject, looking at it from the viewpoints of marriage, extramarital relations, the educational system, home environment, the failure of religion, the tyranny of money, and the rich breeding ground of decomposition which I believe is to be found in syphilophobia, prostatitis, early baldness, peptic ulcer, edentulous cases, true and hysterical impotence, and spreading of the metatarsals." I tried to wrench a tray of Martinis from a man in a white coat, but he would only let me have one. "Let's go over and sit down on that sofa," Peifer said. I followed him, glancing ruefully over my shoulder at my lost chaoticist. "It's a difficult article," I said. "If you use names, it's dangerous, and if you don't, it won't be interesting. You can't very well say that Joseph Doakes, after petering out on page 73 of his unfinished novel, 'Whatever Gods,' a childlike and feathery permutation of his first book, 'Fear Set Free,' is living in sin with his cook and spends his time cutting the pips out of playing cards."

Peifer took my olive. "The article is not to be a gossip column," he said. "It's to be a scholarly treatise. I am interested in exploring the causes of literary collapse, not in collecting scandalous post-disintegration case histories of quixotic individuals who would no doubt have gone to pieces in precisely the same way had they been milliners or pharmacists' mates."

"Then, unhappily," I said, "you cannot follow the old codgers past the hour of their deterioration, and in so doing you will omit a great deal of fascinating sequelae. You are interested only in causation. You would trace the career of, let us say, Bruce Balliol up to that afternoon in June when he abruptly began to write the middle section of 'Love Not the Wind' in the manner of the late Senator Albert J. Beveridge, and realized to his dismay that he was washed up at fifty-six. I would take him through his divorce, his elopement with the hairdresser, and those final baffling years on the peacock ranch."

A grim man I had never seen before walked up to us, dribbling his Manhattan. "Cora in the bells and grass," he said. "Cora with a cherry halfway to her lips." The man walked away. "I like Eve better than Cora," I said. Peifer apparently didn't know the poem the man had paraphrased. "You do?" he said, with his laboratory glint. "You were talking," I said. "Go on." Peifer took a curved briar pipe out of his pocket and rubbed the bowl on his pants leg. He began to chew on the stem of his pipe.

"That was poor old Greg Selby," I said, "a perfect specimen for your analysis. He stopped writing suddenly, a fortnight after his fifty-fourth birthday. Bang!" Peifer started. "Like that," I said. "His felicity of style was the envy and despair of us all, and then abruptly one day he began to write like a doorman cockeyed on cooking sherry." "I never heard of any writer named Greg Selby," Peifer said. I lifted a Martini from a passing tray. "He has never published anything," I said. "He is going to leave all his work to Harvard, to be published a thousand years from now. Greg's writing has what he calls Projected Meaning. He feels that in another millennium the intellectuals will understand it readily enough. I have never made head or tail of any of his stuff myself, but there is no missing the unique quality of the most exquisite English prose of our time."

Peifer made figure eights in the air with his pipe. "He

53

seems a little special," he said. "I'm not interested in idiosyncratic variables, except, perhaps, as footnotes."

"He is a male American writer who petered out in his middle fifties," I insisted. "He fits in perfectly."

"What I have in mind is the published writer of established merit," my companion said as I stopped another Martini tray, "but go on. What happened to this man Selby?"

"His first wife, Cora," I began, "claimed to have discovered that his last book, 'Filiring Gree,' was his next-to-last book, 'Saint Tomany's Rain,' written backward. It was insupportable to Greg that his wife should go through his books like a public accountant investigating a bank ledger. He threw her and her Siamese cats out of the house—the macaw wouldn't go. He had not heard the last of her, however. She called him up every few days and in the falsetto of a little child asked him why he didn't dramatize the Little Colonel stories for Margaret O'Brien. She divorced him, finally, and married a minor-league outfielder."

"This is really terribly special," Peifer complained, signalling a tray of highballs.

"Cora was ordinary enough. It was Eve who was special. She was the author of a number of mystery books. You probably remember 'Pussy Wants a Coroner.' " Peifer replied, a little pettishly, that he did not read mysteries.

"After her marriage to Greg," I went on, "Eve's books took on a curiously Gothic tone; the style was cold and blocky, and the plots had all the flexibility of an incantation. She explained to her alarmed publishers that she was trying to write for the understanding of intellectuals a thousand years ago." Peifer put his drink on the floor and stood up. "I presume you would consider Douglas Bryce a published author of established merit, wouldn't you?" I demanded. I had thought the name up fast. "Well," Peifer said uneasily. He sat down again.

"Doug," I said, "ran out of ideas and his command of

sentence construction at the same time, on a Wednesday. He was fifty-eight. That was a long time ago. He died in 1932, on his chinchilla farm, and only the hatcheck girl, Dolores, was at his bedside. Nell left him after the Lawrence Stone incident."

Peifer recrossed his legs restlessly and reached for another highball. "It would be as hard to find a copy of 'The Tenant of the Room' now as it would be to turn up a first edition of 'V.V.'s Eyes,' " I told him. " 'The Tenant' was Doug's last book. It was a flimsy rehash of his earlier 'A Piece in Bloom.' The love story was a little more disgusting, but in general it was a slight rearrangement of the well-worn characters and incidents. Doug had once had a facile and effective style, but the writing in 'The Tenant' fell well within the capabilities of a shrewd pin boy."

I took another Martini. "Get on with it," Peifer said.

"Nell once told me that after the failure of 'The Tenant,' Doug spent his days making cryptic and vainglorious notes on pieces of Kleenex, doorjambs, the flyleaves of books, and shirt fronts. He would jot down such things as 'Translate Lippmann into Latin,' 'Reply to Shelburne Essays,' 'Refute Toynbee,' 'Collaborate with G.B.S.?', 'Call Gilbert Miller.' Other notes indicated that he planned a history of the New York, New Haven & Hartford in verse, an account of women in sports, to be called 'Atalanta to Babe Didrikson,' and a pageant based on the Tristram legends, in which he proposed to star the late Devereux Milburn."

"I really must go," Peifer said. He stood up and then resumed his seat. "What was the Lawrence Stone incident?" he asked.

"Just before he bought the chinchilla farm, Nell found, scribbled on the bathroom wall, 'The Shore; The Plain; The Mountain, a trilogy by Douglas Bryce.' Under that he had written 'A monumental achievement,' which he had signed 'Van Wyck Brooks.' But he was onto himself at last;

he was tired and he was through and he knew it. The reservoir of his natural talent had run dry and he had been reaching for the waters of the moon. But as I say, he was onto himself. Under it all he had scrawled, almost illegibly, 'a trilogy wilogy by Brycey-Wycey.'"

"Who was this man Stone? And then I must go," Peifer said. "People are beginning to sing."

"Doug had one more project," I said. "He conceived the idea of writing a long biography of a man picked at random in the street. The book was to be called 'Let Twenty Pass.' He stood one day at the corner of Fifth Avenue and Forty-fourth Street, counted off twenty men who walked by going north, and accosted the twenty-first. The twenty-first was a large, preoccupied mining engineer named Lawrence Stone. He called the police and a rather nasty fuss was kicked up in the papers. It came out, you remember, that Stone was quite deaf, and his functional disability had twisted Doug's proposal into a shockingly complex plan to seize the major networks. Dolores was passing when Doug accosted Stone, and her testimony as to what was actually said cleared Bryce. It was a near thing, though."

Peifer twisted around on the sofa, slowly and with difficulty, as if invisible blankets hampered his legs. I saw that his unfriendly stare glittered frostily in almost imperceptibly crossed eyes. I wondered I had not noticed before that his liquor, much of it unburned, had left him, in spite of a fluent grasp on his subject, balanced precariously between command and dissolution. His expression took away all my pride of invention in the garish show of figures I had conjured up to ornament his theme. I had been careless, too, in the name of the mining engineer, and Peifer had caught me out. "I happen to be familiar with Browning," he said with shrewd dignity, "and I happen to know how the line that begins 'Let twenty pass' ends."

I was conscious of a figure at my shoulder. Someone had come to save me. It was the slender lady, my dark lady of

chaos, grown a little mistier with the passing of the afternoon and possessed now of the posture of the rose in a summer wind. I stood up, and Peifer managed it, too. "Nell,"
I said, "may I present Mr. Peifer?" He bowed stiffly. "This
is Nell Bryce," I told him. The game was up, but here I
was, kicking field goals by moonlight. "Peifer here," I said,
"would not have followed Bierce beyond the Rio Grande
or Villon through the *porte* of St. Denis to see in what
caprice or rondeaux their days came to an end."

"Let's phone the police and plague 'em till hell won't
have it," the lady said. It seemed to hurt Peifer like a slap.
He bowed, almost too low to sustain the moral advantage
he undoubtedly held over both of us. "It is a great pity,
Madam," he said, tightly, "that your mythical husband
had the misfortune to encounter an engineer named Stone.
Ah, what a flaw in the verisilimitude was there! It is a great
pity your husband did not have the luck to encounter an
engineer named Costello or McKelway or Shapiro." The
dark lady listened to him with the expression of one who
is receiving complicated directions in a great, strange town.

Peifer turned a cold, uncertain eye on me. "Let twenty
pass," he snarled, "and stone the twenty-first." The dark
lady watched him, on a quick opening play, break between
guard and center of a mixed quartet. "Now, how in the
God's name"—she had a charming diaphragmatic convul-
sion—"did he know my husband was mythical?" It was
too long a story to go into. I took her arm and, in silence, led
her to the telephone to call the police.

Exhibit X

I HAD BEEN a code clerk in the State Department in Washington for four months during the first World War before my loyalty was investigated, if you could call my small, pleasant interview with Mr. Shand an investigation. He had no dossier on Thurber, James Grover, except a birth certificate and draft-board deferment papers. In 1918, Americans naïvely feared the enemy more than they feared one another. There was no F.B.I. to speak of, and I had neither been followed nor secretly photographed. A snooping photographer could have caught me taking a code book home to study one night and bringing it back the next day —an act that was indiscreet, and properly regretted when I learned the rules—but a pictorial record of my activities outside the Bureau of Indexes and Archives in Washington would actually have been as innocent as it might have *looked* damning.

It would have shown me in the company of Mrs. Nichols, head of the information desk at the State, War, and Navy Building (a psychic lady I had known since I was six); George P. Martin, proprietor of the Post Café, and Mrs. Rabbit, his assistant; Frank Farrington, a movie actor who had played the part of a crook named Braine in "The Million Dollar Mystery;" and Jack Bridges, a Los Angeles air-mail flier and Hispano-Suiza expert. I doubt if any such photographs, even one showing me borrowing twenty dollars from Bridges half an hour after meeting him for the first time in my life, would have shaken Mr. Shand's confidence in me.

Mr. Shand called me to his office about a week before I was to sail for France and the Paris Embassy. He was a tall, quiet, courteous gentleman, and he had only one question to ask me. He wanted to know if all my grandparents had been born in the United States. I said yes, he wished me Godspeed, we shook hands, and I left. That's all there was to it. Waking up at night now and looking back on it, I sometimes wonder how I would have come out of one of those three-men inquisitions the Department was caught conducting last year. Having as great a guilt sense as any congressman, and a greater tendency to confession, it might have taken me hours to dredge up out of my mind and memory all the self-indictments that must have been there. I believed then, and still do, that generals of the Southern Confederacy were, in the main, superior to generals of the Northern armies; I suspected there were flaws in the American political system; I doubted the virgin birth of United States senators; I thought that German cameras and English bicycles were better than ours; and I denied the existence of actual proof that God was exclusively a citizen of the United States. But, as I say, Mr. Shand merely asked me about my grandparents, and that was all. I realize now that, as a measure of patriotism, the long existence of my ancestors on American soil makes me more loyal than Virginia Dare or even George Washington, but I didn't give it any thought at the time.

Before I sailed on the S.S. Orizaba, a passenger ship converted into an Army transport and looking rather sheepish about it, I was allowed to spend four days in Columbus, Ohio, and my mother has preserved, for reasons known only to mothers, a snapshot taken of me on the last day of my leave. The subject of the photograph is obviously wearing somebody else's suit, which not only convicts him of three major faults in a code clerk—absent-mindedness, carelessness, and peccability—but gives him the unwonted appearance of a saluki who, through some egregious mischance of nature, has exchanged his own ears for those of a barn owl. If this would not be enough to cause a special agent to phone Hoover personally, *regardez*, as the French Sûreté would say excitedly, the *figure* of this alarming *indiscret*. His worried expression indicates that he has just mislaid a code book or, what is worse, has sold one. Even Mr. Hoover's dullest agent could tell that the picture is that of a man who would be putty in the hands of a beautiful, or even a dowdy, female spy. The subject's curious but unmistakable you-ask-me-and-I'll-tell-you look shows that he would babble high confidences to low companions on his third *pernod à l'eau*. This man could even find some way to compromise the Department of Agriculture, let alone the Department of State.

The picture would have aroused no alarm in the old days, however, for it was almost impossible to be a security risk in the State Department in 1918, no matter how you looked. All our code books except one were quaint transparencies dating back to the time when Hamilton Fish was Secretary of State, under President Grant, and they were intended to save words and cut telegraph costs, not to fool anybody. The new code book had been put together so hastily that the word "America" was left out, and code groups so closely paralleled true readings that "LOVVE," for example, was the symbol for "love."

Whatever slight illusion of secrecy we code clerks may have had was dispelled one day by a dour gentleman who announced that the Germans had all our codes. It was said that the Germans now and then got messages through to Washington taunting us about our childish ciphers, and suggesting on one occasion that our clumsy device of combining two codes, in a desperate effort at deception, would have been a little harder if we had used two other codes, which they named. This may have been rumor or legend, like the story, current at the time, that six of our code books were missing and that a seventh, neatly wrapped, firmly tied, and accompanied by a courteous note, had been returned to one or another of our embassies by the Japanese, either because they had finished with it or because they already had one.

A system of deception as easy to see through as the passing attack of a grammar-school football team naturally produces a cat's-out-of-the-bag attitude. In enciphering messages in one code, in which the symbol for "quote" was (to make up a group) "zoxil," we were permitted to use "unzoxil" for "unquote," an aid to perspicuity that gave us code clerks the depressing feeling that our tedious work was merely an exercise in block lettering. The Department may have comforted itself with the knowledge that even the most ingenious and complex codes could have been broken down by enemy cipher experts. Unzoxilation just made it a little easier for them.

Herbert O. Yardley, one-time chief cryptographer of the War Department, warned the government in a book published nearly twenty years ago that the only impregnable codes are those whose pattern is mechanically jumbled in transmission by a special telegraphic method that reassembles the pattern at the point of reception. To prove his point, Yardley revealed how he had broken the toughest Japanese code five years before. The government must have taken his advice. I doubt that we could have got through a second world war shouting, "zoxil Here we come, ready or not unzoxil."

The State Department, in the happy-go-lucky tradition of the time, forgot to visa my special diplomatic passport, and this was to cause a tremendous *brouhaha* later on, when the French discovered I was loose in their country without the signs, seals, and signatures they so devoutly respect. The captain of the Orizaba wanted nothing to do with me when I boarded his ship, whether my passport was visaed or not. He had no intention of taking orders from the State Department or carrying its code clerks, and who the hell was

61

Robert Lansing, anyway? He finally let me stay on board after I had bowed and scraped and touched my forelock for an hour, but he refused to monkey around getting my trunk on board. When I received it in Paris, more than a year later, everything in it was covered with the melted chocolate of a dozen Hershey bars I had tucked in here and there.

I had been instructed to report to Colonel House at the Hotel Crillon when I got to Paris, but I never saw him. I saw instead an outraged gentleman named Auchincloss, who plainly regarded me as an unsuccessfully comic puppet in a crude and inexcusable practical joke. He said bitterly that code clerks had been showing up for days, that Colonel House did not want even one code clerk, let alone twelve or fifteen, and that I was to go on over to the Embassy, where I belonged. The explanation was, I think, as simple as it was monumental. Several weeks before, the State Department in Washington had received a cablegram from Colonel House in Paris urgently requesting the immediate shipment of twelve or fifteen code clerks to the Crillon, where headquarters for the American Peace Delegation had been set up. It is plain to me now what must have happened. Colonel House's cablegram must have urgently requested the immediate shipment of twelve or fifteen code books, not code clerks. The cipher groups for "books" and "clerks" must have been nearly identical, say "DOGEC" and "DOGED," and hence a setup for the telegraphic garble. Thus, if my theory is right, the single letter "D" sent me to Paris, when I had originally been slated for Berne. Even after thirty years, the power of that minuscule slip of the alphabet gives me a high sense of insecurity. A "D" for a "C" sent Colonel House clerks instead of books, and sent me to France instead of Switzerland. On the whole, I came off far better, as events proved, than the Colonel did. There I was in Paris, with a lot of jolly colleagues, and there was Colonel House, up to his ears in code clerks, but without any code books, or at least not enough to handle the flow of cablegrams to and from the Crillon when the Peace Conference got under way.

That tiny "D" was to involve the State Department, the Paris Embassy, the Peace Conference, and, in a way that would have delighted Gilbert and Sullivan, the United States Navy in a magnificent comic opera of confusion. An admiral of the Navy, for some reason (probably because he had a lot of Navy code books), arbitrarily took over, at the Crillon, the State Department's proud prerogative of diplomatic communication, and a code shambles that might have perplexed Herbert Yardley himself developed when cablegrams in Navy codes were dispatched to the State Department in Washington, which could not figure them out and sent back bewildered and frantic queries in State Department codes, which the admiral and his aides could not unravel. The Navy has always been proud of its codes, and the fact that they couldn't be broken by the State Department only went to show how strong they were, but when communication between the Peace Conference and Washington came to a dead stop, the admiral agreed to a compromise. His clerks, young and eager junior lieutenants, would use the State Department codes. This compounded the confusion, since the lieutenants didn't know how to use the strange codes. The dozen State Department clerks Colonel House had turned away and now needed badly were finally sent for, after a month, but even then they were forced to work under the supervision of the Navy. The Great Confusion was at last brought to an end when the desperate State Department finally turned to a newspaperman for help, and assigned him to go and get its stolen power of diplomatic communication and bring it back where it belonged. Not since an American battleship, many years before, in firing a twenty-one-gun salute in honor of the President of France, had accidentally used real shells and blown the bejeezus out of the harbor of Le Havre had the

63

American Navy so royally loused up a situation. And think of it—a "DOGEC" for a "DOGED" would have sent me to Berne, where nothing at all ever happened.

The last time I saw the old building, at 5 Rue de Chaillot, that housed the chancery of the American Embassy when I was a code clerk was in 1937. Near the high, grilled door, a plaque proclaimed that Myron T. Herrick was our Ambassador during the first World War, thus perpetuating a fond American misconception and serving as a monument to the era of the Great Confusion. The truth is that Herrick served during only the first four months of the war, and from December, 1914, until after the war, in 1919, an unsung man named Willian Sharp was our Ambassador to France. This note of bronze fuzziness cheered me in a peculiar way. It was a brave, cockeyed testament to the enduring strength of a nation that can get more ingloriously mixed up than any other and somehow gloriously come out of it in the end.

As I stood there before the old chancery, I remembered another visit I had made to 5 Rue de Chaillot, in 1925, and for the convenience of the F.B.I., who must already have twenty-three exhibits to fling at me when I am called up before some committee or other, I offer my adventure in 1925 as Exhibit X. Myron Herrick was once more our Ambassador to France, and I was granted an interview with him, or, as Counsellor Sheldon Whitehouse insisted on calling it, an audience. I had given up diplomacy for journalism, as I used to explain it, and I needed material for an article I was writing about Herrick for an American newspaper. I decided I ought to have a little "art" to go along with the story, such as a photograph of the Ambassador's office, a large, bright, well-appointed room on the second floor, facing the street. I knew I couldn't get official permission to take a picture of the room, but this didn't discourage me. I had discovered that the same old French *concierge* lived in the same rooms on the ground floor of the chancery and controlled the opening of the great, grilled door. Remembering that Sunday had always been an off day, with a skeleton staff in charge, I picked out a clear, sunny Sabbath for my exploit. I went to the chancery and pushed the bell, and the *concierge* clicked the lock from her room. I went in, said *"Bonjour, Madame,"* went upstairs, photographed the Ambassador's office, came down again, having been challenged by nobody, said *"Bonjour, Madame"* to the *concierge*, raised my hat politely, and went away.

The Republicans were in charge of the Embassy then, not the Democrats, as in my code-clerk days, but things hadn't changed much. I am a pretty good hand at time exposures, and the photograph came out well. There is still a print of it in the art morgue of an American newspaper, or ought to be, but it is merely a view of a room in the home of whatever French family now lives at 5 Rue de Chaillot.

We probably learned a lot during the recent war, and I doubt if tourists with cameras could get into any of our Embassies today. If this belated confession makes it a bit harder for them, anyway, I shall be very happy indeed. I must close now, since somebody is knocking at the door. Why, it's a couple of strange men! Now, what in the world could *they* want with me?

The Lady on the Bookcase

ONE DAY twelve years ago an outraged cartoonist, four of whose drawings had been rejected in a clump by *The New Yorker*, stormed into the office of Harold Ross, editor

"With you I have known peace, Lida, and now you say you're going crazy."

of the magazine. "Why is it," demanded the cartoonist, "that you reject my work and publish drawings by a fifth-rate artist like Thurber?" Ross came quickly to my defense like the true friend and devoted employer he is. "You mean third-rate," he said quietly, but there was a warning glint in his steady gray eyes that caused the discomfited cartoonist to beat a hasty retreat.

With the exception of Ross, the interest of editors in what I draw has been rather more journalistic than critical.

Home

They want to know if it is true that I draw by moonlight, or under water, and when I say no, they lose interest until they hear the rumor that I found the drawings in an old trunk or that I do the captions while my nephew makes the sketches.

The other day I was shoving some of my originals around on the floor (I do not draw on the floor; I was just shoving the originals around) and they fell, or perhaps I pushed them, into five separate and indistinct categories. I have never wanted to write about my drawings, and I still don't want to, but it occurred to me that it might be a good idea to do it now, when everybody is busy with something else, and get it over quietly.

"All right, have it your way—you heard a seal bark."

Category No. 1, then, which may be called the Unconscious or Stream of Nervousness category, is represented by "With you I have known peace, Lida, and now you say you're going crazy" and the drawing entitled with simple dignity, "Home." These drawings were done while the artist was thinking of something else (or so he has been assured by experts) and hence his hand was guided by the Unconscious which, in turn, was more or less influenced by the Subconscious.

68

Students of Jung have instructed me that Lida and the House-Woman are representations of the *anima*, the female essence or directive which floats around in the ageless universal Subconscious of Man like a tadpole in a cistern. Less intellectual critics insist that the two ladies are actual per-

"That's my first wife up there, and this is the present Mrs. Harris."

sons I have consciously known. Between these two schools of thought lies a discouragingly large space of time extending roughly from 1,000,000 B.C. to the middle Nineteen Thirties.

Whenever I try to trace the true identity of the House-Woman, I get to thinking of Mr. Jones. He appeared in my office one day twelve years ago, said he was Mr. Jones, and asked me to lend him "Home" for reproduction in an art magazine. I never saw the drawing again. Tall, well-dressed, kind of sad-looking chap, and as well spoken a gentleman as you would want to meet.

69

Category No. 2 brings us to Freud and another one of those discouragingly large spaces—namely, the space between the Concept of the Purely Accidental and the Theory of Haphazard Determination. Whether chance is capricious

"For the last time, you and your horsie get away from me and stay away!"

or we are all prisoners of pattern is too long and cloudy a subject to go into here. I shall consider each of the drawings in Category No. 2, explaining what happened and leaving the definition of the forces involved up to you. The seal on top of the bed, then ("All right, have it your way—you heard a seal bark"), started out to be a seal on a rock. The rock, in the process of being drawn, began to look like the head of a bed, so I made a bed out of it, put a man and wife in the bed, and stumbled onto the caption as easily and unexpectedly as the seal had stumbled into the bedroom.

The woman on top of the bookcase ("That's my first wife up there, and this is the *present* Mrs. Harris") was originally designed to be a woman crouched on the top step of a staircase, but since the tricks and conventions of per-

"The father belonged to some people who were driving through in a Packard."

spective and planes sometimes fail me, the staircase assumed the shape of a bookcase and was finished as such, to the surprise and embarrassment of the first Mrs. Harris, the present Mrs. Harris, the lady visitor, Mr. Harris and me. Before *The New Yorker* would print the drawing, they phoned me long distance to inquire whether the first Mrs. Harris was alive or dead or stuffed. I replied that my taxidermist had advised me that you cannot stuff a woman, and that my physician had informed me that a dead lady cannot support herself on all fours. This meant, I said, that the first Mrs. Harris was unquestionably alive.

The man riding on the other man's shoulders in the bar ("For the last time, you and your horsie get away from me and stay away!") was intended to be standing alongside the irate speaker, but I started his head up too high and made it too small, so that he would have been nine feet tall *if I*

"What have you done with Dr. Millmoss?"

had completed his body that way. It was but the work of thirty-two seconds to put him on another man's shoulders. As simple or, if you like, as complicated as that. The psychological factors which may be present here are, as I have indicated, elaborate and confused. Personally, I like Dr. Claude Thornway's theory of the Deliberate Accident or Conditioned Mistake.

Category No. 3 is perhaps a variant of Category No. 2; indeed, they may even be identical. The dogs in "The father belonged to some people who were driving through in a Packard" were drawn as a captionless spot, and the interior

72

with figures just sort of grew up around them. The hippo-potamus in "What have you done with Dr. Millmoss?" was drawn to amuse my small daughter. Something about the creature's expression when he was completed convinced me that he had recently eaten a man. I added the hat and

"Touché!"

pipe and Mrs. Millmoss, and the caption followed easily enough. Incidentally, my daughter, who was 2 years old at the time, identified the beast immediately. "That's a hippotomanus," she said. *The New Yorker* was not so smart. They described the drawing for their files as fol-lows: "Woman with strange animal." *The New Yorker* was nine years old at the time.

Category No. 4 is represented by perhaps the best known of some fifteen drawings belonging to this special grouping, which may be called the Contributed Idea Category. This drawing ("Touché!") was originally done for *The New Yorker* by Carl Rose, caption and all. Mr. Rose is a realistic artist, and his gory scene distressed the editors, who hate violence. They asked Rose if he would let me have the idea, since there is obviously no blood to speak of in the people I draw. Rose graciously consented. No one who looks at "Touché!" believes that the man whose head is in the air

"Well, I'm disenchanted, too. We're all disenchanted."

is really dead. His opponent will hand it back to him with profuse apologies, and the discommoded fencer will replace it on his shoulders and say, "No harm done, forget it." Thus the old controversy as to whether death can be made funny is left just where it was before Carl Rose came along with his wonderful idea.

Category No. 5, our final one, can be called, believe it or not, the Intentional or Thought-Up Category. The idea for each of these two drawings just came to me and I sat down and made a sketch to fit the prepared caption. Perhaps, in the case of "Well, I'm disenchanted, too. We're all disenchanted," another one of those Outside Forces played a part. That is, I may have overheard a husband say to his

74

wife, on the street or at a party, "I'm disenchanted." I do not think this is true, however, in the case of the rabbit-headed doctor and his woman patient. I believe that scene and its caption came to me one night in bed. I *may* have

"You said a moment ago that everybody you look at seems to be a rabbit. Now just what do you mean by that, Mrs. Sprague?"

got the idea in a doctor's office or a rabbit hutch, but I don't think so.

If you want to, you can cut these drawings out and push them around on the floor, making your own categories or applying your own psychological theories; or you can even invent some fresh rumors. I should think it would be more fun, though, to take a nap, or baste a roast, or run around the reservoir in Central Park.

The Ordeal of Mr. Matthews

"THE PRACTICE of wit as a fine art is one with the carriage horse and the dulcimer," I said to the businessman who got stuck with me at a party in the country one afternoon. The sounds of modern teatime—gabble and loud laughter—drifted into the small study where I had found him sitting down over a back copy of *Life*. "For one thing," I went on, "the appointments, the accoutrements, the accessories have vanished like the snows of the famous ballade."

"My name is Matthews," he said, and shifted a glass of ale from his right hand to his left. We shook hands.

"Where now, Matthews," I demanded, "are the long draperies, the bright chandeliers, the shining floors, the high ceilings, the snuffbox, the handkerchief stuck in the sleeve with careless care, the perfect bow from the waist, the formal but agile idiom?"

"Setup is different today," Matthews said.

"Gone," I told him. "Lost in the oblivious plangency of our darkening era, crumbled of their lustre, save for a sparkle here, a twinkle there, in the remembered dust of the stately centuries."

Matthews put the copy of *Life* on the floor and got up. "Think I'll have some more of this ale," he said.

To my surprise, he came back a minute later, with an uncapped bottle and the dogged expression of a man determined to make out the meaning of voices heard dimly beyond a wall.

"The high tradition of wit in court and chancellery," I resumed, "died, I suppose, with Joseph Choate. His weapon was a sabre, not a rapier, but even the clangor of that bold steel did not linger in London Town to inspire with its faraway echoes Walter Page and Joseph Kennedy."

"Lots of energy, Joe Kennedy," Matthews said. "Tackle anything, handle it well."

"Choate lived to see the lights diminish, the magnificence dwindle, and the men decline," I said. "He saw the thrust lose its deftness until there was no longer need for skillful parry and riposte. The querulous and the irritable then had their day, giving way, in our land and time, to the wisecrack and the gag, the leg pull and the hotfoot, the gimmick and the switcheroo."

Matthews grunted and sought sanctuary in the close examination of a cigar.

"For the exercise of wit in the grand manner," I told him, "for the slash supreme, the stab sublime, or, if you prefer Untermeyer, the devastating crusher, one has to go back to the golden age of John Wilkes and Benjamin Disraeli."

Matthews lighted his cigar. "What'd you say it was Sam Untermyer said?" he asked.

"Not Sam," I said. "Louis."

A woman appeared at the door of the study. "Have you seen Nora?" Matthews asked her.

"She's in the dining room with Ed and Carl, having fun and laughs. Don't you want a drink, Mr. Thurber?"

"I'm on the wagon," I said. Matthews looked at me as if he didn't believe it. The woman went away. "Who was that?" I asked.

"Our hostess," he said simply. He tried a sudden tack. "Ed's certainly brought that business of his up from nowhere."

I quickly bypassed the looming discussion of Ed's acumen and went on talking. "Both Wilkes and Disraeli enjoyed, of course, those unique advantages of décor and deportment which were so conducive and becoming to the brilliant verbal duel. Wilkes, for example, had that most superb of foils, that greatest straight man in the history of wit, Lord Sandwich, almost always at his side in resplendent assemblages. At one of these, with all the important ears in town cocked, Sandwich accosted Wilkes with 'You will die of a pox, sir, or on the gallows,' to which Wilkes replied, 'That depends, sir, on whether I embrace your mistress or your principles.' "

Matthews turned his glass in his hand. "Had 'em more openly in those days, of course—mistresses," he said.

I let that pass. "Then there was old Disraeli," I said, "whose guardian angel, in the guise of one eager lady or another, was forever at his shoulder ready to pounce upon him during one of those happy silences with an inspired and perfect question. At one gathering she broached him with 'What is the difference between a misfortune and a calamity?' Disraeli favored her with his famous smile and replied, 'If Mr. Gladstone were to fall in the Thames, it would be a misfortune, but if someone were to pull him out, it would be a calamity.' " I didn't wait for Matthews' comment on this.

"The Disraeli woman," I went on, "with her mature intelligence, her arresting carriage, her eager interest in definition and discrimination, is extinct, or as near as makes no difference, in God's country today. The curiosity of the American woman, cabined and confined, rarely takes provocative or stimulating shape. It is all but impossible, for instance, to conceive of a lady upping to Swope, say, at the bar in '21,' with a question calculated to evoke an immortal reply. For one thing, the cramped and noisy setting is distinctly unpropitious, since it is far removed indeed from the resplendent assemblage, with its gracious and convenient lulls in conversation. One would have to say to our hypothetical lady, 'How's that?' or 'I beg your pardon?', and the precise timing so essential to the great retort would be irreparably ruined."

A woman came into the study with a cocktail in her hand.

"Don't you think we ought to be getting along, Nora?" Matthews asked.

"Nonsense," she said. "It's early."

"This is Mr. Thurber," he told her. "My wife." I stood up. "Mr. Thurber has been telling a story about Gerard Swope."

"Not Gerard," I said. "Herbert Bayard."

"Oh," said Matthews.

"That's nice," said his wife, and she went away.

"Only yesterday," I said, sitting down, "my secretary straightened up the room I work in—and an imposing task it was, to be sure. She separated answered and unanswered mail, soiled handkerchiefs and telegrams, dog drawings and razor blades, and in the process she came up with a folder of news clippings marked 'Things You Said.' "

"Things you said yourself, eh?" Matthews' eyes narrowed a little.

"Well, so the record shows." I sighed. "It all supports our theory of the changing setup, the deterioration of the players and the scene, the passing of the ancient glories. I have the contents of the folder fairly well in mind. They're skimpy enough, God knows. The first item is a clipping from the Chicago *Sun*."

"Field," said Matthews. "Big operator."

"It seems that Freddy Wakeman, the millionaire novelist, told the *Sun's* Spectorsky an anecdote about me when I was in Bermuda. A dewy young thing came up to me in a bar in Somerset, the story goes, and asked me why I had sold a certain piece of mine to the movies. Quick as a flash, I answered, 'M-o-n-e-y.' "

"Government probably got most of it," Matthews said.

The man was beginning to make me nervous. "The point is not in the financial transaction itself," I said testily. "The point is in the payoff at the bar down there in Somerset. I

79

spelled it out. There is no surer way to blunt the crusher and destroy the devastation."

"You don't have any recollection of the incident, eh?" Matthews asked shrewdly.

"None," I said. "Of course, I was fifty-one at the time, and perhaps a little cockeyed. If I spelled out the payoff, it is an indictment of my slowing mind or a proof of my decrepitude."

Matthews sat forward in his chair, as if poised for flight. "How big a folder'd you say this was?" he asked.

"Sparse," I snapped. "It won't detain you long. Why don't you get some more ale?"

"I believe I will," he said, and went away.

When Matthews came back, I began again. "Well, it seems I came out of this movie theatre with a group of friends—I always attend the cinema in the bosom of my circle—and one of them said, 'I think that picture stinks,' to which I instantly replied, 'I didn't think it was that good.' " I got out a cigarette and lighted it.

"My wife and daughter are crazy about this James Mason," Matthews said.

"The anecdote limps so obviously that I feel myself, now and then, attempting to repair or recap it," I went on. "Like this, for example: 'If a picture worse than stinks,' put in Louis Sobol, who was also there, 'metrofaction may be said to have set in.' "

"What was that?" asked Matthews.

I exhaled slowly. "Nothing," I said. "But if you have already been blinded by the brilliance, shade your mental eyes against what is still to come. In the summer of 1946, some months after the movie episode, a sensitive *Time* reporter got me on the long-distance phone to chat about the I.C.C. He said, 'Do you know Jo Davidson?' "

"No," said Matthews, "I don't."

"The reporter asked *me* that," I snarled. "The files of *Time*, forever antic and forever wrong, reveal that I shot back, 'I met him once. He has a beard.' "

Matthews shifted his glass to his left hand and adjusted his tie.

"The *Time* man omitted to report, for some obscure reason, that I thought Mr. Davidson was head of the Interstate Commerce Commission. It's too bad, because Timen and Tiwomen—in fact, the whole Lucempire—would still be laughing."

"Never miss an issue of *Time* if I can help it," Matthews said.

"As keen as my famous Davidson quip was," I said, "I was to top it in that same remarkable year. A few months later, Earl Wilson, the sympathetic columnist of the New York *Post*, called on me at my office in the city. When he came in, I was drinking black coffee. My greeting was what I can only describe as a staggeroo. 'I'm having some formaldehyde,' I'm supposed to have said. 'Will you join me?' "

Matthews took out another cigar and gave it a squirrelly inspection.

"Well, sir, to get on with the folder," I began again, "it seems that I came out of a movie theatre last July after seeing a picture based rather insecurely on a piece I wrote years ago. On this occasion, the story goes, I emerged in the company of a distinguished group of New York cognoscenti. 'Did anybody catch the name of that picture?' I asked drolly. Bennett Cerf, a wit in his own right, and in several other persons', printed my comment in his column. The town is still chuckling."

Matthews lighted his cigar and seemed to be trying to hide behind it.

"The most recent and, you will be glad to hear, the final item in the folder," I said, "appeared in an issue of the *Hollywood Reporter*. I think I can quote it exactly. 'His'— mine, that is—'favorite line about Hollywood is "Look what they did to Maurice Costello." ' I take it that one repeats one's favorite line as one rereads one's favorite book. The appalling thought has occurred to me that at some party or other I may have repeated the line several times to the same person. I wonder that no one has shouted at me, 'Will you, for the love of God, stop saying that!' "

"What's going on in here? Are you two fighting?" It was Nora back again, with a fresh cocktail.

"No," I said. "You overheard an inner quote."

"Some woman yelled at him at a party," Matthews explained.

"The wretch!" cried Nora.

"We must be charitable," I said. "After all, she had been through a lot."

"Nora, don't you think—" Matthews began.

"It's the shank of the afternoon," she said, and left the room. Matthews finished his ale and puffed at his cigar. He was getting fidgety.

"So endeth," I sighed, "the paltry, the pathetic folder."

Matthews' elbows seemed about to lift him out of his chair, but he relaxed when I began again.

"One of my colleagues is reported to have watched, on a Long Island estate, the transplanting of a great elm. 'This little job,' his host told him, 'is costing me two hundred thousand dollars.' 'Shows what God could do if he had money,' my friend commented. He modestly disclaims the observation, but the point I want to make is this. If it had been hung on me, the story would go: ' "This little job is costing me two hundred thousand dollars." "That," remarked Thurber, "is a lot of money." ' "I resent, Matthews," I added angrily, "what has all the appearance of a conspiracy to place on my shoulders the mantle of Calvin Coolidge."

Matthews frowned for a long moment. "Things you really said never got printed, eh?" he shrewdly inquired.

I laughed modestly and put on an expression of feigned embarrassment. "Well, they don't exactly ripple off my tongue," I said. "I'm no Jack Warner. But as a matter of fact, since you ask, there *was* one. This happened—oh, fifteen years ago. I had completely forgotten about it until something reminded me of it about six months ago. A tall, thin, serious-looking man came into the reception room of the magazine I worked for and asked for me. He told me he represented a publisher of high-priced special editions. He said his firm had hit on the idea of having me do new illustrations for 'Alice in Wonderland.' I said, 'Let's keep the Tenniel drawings and I'll rewrite the story.' The chap bowed and went away."

Matthews scowled. "Fellow thought you were an artist instead of a writer, eh?" he brought out finally.

"Precisely," I said. "Well, as it happened, there was no one but this man and me in the reception room at the time. I never have any luck that way. However, I sauntered into the office of a colleague and told him what I had said. Weeks went by, then months, and years, but no one ever spoke to me about the incident. My colleague, absorbed with some problem of his own, had apparently not listened to what I told him. The tall, thin man obviously never repeated the bit of dialogue, either."

"Turned down, probably disappointed," said Matthews.

"When I was reminded of the incident six months ago," I went on, "I told it to a writer friend of mine. He put it in the first act of a play he was writing, giving me credit by name and retelling the story perfectly."

"What play was that?" asked Matthews.

"It was never produced," I said.

Matthews pushed himself up out of his chair, mumbled something about having to see Ed, and walked away—swiftly, I thought, for a man of his bulk. He had pretty well worn me out.

A middle-aged woman flounced into the room and sat down in the chair he had left. "What do you know about Putney?" she yelped.

"Everything," I lied, hastily, but it was no good. She told me about Putney until it was time to leave.

Another woman came up to me before I could find my hostess or my hat. "John Matthews has been telling us a perfectly wonderful story, Mr. Thurber," she squealed, "about how you absolutely refused to rewrite 'Alice in Wonderland,' in spite of all the money they offered you."

"M-o-o-l-a," I said, coldly.

"Well, I think it was perfectly wonderful of you, I really do!"

"It was nothing at all," I said. "Anybody would have done the same thing."

She shrieked, "You're much too modest, Mr. Thurber, really!"

"I'm not modest, Madam!" I snarled. "I'm simply too g-o-d-d-a-m-n unlucky for words." I felt my wife's firm, familiar grip on my arm.

"Come on," she said. "It's time to go. I said good-bye to Harriet for you." She found my hat and we went out and got in the car.

"What were you shouting at Ida Barlow for?" she asked, starting the engine.

"Madam," I said, "if a man shouts at Ida Barlow, he makes an ass of her, but if he does not shout at Ida Barlow, he makes an ass of himself. Ask me anything and I'll give you a comeback."

"How did you manage not to fall off the wagon?" she asked. "I was sure you were going to when I saw you were stuck with John Matthews."

"Putney anything else would have been as bad," I said. She glanced at me with a hint of concern. "Ask me why I didn't fall off the wagon," I demanded.

She sighed. "All right, why didn't you fall off the wagon?"

"They didn't have any formaldehyde," I chortled.

It didn't strike her as funny, for some reason, but I had to laugh. I laughed most of the way home.

84

The Dewey Dewey Fog

IF 1948 DOES not mend its political strategies, and quickly, too, it is likely to go down in history as the Presidential Year of the Confused Identities or—and I hate this as much as you do—the Presidential Year of the Dewey Dewey Fog. The latter phrase happens to possess rather more aptness than mischief, and I trust that readers of all parties will excuse it.

I first noticed that there was something oblique about the political situation one night while listening to Quincy Howe's summary of the news over WCBS. He told how he had discovered Governor Dewey in the act of donning certain light and shining political garments that looked very much like those designed by Franklin D. Roosevelt. And Mr. Howe ended his remarks with the sentence "We thus see Dewey trying to out-Truman Truman, which will, of course, lead Truman to out-Dewey Dewey."

I happen to be fairly smart when it comes to political dialectic, but the sudden appearance of three Trumans and three Deweys in one sentence mixed me up. I do not accuse Mr. Howe of trying to out-Crisler Crisler, but there *was* a hint of razzle-dazzle, or Michigan-backfield attack, in this explanation of the new 1948 crisscross political strategy. I lost sight of the point for a moment, the way Southern California lost sight of the ball in the Rose Bowl when they saw what must have looked to them like three Yergeses and three Weisenbergers trying to out-Chappuis Chappuis.

The next day the situation was further complicated by

what I can only call a double end-around play. I quote from the *Herald Tribune:* "The shout of 'Wallace-ism' was raised by other Republican senators and representatives in such words as these: Representative Russell V. Mack, Republican, of Washington: 'It looked to me as if President Truman was trying to out-Wallace Wallace . . .'" And the *Times* printed this: "Representative Charles A. Halleck, House majority leader, called the message [Truman's] 'a purely political document designed to out-Wallace Wallace . . .'" The fair-minded critic will not draw the inference that Mack and Halleck are trying to out-Howe Howe. The thing is simply in the air. Everybody's doing it.

Now, it seems to me that Dewey is going to be thrown for a heavy loss, maybe even back of the '44-yard line, if he doesn't change his tactics. For if Dewey is trying to out-Truman Truman and Truman is trying to out-Wallace Wallace, a lot of voters will jump to the conclusion that Dewey Dewey—I mean Dewey—is trying to out-Wallace Wallace. As a matter of fact, he probably intends only to out-Truman the Truman who is trying to out-Roosevelt Roosevelt, and not the Truman who is trying to out-Wallace Wallace, but this may not be clear to the Frightened Fringe, that formidable body of voters who are afraid they may inadvertently cast their ballots for a man who wants to out-Stalin Stalin.

It seems to me that Dewey must reverse his field and try to out-somebody somebody else. The question then arises: out-who whom? Taft is the only man who can successfully out-Taft Taft, and it would scarcely be advisable to out-Eisenhower Eisenhower now that Eisenhower has decided not to Eisenhower. This doesn't seem to leave Dewey much choice in the present field of candidates, and he may find himself in the end with nothing better to do than out-Coolidge Coolidge.

Political historians will tell you that the Out Strategy has been used before in Presidential campaigns, but never,

86

of course, to such a bewildering extent. Harding, for example, set out to out-McKinley McKinley but succeeded only in out-Granting Grant. In 1944, when Bricker was campaigning for first place on the Republican ticket, he also tried to out-McKinley McKinley. McKinley's one contribution to political maneuvering was the conceit of speaking from his front porch, a rostrum designed to enhance the homey and wholesome character of the man whose favorite flower was the homey and wholesome white carnation. Bricker actually did out-McKinley McKinley, by installing a front porch inside an auditorium, so that his listeners could sit down. McKinley's audiences had had to stand up on the front lawn of the McKinley home. Bricker's achievement in out-McKinleying McKinley got him nowhere, because, almost fifty years after McKinley's death, the people had forgot what it was to McKinley, let alone to out-McKinley McKinley, and the practice of out-McKinleying McKinley fell into high disfavor. Many observers thought, when Bricker mucked up the Out Trend by moving the McKinley porch indoors, that this bewildering strategy was gone forever, and its sudden revival this year, after the brilliant Roosevelting of Roosevelt, has alarmed the shrewder counsellors of both major political parties. The followers of Wallace do not worry, because they know that their leader will go all the way to Election Day crying simply, "Look, Mama, I'm Wallacing."

What this Presidential Year needs, I think, is some bright symbol or other in the grand old tradition of the log cabin and the whiskey barrel, the white plume of Henry of Navarre, the shining sword at Armageddon, and the brown derby of the Happy Warrior. Personally, in preference to the monstrous mechanism of identification, I would settle, God help me, for a dark whisper, a little mud, or the grass in the streets.

A Guide to the Literary Pilgrimage

IN A CERTAIN restaurant on Third Avenue, whose proprietors are patrons of the arts, I was standing at the bar one evening, smiling in my beer, when a short, bald, middle-aged man appeared at my shoulder and said, "What sets *you* off from the other temperaments in this ateleer, Mac?" I could have run the fellow through with that cold, steady stare of mine which has been called "brown ice," but I found, a little to my surprise, that I had an answer to his question. "I am the only living writer," I said, "who has not called on George Bernard Shaw and who does not want to call on George Bernard Shaw." The character at my shoulder, who had expected to call forth from me a foolish grin and a few stammered words, slunk sheepishly down the bar to insult a rather peaked etcher who was quietly cursing to himself. I was left to examine, the way a squirrel examines a nut, the sudden little definition of singularity which I had tossed off. I could find no flaws in it.

It is not that I have anything against George Bernard Shaw or fail to appreciate his genius. It is neither an emotional blockage nor a mental judgment which stands in the way of my wanting to call on him. It is, I think, a purely nervous apprehension. I am afraid, perhaps, that I would sit in the great man's study gaping like a badly carved jack-o'-lantern, squirming and stammering like the hobbledehoy I really am under my well-groomed exterior, behind my mask of cold indifference.

On top of this singularly personal attitude toward calling on Shaw, there has been superimposed a pattern of actual experience—not my own experience, to be sure, but that of two other writers, Ralph Waldo Emerson and a man whom I shall call Mitchell Morris. The adventures of these two gentlemen in the homes of the literary great have persuaded me of a basic and unfortunate fact about the literary pilgrimage: it almost never comes off very well.

Emerson may have founded the American cult of the literary pilgrimage; at any rate, he risked a tricky stomach on a sailing ship more than a hundred years ago to pay his respects to Wordsworth, Coleridge, Carlyle, and Landor. He found in Carlyle a man who was to become a lifelong friend (they even kind of romped together, a thing I would have gone a long way to see), but he didn't do so well with the others. Wordsworth, who had just broken a front tooth, recited two sonnets while he and his guest both stood looking at each other—surely one of the most uncomfortable moments in the annals of the literary pilgrimage. Coleridge wore green spectacles and argued querulously about Unitarianism. Landor disagreed about almost everything his visitor brought up, from military leaders through Southey to the Latin poets.

The case of my writer friend, Mitchell Morris, was more recent and quite different. Morris called on the late William Bolitho at his villa in southern France about fifteen years ago. After my friend had presented himself, Bolitho said, "I will talk for an hour and you will talk for an hour."

The Bolitho system of literary communion has never seemed sound to me. If I were the man told off to speak last, I would not be able to take in what the other man was saying because I would be trying to think of something to say when my own turn came. This would lead to the stiff posture, the horrible smile, the inattentive monosyllabic interjection, and the glazed expression of the eye. When my host's hour was up, I am afraid I would only be able to repeat, over and over, "This is a mighty nice place you've got here."

If the adventures of Emerson and Morris in the living rooms of the great serve to prove that the literary communion of literary men is by no means a pleasurable and relaxing way to pass an afternoon, the experience of another writer I know who called on André Gide in North Africa recently establishes the rare and pleasant exception to the rule. The distinguished old Frenchman, it came out, was, at the moment, immersed in a profound study of the works of the American intellectual, Dashiell Hammett. Now, the works of Dashiell Hammett happen to constitute a field in which I can hold my own with anyone, a field in which, on one occasion, I even held my own with the celebrated author himself.

I should explain, at this point, that Mr. Hammett and I did not meet by appointment. He did not call on me and I did not call on him. We ran into each other at Tony's, once the fashionable meeting place of the literati of two continents. In Tony's in the old days, literary communion was informal to the point of rough-and-tumble, and a writer did not sit at the feet of another writer unless he was knocked there.

Well (to get farther and farther away from my friend's call on Gide), Hammett was pleased to announce that the only author whose writing had influenced his own was the late Henry James. It chanced that the subtle but notable similarities between "The Maltese Falcon" and "The Wings of the Dove" had been apparent to me long before they were exposed by Henry Morton Robinson. My own monograph on this curious literary resemblance, "Could Dashiell Hammett Have Created Sam Spade and Ned Beaumont if Henry James Had Not Created Merton Densher and Lambert Strether?", had, unfortunately, been stored in a warehouse in Bridgeport which burned down in 1934.

Furthermore, it would be just my luck, if I called on Gide, to catch him during a period of Hammett-fag, so that he would be in no mood to listen to the brilliant and carefully prepared parallel I can draw between "The Glass Key" and "The Golden Bowl." Monsieur Gide would probably open up on me by saying, "You are familiar, of course, with the works of Aristide Luchon?" It is my embarrassed tendency in such cases to reply, "Yes. Oh, yes, indeed." Surely no one can imagine a more awful way to spend an afternoon than by attempting to discuss novels or plays one has never read, written by a man one has never heard of.

My fear about Shaw is that he might, to get back at me for some casual mention of the resemblance between "The Thin Man" and "The Sacred Fount," *invent* out of thin air a writer named Aristide Luchon. In all the calendar of dirty tricks one writer can play on another, this is the dirtiest. I believe that Shaw would be capable of such black deviltry. In fact, I sometimes see him, in my dreams, leaning toward me and saying, "Do you agree with me that the character of Mathilde in Luchon's 'Dormer Avant le Coucher du Soleil' is badly thought out?" I ride into that with all the reckless courage of Senator Bricker, crying, "I do, indeed!" and the fat is in the fire, the cat out of the bag, the jig up, and my audience with Shaw at an end. His satanic laughter, as I run full upon his rapier, rings through my nightmares and brings me, panting and terrified, awake.

These nightmares inspired me to work on a set of rules called "The Young Writer's Guide to the Literary Pilgrimage." The rules are by no means complete, but if they serve to lighten in any way the burden of the visiting—or of the visited—author, I shall be amply repaid for my pains.

Rule I. Bear in mind always that you are the minor artist and that the man you are calling on is the major artist.

91

Otherwise, he would be calling on you. He is not going to write an article about your visit to him; hence, who you are and what you have written will serve only to embarrass him. Thus, it is extremely bad form to present yourself with a loud, proud "I am George Benton Fields." The great man might respond with a pseudo-hearty "Well, I should say you are!" * and the interview would be off to an awkward start. It is equally unfortunate and dangerous to open up with a muttered "My name is Fields, sir." Your host might bellow irritably, "Speak up, man!", or he might address you all afternoon as Mr. Fieldser, which would be most uncomfortable.

Sedulously avoid any of the three principal forms of the General or Indefinite Introduction. These are as follows: 1. The Modest or Casual Presentation: "I am a writer from Seattle, Washington." 2. The Self-Derogatory Introduction: "I am a broken-hearted bum from Warren, Ohio." 3. The Flippant or Facetious Identification: "I am a little stiff from Bowling Green, and my actuary gives me only thirty-five years to live." In the first place, you will have made an appointment (if not, you might as well get back on your bicycle), so the Master will know who you are and what you want, in a general sort of way. Just say "How do you do, sir?" and let him take the lead from there.

RULE II. Do not attempt to impress the great man with some observation or aphorism of your own which you have carefully polished up for the occasion, such as "The noblest study of mankind is insects," or "The César Franck D Minor Symphony is a fraternity whistle," or "Clover leaves rarely strike four times in the same place," or "There are two ways to get a subject down—pat and mike." The ice may never be broken if you start out like that.

RULE III. Do not come out with (and this is especially directed to the visiting female author) "I have simply *de-*

---

* A comeback made by the late Clare Briggs when a total stranger approached him with "I am Henry Preston Barnes."

voured every line you have ever written, and I *adore* them all!" If, by the end of the afternoon (or of the first five minutes), the great man comes to the conclusion that you are an indiscriminating ass, he may be moved to do some rash and deplorable violence to his novels or plays. Many a distinguished author in his advanced years has completely revised the entire body of his work, usually for the worse. The reason has long remained a mystery, but in the lady who devours and adores every line, I think we have the answer.

RULE IV. Keep all critics' names out of the conversation. Do not say, "As Van Wyck Brooks [or Bernard De Voto] so aptly put it . . ." It is more than likely that the mention of the name of any critic since Sainte-Beuve has been strictly forbidden in the shrine for more than forty years.

RULE V. Be careful, if you mention any of the writer's works (and you better had), not to confuse him with some other writer. H. G. Wells once said that most of the people who visited him informed him that his best novel by far was "The Old Wives' Tale."

RULE VI. For God's sake don't recite anything. What do you suppose Wordsworth would have thought if Emerson had recited a couple of his own poems to *him* (Wordsworth)?

RULE VII. Don't bring the celebrated artist a letter of introduction from Herbert Bayard Swope, Clarence Budington Kelland, Robert Alphonso Taft, Gene Tunney, George Palmer Putnam, H. V. Kaltenborn, Dan Golenpaul, or some Scarsdale woman who claims she met the old boy on a ship during a frightful crossing to Pernambuco. It is better not even to mention this woman's name or the name of the ship (or Pernambuco or Scarsdale).

RULE VIII. Do not come into the Presence bearing gifts. He has almost everything, doesn't need anything, and likes practically nothing. Furthermore, it is very hard for him to say "Thank you." In the case of a great many offerings, I

93

don't blame him. Here is a list of gifts which should especially be excluded: a clipping of an article written by the eminent gentleman for a school paper when he was fifteen; a copy of one of his plays done on the head of a tenpenny nail; a copy of one of his plays translated into Shawnee by an employee of the Department of the Interior; a paragraph laboriously constructed by rearranging all the words in the titles of all his books and intended to supply a key to What He Has Been Trying to Say; any caricatures, effigies, or likenesses of the great man, particularly those made out of typewriter punctuation marks, embroidery floss, field-corn kernels, buckeyes, matches, toothpicks, pipe cleaners, paper clips, tiddlywinks, dice, pigeon feathers, spools, milk-bottle caps, cigar bands, BB shot, or potatoes. The value of these objects is not enhanced by the fact that they were made by a child under seven, a woman over ninety, a Camp Fire Girl, Mayor O'Dwyer, the seventh daughter of a seventh daughter, or a midget.

RULE IX. Do not take with you your friends and neighbors, Mr. and Mrs. Howard M. Phillips, who happen to be travelling with you. If I know Mrs. Phillips, and I think I do, she will tell about her niece who, though only nine, writes verse and composes music. She will try to read some of the poems, which she always carries in her handbag, and, if there is a piano, she may even play one of the child's sonatas.

RULE X. If, on your arrival, the door is opened by a member of the literary figure's household who says that the Master will not be able to see you for forty-eight hours, do not hang around the house or the neighborhood. Go away.

RULE XI. If, in such a case, you do go away, do not leave behind, for the distinguished writer to read, a thousand-word note written in longhand and beginning, "In 1908, when my brother-in-law was an oiler on a Danish cattle boat, he found one of your," etc., etc., etc. Don't leave any note at all. Just go away.

94

RULE XII. And stay away.

If you are protesting that my Guide to the Literary Pilgrimage does not so much present my reasons for not wanting to call on Shaw as it does his probable reasons for not
wanting me, or you (or your Aunt Clara, who once had a
piece in *Harper's* "Lion's Mouth"), to call on him, I can
only point out that my reluctance to make the pilgrimage
is implicit in the very nature of the rules. Beyond the suggestion that the visitor should begin with a simple "How
do you do, sir?" the rules do not offer any instructions as to
what to say. This is because I have not been able to think
of anything to say in the presence of George Bernard Shaw,
and I do not believe that Shaw would be amused by anyone
who just sat there and said nothing.

The only famous writer I have ever heard of who did
not expect his companion to say anything at all was the
late Hendrik Willem van Loon. A friend of mine, who
used to ride with van Loon from Stamford to New York
several times a week, determined one day on a test. He decided to greet van Loon on the Stamford platform on this
particular morning simply with a smile and a handshake
and to leave him in Grand Central station the same way,
having said no word. He wondered if the great man would
catch on to the fact that his companion had not once opened
his mouth. The next morning, he again came up to van
Loon on the Stamford platform and said, "That was a fine
discussion we had on the train yesterday." "It was, indeed,"
said van Loon. "I enjoyed it a great deal."

That would surely be too much to expect of Mr. Shaw.
Or perhaps I should say too much for Mr. Shaw to expect
of me. In any event, I have written enough about what I
do not intend to say on a literary pilgrimage I am never
going to make.

Prehistoric Animals of the
Middle West

MANY RESIDENTS of that broad, proud region of the
United States known as the Middle West are, I regret to
say, woefully ignorant of, not to say profoundly incurious
about, the nature and variety of the wild life which existed,
however precariously in some instances, in that part of
North America before the coming of the Red Man (*Homo
Rufus*) or of anybody else.

The only important research which has been done in
this fascinating field was carried on for the better part of
thirty-two years by the late Dr. Wesley L. Millmoss.* For
the last twenty years of the great man's life, I served as
his artist, companion, counsellor and assistant. In this last
capacity, I did a great deal of heavy lifting, no doubt more
than was good for me. During the years I spent with Dr.
Millmoss, he devoted most of his time to digging in all parts
of the Middle West for the fossilized remains of extinct
animals. From bits of a thigh bone, or one vertebra, he
would reconstruct the whole animal. My drawings of his
most famous reconstructions accompany this treatise.

For the past twelve years I have striven without success
to have his findings, together with their accompanying illus-
trative plates, published in one or another of the leading
scientific journals of this and other countries. I lay my fail-

* While on a field trip in Africa in 1931, Dr. Millmoss was eaten by a
large piano-shaped animal, to the distress of his many friends and colleagues.

96

ure directly at the door of Dr. Wilfred Ponsonby who, at the meeting of the American Scientific Society in Baltimore in 1929, made the remark, "The old boy (Dr. Millmoss) has never dug up half as many specimens as he has dreamed up."

Although Dr. Millmoss, quite naturally, was unable to perceive the wit in this damaging observation, which hung like a cloud over his last days, he was not without a sense of humor, and I believe, if he were alive today, he would take no little satisfaction in the fact that for the last five years Dr. Ponsonby has labored under the delusion that he is married to a large South African butterfly.

However, this is scarcely the place for an exploration of the little feuds and fantasies of the scientific world. Let us proceed to an examination of the remarkable fauna of the prehistoric Middle West. If in doing so, I present no formal defense of the Millmoss discoveries, put it down to a profound reverence for the memory of Wesley Millmoss, who used so often to say, "A Millmoss assumption is more important than a Ponsonby proof."

All the plates reproduced here were drawn by me from photographs of original life-size models constructed by Dr. Millmoss out of wire, *papier mâché* and other materials. These models were all destroyed by fire in 1930. "All that I have to show for them," the good doctor once told a friend, "is two divorces."

According to all scientists except Dr. Millmoss, the famous mounds of Ohio were built by an early race of men known as Mound Builders. The doctor, on the other hand, contended that the mounds were built by the Mound Dweller (Plate I). This primitive creature was about the size of the modern living room. The Mound Dweller's body occupied only one third of the space inside his shell, the rest of which was used to carry the earth as he dug it up. The creature's eye was an integral part of its shell, a mistake made by Mother Nature and not, as has been claimed,* "a bit of Millmoss butchery-botchery." The Mound Dweller is of interest today, even to me, principally because it was my friend's first reconstruction, and led to his divorce from Alma Albrecht Millmoss.

Plate I.

In Plate II, I have drawn the Thake, a beast which Dr. Millmoss was wont to refer to lovingly as "Old Laughing Ears." It represents perhaps the most controversial of all the ancient creatures reconstructed by the distinguished scientist. Dr. Millmoss estimated that the Thake had inhabited the prairies of Illinois approximately three million years before the advent of the Christian era. Shortly after Dr. Millmoss gave his model of the Thake to the world, Dr. Ponsonby, in a lecture at Williams College that was notable for its lack of ethical courtesy, asserted that the Thake bones which Dr. Millmoss had found were in reality those of a pet airedale and a pet pony buried together in one grave by their owner, *circa* 1907. My own confidence in the authenticity of the Thake has never been shaken, although occasionally it becomes a figure in my nightmares, barking and neighing.

Plate II.

In Plate III, we have the Queech, also known as the Spotted, or Ringed, Queech—the only prehistoric feline ever discovered by Dr. Millmoss in his midwestern researches. I find no record in the doctor's notes as to the probable epoch

*Dr. W. Ponsonby, in the *Yale Review*, 1933.

in which it flourished. Like so many of Dr. Millmoss' restorations, the Queech was made the object of a particularly unfriendly and uncalled-for remark by Dr. Ponsonby. At a dinner of the New York Society of Zoologists, held at the

Plate III.

old Waldorf-Astoria some fifteen years ago, Ponsonby observed, "There is no doubt in my mind but that this pussy cat belongs to the Great Plasticine Age."

As to the authenticity of the Cobble-tufted Wahwah (Plate IV), even the sardonic Dr. Ponsonby could offer no slighting insinuations.* Like all other scientists, he was forced tacitly to admit the brilliant precision with which the old master had restored this antediluvian fowl. The Wahwah bird, in spite of its mammoth size, measured nothing at all

Plate IV.

from wing tip to wing tip, since it had only one wing. Because of its single wing, its obviously impractical feet and its tendency to walk over high rocks and fall, it is probable,

Author's Note: My research staff has since established that Dr. Ponsonby was enjoying a two-year sabbatical in Europe at the time the Wahwah model was completed.

Dr. Millmoss believed, that the species did not exist for more than a hundred and seventy-five years. Dr. Millmoss once told me that, if the bird made any sound at all,

it probably "went 'wah-wah.'" Since this embarrassed me for some reason, the celebrated scientist did not press the point.

In Plate V, we come upon my favorite of all the Millmoss discoveries, the Hippoterranovamus. One of Nature's most colossal errors, the Hippoterranova-

Plate V.

mus ate only stork meat and lived in a land devoid of storks. Too large to become jumpy because of its predicament, the 'novamus took out its frustration in timidity. It almost never came out completely from behind anything. When I asked Dr. Millmoss how long he figured the 'novamus had existed as a species, he gave me his infrequent but charming smile and said in his slow drawl, "Well, it never lived to vote for William Jennings Bryan." This was the only occasion on which I heard the great man mention politics.

Plates VI and VII represent, respectively, the Ernest Vose, or Long-necked Leaf-eater, and the Spode, or

Plate VI.

Wood-wedger. Neither of these animals has ever interested me intensely, and it is only fair to say that I am a bit dubious as to the utter reality of their provenance. At the time he constructed these models, Dr. Millmoss was being divorced by his second wife, Annette Beggs Millmoss, and he spent a great deal of his time reading children's books and natural histories. The tree at the back of the Spode is my own conception of a 3,000,000-year-old tree. The small animal at the feet of the Ernest Vose is a Grod. Dr. Millmoss' notes are almost entirely illegible, and I am not even sure that Ernest Vose is right. It looks more like Ernest Vose than anything else, however.

The final plate (Plate VIII) was one of the last things Wesley Millmoss ever

Plate VII.

did, more for relaxation, I think, than in the interests of science. It shows his idea, admittedly a trifle fanciful, of the Middle-Western Man and Woman, three and a half million years before the dawn of history. When I asked

Plate VIII.

him if it was his conviction that Man had got up off all fours before Woman did, he gave me a pale, grave look and said simply, "He had to. He needed the head start."

Even in death, Dr. Wesley Millmoss did not escape the sharp and envious tongue of Dr. Wilfred Ponsonby. In commenting upon the untimely passing of my great employer and friend, the *New York Times* observed that explorers in Africa might one day come upon the remains of the large, piano-shaped animal that ate Dr. Millmoss, together with the bones of its distinguished and unfortunate prey. Upon reading this, Ponsonby turned to a group of his friends at the Explorers' Club and said, "Too bad the old boy didn't live to reconstruct *that*."

Here Come the Tigers

IT WAS AFTER midnight and I had got up to turn off the radio and go to bed when a baritone began to sing "Bye-Bye, Blackbird" with the rueful reverence the song deserves. I sat down again, and I was lost. If I had shut off the radio, turned out the lights, and locked the door, Jordan and Hayes would have driven up to a dark house and gone away, or if they had hammered on the door, I would have let them hammer till they got discouraged and drove off. The lights were on, though, and the door was unlocked. The tires of a car swashed over the gravel of the driveway and came to a sudden, complaining stop. My door opened and they tumbled in without knocking, like a pair of comics taking an encore. I turned off the radio and reached for the light switch.

"Hold!" Jordan cried. "Stay that naughty hand!"

I took my hand off the switch. "I'm tired," I said, "and Alice is asleep."

"Sleep! Sleep—on a night of wild discovery!" Jordan moaned. He went over to the bar in a corner of the living room and began mixing a bourbon-and-soda. Hayes took Jordan's place at the bar when his companion flopped into a chair and swung one leg over an arm. "We have discovered a new dimension of meaning," Jordan said. He took a great gulp of his drink. "And a new plane of beauty."

"You want a drink?" Hayes asked me.

"It's late," I said, "and I'm tired."

Jordan snorted, choked on his whiskey, and coughed for

103

a full minute. "The man wants torpor," he spluttered finally. "On a night like this, the man wants torpor."

"Torpor is a good word," Hayes said. He sat on the arm of a chair. "Shall we take it apart for him?"

"You guys are stiff," I said.

Jordan frowned, finished his drink, and went back to the bar. "Stiff is better," he said. "I think stiff is probably perfect. Let me get at it." He dropped into the chair again, with a new highball.

I stared at the ceiling. If I didn't humor them, they might go away.

"We're starting too high," Jordan said. "We're the hell too high. He won't get it. Look at him."

"Nuts," I said coldly.

"Let me unwrap stiff for you," Jordan said. "God knows that ought to be simple enough. Listen to this. It's perfect. Stiff, tiff, fists, fits."

"He means that the mood and tone and color of a word are echoed in its component parts," Hayes said. "Tiff is argument, fist is fight, fits—fits—"

"Don't make it glare," Jordan said. "You're making it glare. Let him feel it. You got to feel it."

"Look—" I began wanly.

Jordan regarded me sorrowfully and shook his head. "He's going to compare it to Joyce or Dada or Gertrude Stein," he said. "He is an enemy of the new dimension. Oh, no, he can't be," he added. "Not in *this* house, he can't be." He had some trouble getting up, but he made the bar.

"It's *his* house," Hayes said.

I was glad he was soberer than Jordan, who after a moment of deep thought said, "Last place in the world a man should make an ass of himself. Host, you know. and all that."

"Where have you guys been?" I asked.

Jordan looked at Hayes and shrugged, splashing a dollop of his new drink on the carpet. "We have been in a new dimension of meaning and beauty," he said, "but I doubt if you could understand it."

"Well, what the hell is it?" I demanded. I went to the bar and poured myself a short drink. "Are you going to crawl around it all night, or are you coming out with it?"

"Tell him the quatrain," Jordan said. "I want him to hear the quatrain."

Hayes studied the floor for a while. Then he recited the quatrain:

"There are lips in pistol
And mist in times,
Cats in crystal,
And mice in chimes."

I stared coldly at Jordan's transfigured face. "Is this the spearhead of the New Beauty?" I asked.

Jordan globbered his drink down, ran his hand through his hair, and glared at me demoniacally. "Shows what What's-his-name of 'Christabel' and Keats of 'Eve of St. Agnes' could have done if the goddam fairy casements had opened on this lovely dimension!" he shouted.

"Coleridge," Hayes said. He was nursing his drink along, and seemed to be getting sober.

Jordan went to the bar and sloshed out more bourbon. "Well?" he demanded, but he didn't wait for me to answer. "We were unlocking animals from almost every word you can think of when we got to cats in crystal and mice in chimes. Tell him some of 'em, Tom. You got 'em all written down."

Hayes put his drink on the floor and pulled a piece of folded cardboard out of his pocket. I saw that it was a dinner menu with pencil scribblings on the back. "There's the wolf in flower, the gander in danger, and the frog in forget," he said. "There's the emu in summer, the ant in autumn, the wren in winter, and the pig in spring." He turned the cardboard upside down and scowled at it. "There's the gnu in jungle," he went on, "the swan in answer, and the toad in toward." He put the menu down, and

I thought he looked a little unhappy, as if the whiskey and the spell of the new dimension were wearing off at the same time.

Jordan kept snapping his fingers, trying to remember other beasts in other words.

"Try to find the tiger in a six-letter word," Hayes said to me. "It isn't easy. There are three six-letter words with tiger, but it isn't easy."

"It's not a game, it's more than a game," Jordan said severely. "Let's not get back to the game."

"It began as a game," Hayes said to me. "It's an old word game. You try to see how many words you can make out of another word."

"We played it a million times before," Jordan said, "but tonight, for the first time, I see what we got, like Emily What's-her-name hearing the river in the trees. You might hear the wind in the trees all your life and never hear the river. Give me that thing, Tom." He reached out and took the menu from Hayes, and began turning it slowly in his big hands. The writing on the back apparently ran in all directions. He sighed dolefully and handed it back to Hayes. "There's practically a sentence in woman," he said. "It's perfect in mood and tone. In mood and tone it's practically perfect. See if you can find the sentence, Tom."

Hayes patted away an incipient yawn. "Woman: moan now won wan man," he chanted, and then the yawn got the best of him.

"What'd I say it had in it, Tom?"

Hayes consulted the back of the menu. "The thunder of Genesis," he announced finally, "it says here."

"It's practically Biblical," Jordan said, "with only five letters." He went to the bar again. "Who wants a drink?" he asked. Neither of us said anything. Hayes had slumped a little in his chair. I leaned back, gazed at the ceiling, and hunted the tiger. For the next five minutes, I heard the sound of Jordan's voice but I didn't take in the sense. I found the roach in orchard, the horse in shore, the owl in wobble, the stag in ghastly, and the bear and zebra in brazen, but no glimmer of a tiger anywhere.

"It's like little boxes, one inside each other," Jordan was saying when I came out of my own jungle of words. "You lift out concentric meanings of practically identical mood and tone. Yet people have let the component parts of words go for a thousand years. They lose the depth and the roundness and the whole quality." He turned to Hayes. "Take pistol apart for Jim," he begged. "Take pistol apart." I got up and went to the bar and poured out a stiff rye. "Go ahead," I said.

"It kind of rips and squirts and goes all to hell, the way pistol should," Jordan said by way of foreword.

"Shoot," I said.

"No gags," Jordan implored me. "For God sake, no gags."

"Pistol," Hayes began. "Slip, spit, split, spilt, spoil, spoilt, slop, slot, tips, tops, spot, pots, stop."

"You see what I mean?" Jordan asked. I visualized the word and studied it for a while.

"He left out oils and soil," I said finally, "and what are Lois and silo doing in pistol?"

Jordan turned to Hayes, who had shut his eyes. "Didn't I tell you we'd be up against that?" he demanded. "What'd I say we'd be up against, Tom?"

"The obscurantism of the explicit," Hayes brought out after frowning over it.

"That's it! That's what I said we'd be up against, like in chalice."

Hayes decided to try another drink, and he went over and poured himself a short one. "You get lace and hail and ice and Alice in chalice," he said, "but you got lice to account for."

"So what?" said Jordan. "So what the hell?" He spread his hands.

"What about the rats in crystal, with the cats?" I asked.

"Jordan hasn't got the technic and ethic worked out yet," Hayes told me.

"I can handle the rats," Jordan said.

"And the salt and the slat and the cyst and the cart?" I asked.

"Yeh, and the star and the cry and the satyr. They all mix into crystal."

Hayes yawned openly. He was drinking slowly. "It seems a little thin, somehow," he said. "I mean the whole thing, in times like these."

"What does?" Jordan stared at him blankly.

I saved an argument by suddenly running across Roget in forget. "If there were no forget," I said to Jordan, "it would not be necessary to create Roget."

"I don't think you get the idea," he said. "I don't think he gets the idea, Tom. What was it I said earlier this evening? I said, 'Tom, he'll never get it in a million years.' I said, 'Tom, the obscurantism of the explicit is what's going to louse up this lovely thing.' Didn't I say that, Tom?"

"Yes," Hayes said, tapping another yawn.

"Do hotels for him, Tom. Maybe that'll give him the idea."

"Hotels," Hayes read. "Sot, lost, hose, stole, shoe. Hotel so hot she shot host. . . . I'm tired." He sagged in his chair.

"A lost mood, see?" Jordan tried to express it with a gesture of his hands. "You got to feel it like a child. Do you feel it?"

"I certainly do," I said.

"What are you tired for, Tom?" Jordan gave his friend a worried glance.

"I don't know," Hayes said. "It just seems a little thin, somehow."

"What does?"

"Mice in chimes. It seems a little thin."

"What's he talking about?" Jordan asked me.

"I mean when you get to thinking of the hare twisting in the frozen grass and the mastiff bitch in the moonshine cold," Hayes said.

"What the *hell's* he talking about?" Jordan almost wailed.

"What's-his-name and Keats," I said.

Jordan made a small, despairing gesture. "Do phrase," he pleaded.

"Oh, for God sake!" Hayes got up and went to the radio.

"Don't wake Alice," I said.

"Do phrase and then we'll get the hell out," Jordan said.

"Do phrase," I insisted quickly.

"Explain about it first in its own words," Jordan said. "You know."

"O.K., O.K." Hayes sighed and sat down. "You don't have to dwell on the parse phase, the sharp rasp, the rape shape," he droned.

"Now show him where Tenniel and What's-his-name, the *douanier*, come in," Jordan said eagerly.

"In the apes and the asp and the hares," Hayes went on. "In the peas and the pears and the tea, in the seraph and the harp."

Jordan's eyes glowed, like a cat's in a barn. "Tenniel and What's-his-name, the *douanier*," he said in a throaty voice.

"Come on, let's go, I got to go," Hayes said, getting up.

"You didn't have a hat," I told him.

"Take the oranges and gibbons of What's-his-name," Jordan went on, in a rapt croak.

"Rousseau, for God sake," Hayes said. "Come on."

Jordan got to his feet. His eyes moved slowly around the room.

"You didn't have a hat," Hayes said. "Come on."

He got Jordan just outside the living-room door. Four

more steps would have taken them through the hall to the front door.

"Where do you get the tea in phrase?" I asked suddenly. "There isn't any 't' in phrase."

Jordan turned and loped back to his chair and sat down hard, like a tired setter. "A posset for the highway!" he bawled.

"You asked for this," Hayes told me wearily.

"Mix him a short one," I said.

Hayes went slowly back into the living room and I closed the door behind him. I knew Alice was standing at the head of the stairs in the dark. "What *is* it?" she whispered.

"A posset for the highway," I told her.

"Jink Jordan? Oh, no!" She went back to her room.

I lingered in the hall, hoping they would come out, but Jordan's voice was loud and argumentative. "Will you stop saying it's thin, for God sake?" he shouted.

"All right, all right, it's exiguous, then," Hayes said.

"It's exiguous because it's undeveloped, that's why," Jordan replied. "You can't develop a thing like this in one night."

I went back into the room and shut the door behind me. Jordan was sitting in the chair I had been in, pulling some papers out of his inside coat pocket.

"Put that stuff away," Hayes commanded him sharply.

"Just a second," Jordan said. "I knew we'd left something out. How in the hell could you let me leave Blake out?" He began to pore over a pencilled scrawl on the back of a typewritten page. "We proved Blake had it," he said loudly. "We proved Blake knew all about it, and here it is!"

Hayes grabbed the sheet of paper away from him. "If I read it, will you get up and go home?" he asked. "And don't drink that so fast."

"Read it," Jordan said, waving his glass. "Wait a minute!" He pointed a finger at me. "How many tigers are there in—what's the line, Tom?"

" 'Tiger! Tiger! burning bright in the forests of the night,' " Tom recited.

"One tiger," I said. "How many Toms are there in 'Tom, Tom, the piper's son'?"

Jordan set his drink down and waved his arms despairingly. "Journalist!" he said bleakly.

"This is kind of interesting," Hayes said hurriedly. "There are actually five tigers in the first two lines of the poem—that is, the necessary letters are repeated often enough to spell the word five times, three times in addition to 'tiger, tiger,' with a couple of 't's and an 'i' left over."

Jordan finished his drink in a gulp. "Nursery rhymes!" he said bitterly.

"In those two lines," Hayes cut in, "Blake used only twelve letters of the alphabet, so Jink thinks he was on to the new dimension."

"Thinks!" Jordan cried.

"Wordsworth, who was not on to it," Hayes continued, "used nineteen letters in 'She dwelt among the untrodden ways, beside the springs of Dove.' "

Jordan shook his head at me slowly. "It'll take me ten years to work this thing out," he snarled, "and you giggle at it like a girl. Tell him about Planters Peanuts, Tom."

Hayes handed the sheet of paper back to Jordan and ran his hand over his forehead. "There are nine letters in Planters Peanuts, or only three fewer than Blake used in those two lines. Come on, let's go."

"One more, maybe?" Jordan said, holding out his glass.

"I'm going," Hayes snapped. "I'll wait just two minutes for you in the car." He walked over and opened the door, closed it behind him, went out the front door, got in the car, and slammed the car door shut.

"There goes one of the sweetest characters in the whole world," Jordan said.

I started turning out the table lamps, and Jordan got to his feet. "So long, Jink," I said. He walked slowly to the door, opened it, and said over his shoulder, "Not in a million years." The only light left on now was the one in the hall. Jordan closed the front door after him with great care. After a moment, the engine started and the car drove off.

Half an hour later, in bed, I had almost dropped off when, in the narrow strip of lucidity between the bright compound of consciousness and the dark jungle of sleep, I remembered, with a start like a gunshot, the tiger in the three six-letter words. I tried all the permutations I could think of, using one consonant after another, from "b" to "z." I couldn't fit the tiger into any six-letter word except tigers, and that obviously didn't count. I began all over again: tibger, bitger, grebit, trebig, briget, ticger, grecit, gercit, tidger, gertid, dregit.

The dawn was fluttering at the window when I finally found the three words, one after another, with tiger in them.

Alice woke up. "Haven't you been to sleep *yet?*" she asked.

"Gaiter, goiter, aigret," I said. "Avoid the consonants. It's as simple as that."

"Go to sleep," she said.

I managed it finally. It wasn't easy.

(AUTHOR'S NOTE: Shortly after the foregoing story appeared in *The New Yorker* the editors received and passed on to me a letter written by Mr. George Rose Smith, an eminent tiger hunter of Little Rock, Arkansas. Mr. Smith's letter went in part as follows: "In James Thurber's recent story, Here Come the Tigers, his friends assured him that there are three six-letter words containing the letters t-i-g-e-r. Thurber spent a sleepless night in tracking down the tigers in gaiter, goiter and aigret, and apparently concluded that he had exhausted the possibilities . . . Disturbed by the thought that the tiger is as near to extinction as Thurber intimates, I sent two native beaters through the Websterian veldts and quickly bagged the limit of ten.

"The girt group of words is infested with the beasts, both girted and begirt being perfectly good usage. For some reason engirt is branded as obsolete, though it happens that we in the South have occasion to use it almost daily. The prefix re- conceals two fine tigers, in regilt and regift. In the latter the prefix is used in the sense of 'back to an original or former position,' so that regift is closely allied to the familiar concept of an Indian giver . . .

"The suffix -er is also good for two tigers. Tigger is an attractive word, which the lexicographer (probably late for a date) hurriedly defined as 'one who tigs.' Tig itself means to run about, as cattle pestered by flies. Pestered by tigers is doubtless historically correct, but such tigging doesn't become habitual. Our lexicographer spent more time on tinger, defining it as 'one who or that which tinges.' We do not seem to have any word for one who, or even that which, tings. Perhaps the best choice would be ting-er, the hyphen giving a subtle indication of the tiger's stripes. The definition of gitter, a foreign word for a kind of grating, already carries this connotation of straight lines.

"A rare tiger is preserved in the Scotch word erting, which means urging on—a derivation from a root meaning to tease or provoke. This ancient custom of teasing or provoking tigers, while not mentioned in modern histories of Scotland, was probably a tribal method of demonstrating bravery.

"Thurber and his companions were interested in finding animals in odd places, as the mice in chimes and the cats in crystal, but they completely overlooked the tiger in a six-letter animal, the common or garden variety of grivet. As every schoolboy knows, the grivet is an intelligent and docile monkey, having a dull olive-green back. . . .")

Look Homeward, Jeannie

THE MOOT and momentous question as to whether lost
dogs have the mysterious power of being able to get back
home from distant places over strange terrain has been
argued for years by dog owners, dog haters, and other persons who really do not know much about the matter. Mr.
Bergen Evans in his book, "The Natural History of Nonsense," flatly sides with the cynics who believe that the lost
dog doesn't have any more idea where he is than a babe in
the woods. "Like pigeons," wrote Mr. Evans, "dogs are
thought to have a supernatural ability to find their way
home across hundreds, even thousands, of miles of strange
terrain. The newspapers are full of stories of dogs who
have miraculously turned up at the doorsteps of baffled
masters who had abandoned them afar. Against these
stories, however, can be set the lost and found columns of
the same papers, which in almost every issue carry offers
of rewards for the recovery of dogs that, apparently,
couldn't find their way back from the next block." Mr.
Evans, you see, touches on this difficult and absorbing subject in the uneasy manner of a minister caught alone in a
parlor with an irritable schnauzer.

Now I don't actually know any more than Mr. Evans
does about the dogs that are supposed to return from
strange, distant places as surely as an Indian scout or a loco-
motive engineer, but I am not prepared to write them off
as fantasy on the strength of armchair argument. Skepti-
cism is a useful tool of the inquisitive mind, but it is scarcely

a method of investigation. I would like to see an expert reporter, like Alva Johnston or Meyer Berger, set out on the trail of the homing dog and see what he would find.

I happen to have a few haphazard clippings on the fascinating subject but they are unsupported, as always, by convincing proof of any kind. The most interesting case is that of Bosco, a small dog who is reported to have returned to his house in Knoxville, Tenn., in the winter of 1944 from Glendale, Calif., thus setting what is probably the world's distance record for the event, twenty-three hundred miles in seven months. His story is recorded in a book called "Just a Mutt," by Eldon Roark, a columnist on *The Memphis Press-Scimitar*. Mr. Roark says he got his tip on the story from Bert Vincent of *The Knoxville News-Sentinel*, but in a letter to me Mr. Vincent says he has some doubts of the truth of the long trek through towns and cities and over rivers and deserts.

The dog belonged to a family named Flanigan and Mr. Vincent does not question the sincerity of their belief that the dog who turned up on their porch one day was, in fact, Bosco come home. The dog bore no collar or license, however, and identification had to be made on the tricky basis of markings and behavior. The long-distance record of Bosco must be reluctantly set down as a case that would stand up only in a court of lore.

Far-traveling dogs have become so common that jaded editors are inclined to turn their activities over to the society editors, and we may expect before long to encounter such items as this: "Rex, a bull terrier, owned by Mr. and Mrs. Charles L. Thompson of this city, returned to his home at 2334 Maybury Avenue yesterday, after a four months' trip from Florida where he was lost last February. Mr. and Mrs. Thompson's daughter, Alice Louise, is expected home tomorrow from Shipley, to spend the summer vacation."

Incidentally, and just for the sake of a fair record, my two most recent clippings on the Long Trek deal with cats, as follows: Kit-Kat, Lake Tahoe to Long Beach, Calif., 525 miles; Mr. Black, Stamford, Conn., to Atlanta, Ga., 1,000 miles.

The homing dog reached apotheosis a few years ago when "Lassie Come Home" portrayed a collie returning to its young master over miles of wild and unfamiliar terrain in darkness and in storm. This million-dollar testament of faith, a kind of unconscious memorial to the late Albert Payson Terhune, may possibly be what inspired Bergen Evans' slighting remarks.

I suspect that Professor Evans has not owned a dog since Brownie was run over by the Chalmers. In the presence of the "lost" dog in the next block, he is clearly on insecure ground. He assumes that the dog does not come back from the next block because it can't find its way. If this reasoning were applied to the thousands of men who disappear from their homes every year, it would exonerate them of every flaw except disorientation, and this is too facile an explanation for man or beast. Prince, the dog, has just as many reasons for getting and staying the hell out as George, the husband: an attractive female, merry companions, change of routine, words of praise, small attentions, new horizons, an easing of discipline. The dog that does not come home is too large a field of research for one investigator, and so I will confine myself to the case history of Jeannie.

Jeannie was a small Scottish terrier whose nature and behavior I observed closely over a period of years. She had no show points to speak of. Her jaw was skimpy, her haunches frail, her forelegs slightly bowed. She thought dimly and her coordination was only fair. Even in repose she had the strained, uncomfortable appearance of a woman on a bicycle.

Jeannie adjusted slowly and reluctantly to everything, including weather. Rain was a hand raised against her personally, snow a portent of evil, thunder the end of the world. She sniffed even the balmiest breeze with an air of

116

apprehension, as if it warned of the approach of a monster at least as large as a bus.

Jeannie did everything the hard way, digging with one paw at a time, shoving out of screen doors sideways, delivering pups on the floor of a closet completely covered with shoes. When she was six months old, she tried to bury a bone in the second section of *The New York Times*, pushing confidently and futilely at the newsprint with her muzzle. She developed a persistent troubled frown which gave her the expression of someone who is trying to repair a watch with his gloves on.

Jeannie spent the first two years of her life in the city, where her outdoor experiences were confined to trips around the block. When she was taken to the country to live, she clung to the hearth for several weeks, poking her nose out now and then for a dismaying glimpse of what she conceived to be God's great Scottie trap. The scent of lawn moles and the scurry of squirrels brought her out into the yard finally for tentative explorations, but it was a long time before she followed the woodchuck's trail up to the edge of the woods.

Within a few months Jeannie took to leaving the house when the sun came up and returning when it began to get dark. Her outings seemed to be good for her. She began to look sleek, fat, smug, and at the same time pleasantly puzzled, like a woman who finds more money in her handbag than she thought was there. I decided to follow her discreetly one day, and she led me a difficult four-mile chase to where a large group of summer people occupied a row of cottages near a lake. Jeannie, it came out, was the camp mascot. She had muzzled in, and for some time had been spending her days shaking down the cottagers for hamburgers, fried potatoes, cake and marshmallows. They wondered where the cute little dog came from in the morning and where she went at night.

Jeannie had won them over with her only trick. She could

sit up, not easily, but with amusing effort, placing her right forefoot on a log or stone, and pushing. Her sitting-up stance was teetery and precarious, but if she fell over on her back or side, she was rewarded just the same, if not, indeed, even more bountifully. She couldn't lose. The camp was a pushover.

Little old One Trick had a slow mind, but she gradually figured out that the long trip home after her orgies was a waste of time, an unnecessary loop in her new economy. Oh, she knew the way back all right, Evans—by what improbable system of landmarks I could never guess—but when she got home there was no payoff except a plain wholesome meal once a day. That was all right for young dogs and very old dogs and spaniels, but not for a terrier who had struck it rich over the hills. She took to staying away for days at a time. I would have to go and get her in the car and bring her back.

One day, the summer people, out for a hike, brought her home themselves, and Jeannie realized the game was up, for the campers obviously believed in what was, to her, the outworn principle of legal ownership. To her dismay they showed themselves to be believers in one-man loyalty, a virtue which Jeannie had outgrown. The next time I drove to the camp to get her she wasn't there. I found out finally from the man who delivered the mail where she was. "Your little dog is on the other side of the lake," he said. "She's stayin' with a school teacher in a cottage the other side of the lake." I found her easily enough.

The school teacher, I learned, had opened her door one morning to discover a small Scottie sitting up in the front yard, begging. The cute little visitor had proceeded to take her new hostess for three meals a day, topped off now and then with chocolates. But I had located her hiding place, and the next time she disappeared from home she moved on to fresh fields. "Your little dog's stayin' with some folks over near Danbury," the mailman told me a week later. He explained how to get to the house. "The hell with it," I said, but a few hours later I got in the car and went after her, anyway.

She was lying on the front porch of her current home in a posture of truculent possession. When I stopped the car at the curb she charged vociferously down the steps, not to greet the master, but to challenge a trespasser. When she got close enough to recognize me, her belligerence sagged. "Better luck next time," I said, coldly. I opened the door and she climbed slowly into the car and up onto the seat beside me. We both stared straight ahead all the way home.

Jeannie was a lost dog, lost in another way than Evans understands. There wasn't anything to do about it. After all, I had my own life to live. Before long I would have had to follow her as far as Stamford or Darien or wherever the gravy happened to be thickest and the clover sweetest. "Your little dog"—the mailman began a few days later. "I know," I said, "thanks," and went back into the house. She came home of her own accord about three weeks later and I think she actually made an effort to adjust herself to her real home. It was too late, though.

When Jeannie died, at the age of nine, possibly of a surfeit of Page & Shaw's, I got a very nice letter from the people she was living with at the time.

A Call on Mrs. Forrester

(After rereading, in my middle years, Willa Cather's "A Lost Lady" and Henry James's "The Ambassadors")

I DROPPED off a Burlington train at Sweet Water one afternoon last fall to call on Marian Forrester. It was a lovely day. October stained the hills with quiet gold and russet, and scarlet as violent as the blood spilled not far away so many years ago along the banks of the Little Big Horn. It had been just such a day as this when I was last in Sweet Water, fifteen years before, but the glory of the earth affected me more sharply now than it had when I was midway through my confident thirties. October weather, once a plentiful wine, had become a rare and precious brandy and I took my time savoring it as I walked out of the town toward the Forrester house. Sweet Water has changed greatly since the days when Frank Ellinger stepped down from the Burlington and everybody in the place knew about it. The town is large and wealthy now and, it seemed to me, vulgar and preoccupied. I was afflicted with the sense of having come into the presence of an old uncle, declining in the increase of his fortune, who no longer bothered to identify his visitors. It was a relief to leave the town behind, but as I approached the Forrester house I felt that the lines of my face were set in brave resolution rather than in high anticipation. It was all so different from the free, lost time of the lovely lady's "bright occasions" that I found myself making a little involuntary gesture with my hand, like one who wipes the tarnish from a silver spoon, searching for a fine forgotten monogram.

I first met Marian Forrester when I was twenty-seven, and then again when I was thirty-six. It is my vanity to believe that Mrs. Forrester had no stauncher admirer, no more studious appreciator. I took not only her smallest foible but her largest sin in my stride; I was as fascinated by the glitter of her flaws as by the glow of her perfections, if indeed I could tell one radiance from the other. There was never anything reprehensible to me in the lady's ardent adventures, and even in her awfullest attachment I persisted in seeing only the further flowering of a unique and privileged spirit. As I neared her home, I remembered a dozen florid charities I had invented to cover her multitude of frailties: her dependence on money and position, her admiration of an aristocracy, half false and half imaginary, her lack of any security inside herself, her easy loneliness. It was no use, I was fond of telling myself, to look for the qualities of the common and wholesome morning glory in the rare and wanton Nicotiana. From the darkest earth, I would add, springs ever the sweetest rose. A green isle in the sea, if it has the sparkling fountain, needs not the solemn shrine, and so forth and so on.

I had built the lady up very high, as you see. I had commanded myself to believe that emotional literacy, a lively spirit, and personal grace, so rarely joined in American females, particularly those who live between Omaha and Denver, were all the raiment a lady needed. As I crossed the bridge, with the Forrester house now in full view, I had, all of a sudden, a disturbing fancy. There flashed into my consciousness a vivid vision of the pretty lady, seated at her dressing table, practicing in secrecy her little arts, making her famous earrings gleam with small studied turnings of her head, revealing her teeth for a moment in a brief mocking smile, and, unhappiest picture of all, rehearsing her wonderful laughter.

I stopped on the bridge and leaned against the rail and felt old and tired. Black clouds had come up, obscuring the sun, and they seemed to take the mushroom shape of atomic dust, threatening all frail and ancient satisfactions. It began to rain.

I wondered what I would say to Marian Forrester if she appeared at the door in one of her famous, familiar postures, *en déshabillé*, her hair down her back, a brush in her hand, her face raised in warm, anachronistic gaiety. I tried to remember what we had ever talked about, and could think only of the dreadful topic of grasping women and eligible men. We had never discussed any book that I could recall, and she had never mentioned music. I had another of my ungallant fancies, a vision of the lovely lady at a concert in the town, sitting with bright eye and deaf ear, displaying a new bonnet and gown, striving, less subtly than of old, to capture the attention of worried and oblivious gentlemen. I recalled with sharp clarity a gown and bonnet she had once worn, but for the life of me I could not put a face between them. I caught the twinkle of earrings, and that was all.

The latest newspaper lying open on a chair, a note stuck in a milk bottle on the back porch, are enough to indicate the pulse of a living house, but there would not even be these faint signs of today and tomorrow in Marian Forrester's house, only the fibrillation of a yesterday that had died but would not stay dead. There would be an old copy of *Ainslee's* on the floor somewhere, a glitter of glass under a broken windowpane, springs leaking from a ruptured sofa, a cobweb in a chandelier, a dusty etching of Notre Dame unevenly hung on the wall, and a stopped clock on the marble mantel above a cold fireplace. I could see the brandy bottle, too, on a stained table, wearing its cork drunkenly.

Just to the left of the front door, the big hall closet would be filled with relics of the turn of the century, the canes and guns of Captain Forrester, a crokinole board, a diavolo, a frivolous parasol, a collection of McKinley campaign buttons, a broken stereopticon, a table tennis net, a top-pled stack of blue poker chips and a scatter of playing cards, a woodburning set, and one of those large white artificial Easter eggs you put to your eye and, squinting into it, behold the light that never was, in a frosty fairyland. There would be a crack in the crusty shell, and common daylight would violate the sanctuary of the yellowed and tottery angels. You could find, in all the litter, as measuring sticks of calamity, nothing longer than an envelope firmly addressed in a gentleman's hand, a canceled check, a stern notice from the bank.

The shade of one upstairs window was pulled all the way down, and it suddenly had the effect of making the house appear to wink, as if it were about to whisper, out of the corner of its door, some piece of scandal. If I went in, I might be embarrassed by the ungainly sounds of someone moving about upstairs, after the lady had descended, sounds which she would cover by riffling nervously through a dozen frilly seasons of her faded past, trying a little shrilly to place me among the beaux in some half-remembered ballroom. I was afraid, too, that I might encounter in some dim and dusty mirror a young man frowning disapproval of an older self come to make a judgment on a poor lady not for her sake and salvation but, in some strange way, for his own. And what if she brought out, in the ruins of her famous laughter, what was left of the old disdain, and fixed me shrewdly for what I was, a frightened penitent, come to claim and take away and burn the old praises he had given her? I wouldn't succeed, of course, standing there in my unbecoming middle years, foolishly clutching reasons and arguments like a shopper's husband loaded down with bundles. She would gaily accuse me of being in love with another and, with the ghost of one of her poses of charming bewilderment, would claim a forfeit for my cruelty and insist that I sit down and have a brandy. I would have one

—oh, several—and in the face of my suspicions of the presence of a man upstairs, my surrender would compromise the delicacy of my original cool intentions, and the lost individual would be, once again as always in this house, myself. I wondered, standing there in the rain, how it would all come out.

She would get the other lady's name out of me easily enough, when the brandy began to ebb in the bottle, and being Marian Forrester, for whom jealousy was as simple as a reflex, she would be jealous of the imaginary relations of a man she could not place, with a woman she had never heard of. I would then confess my love for Madame de Vionnet, the lady of the lilacs, of Gloriani's bright Sunday garden, of the stately house in the Boulevard Malsherbes, with its cool parlor and dark medallions. I would rise no doubt to the seedy grandiloquence of which I am capable when the cognac is flowing, and I could hear her pitiless comment. "One of those women who have something to *give*, for heaven's sake!" she would say. "One of those women who save men, a female whose abandon might possibly tiptoe to the point of tousling her lover's hair, a woman who at the first alarm of a true embrace would telephone the gendarmes." "Stop it!" I heard myself shout there in the rain. "I beg you to remember it was once said of Madame de Vionnet that when she touched a thing the ugliness, God knows how, went out of it." "How sweet!" I could hear Mrs. Forrester go on. "And yet, according to you, she lost her lover, for all her charm, and to a snippet of an applecheek from New England. Did the ugliness go out of *that?* And if it did, what did the poor lady do with all the prettiness?"

As I stood there in the darkening afternoon, getting soaked, I realized sharply that in my fantasy I had actually been handing Marian Forrester stones to throw at the house in Paris, and the confusion in my viewpoint of the two

124

ladies, if up to that moment I had had a viewpoint, over-whelmed me. I figured what would happen as the shadows deepened in the Forrester house, and we drank what was left of the brandy out of ordinary tumblers—the ballons of the great days would long since have been shattered. Ban-ter would take on the sharp edge of wrangling, and in the end she would stand above me, maintaining a reedy balance, and denounce the lady of the lilacs in the flat terms she had overheard gentlemen use so long ago over their cigars and coffee in the library. I would set my glass down on the sticky arm of the chair and get up and stalk out into the hall. But though she had the last word, she would not let me have the last silence, the gesture in conclusion. She would follow me to the door. In her house, by an ancient rule, Marian Forrester always had the final moment— standing on the threshold, her face lifted, her eyes shining, her hand raised to wave good-bye. Yes, she would follow me to the door, and in the hall—I could see it so clearly I shivered there on the bridge—something wonderful would happen. With the faintest of smiles and the slightest of murmurs I would bow to my hostess, open the door and walk, not out into the rain, but into that damn closet, with its junk and clutter, smashing the Easter egg with my shoe, becoming tangled in the table tennis net, and holding in my hand, when I regained my balance, that comic parasol. Madame de Vionnet would ignore such a calamity, she would pretend not to see it, on the ground that a hostess is blind—a convention that can leave a man sitting at table with an omelet in his lap, unable to mention it, forced to go on with the conversation. But Marian would laugh, the lost laugh of the bright occasions, of the day of her shameless passion in the snow, and it would light the house like can-dles, reducing the sounds upstairs, in some miraculous way, to what they really were, the innocent creaking of the old floor boards. "What's all this about saving men?" I would cry. "Look who's talking!" And, still holding the parasol, I would kiss her on the cheek, mumble something about coming back some day, and leave, this time by the right door, finding, as I went to rejoin myself at the bridge, a poker chip in the cuff of my trousers.

It seems like a long time ago, my call on Mrs. Forrester. I have never been back. I didn't even send her a Valentine last February. But I did send a pretty book of impeccable verses to Madame de Vionnet, writing in the inscription something polite and nostalgic about "ta voix dans le Bois de Boulogne." I did this, I suppose, out of some obscure guilt sense—these things are never very clear to any man, if the truth were told. I think the mental process goes like this, though. Drinking brandy out of a water glass in the amiable company of a lady who uses spirits for anodyne and not amenity, a timid gentleman promises his subconscious to make up for it later on by taking a single malaga before *déjeuner à midi* with a fastidious lady, toying with aspic, discussing Thornton Wilder, praising the silver point in the hall on the way out, and going home to lie down, exhausted but somehow purified.

I will carry lilacs, one of these summers, to the house in the Boulevard Malesherbes, and take Madame de Vionnet to a matinee of "Louise," have a white port with her at one of the little terraces at the quietest corner of the Parc Monceau, and drop her at her door well before the bold moon has begun to wink at the modest twilight. Since, in the best Henry James tradition, I will get nothing out of this for myself, it ought to make up for something. I could do worse than spend my last summers serenely, sipping wine, clop-clopping around town, listening to good music, kissing a lady's hand at her door, going to bed early and getting a good night's sleep. A man's a fool who walks in the rain, drinks too much brandy, risks his neck floundering around in an untidy closet. Besides, if you miss the 6:15, the east-

126

bound Burlington that has a rendezvous with dusk in Sweet Water every day except Sundays and holidays, you have to wait till midnight for the next train east. A man could catch his death, dozing there in that cold and lonesome station.

The Beast in the Dingle

(With quite the deepest of bows to the master, Henry James)

HE HAD BROUGHT himself so fully in the end, poor Grantham, to accept his old friend's invitation to accompany her to an "afternoon" at "Cornerbright" that now, on the very porch of the so evident house, he could have, for his companion, in all surrender, a high, fine—there was no other word for it—twinkle. Amy Lighter perfectly took in, however, as, for his constant wonder, she always perfectly took in, the unmade, the wider gesture, the unspoken, the wonderful "oh." "You could, you know," she magnificently faced him with it, "run." He promptly matched, he even, for his, as he had once, falling into her frequent idiom, beautifully brought himself to say, money, exceeded her directness, pressing, for all answer, the bell. In the darkly shining, the unfamiliar hallway, our poor brave gentleman, a moment later, found himself, for all his giving up to it, for all his, in point of fact, "sailing" into it, reaching out, as for an arm relinquished. "Let me," it was as though she softly unwrapped it for him, "save you." It needed nothing more to bring him out of it, to bring him, indeed, whole, so to say, hog, *into* it. "Lose me!" he fairly threw it at her. "Lose me!" And managing the bravest of waves, he magnificently set his face to his prefigured predicament.

He had in the fullest degree, now, the sense of being cut adrift, and it was with all jubilant sail set that he made for, saluted, and swept past his clearly astonished hostess. He was bound for, as by, it came to him, a scanned and ordered chart, a paper signed and sealed, the woman in, it had been his little wager, brown, the woman who, he had figured it for Miss Lighter, out of the depths of a mysterious desolation, was somewhere all set to pounce upon him. "Oh, not," his companion had charmingly wailed, "in this, of all seasons, brown." He had not even turned it over. "The color," he had promptly assured her, "the certain, the unavoidable color of dilemma." His companion had, on this, fully taken in his apprehension; she had walked, as it were, around and around it. "She may, of course," Amy Lighter had finally brought out for him, "be charming. I can see her, quite clearly, in the quietest of blues. She might even, you know, beautifully listen."

"Oh, listen!" he gave it back to her. "She will tell me about her children, a boy and a girl. She will have, I quite see it, the little girl, braces on her teeth."

"Beat her, then," Amy Lighter had smiled, "to it. Talk, if you will, her head off. Give her," she had added, after a moment, "the works." Our poor sensitive gentleman could only draw, at this, quite collapsing in his chair, the longest of sighs.

If Charles Grantham's course, before the quickening wind of apprehension remembered and renewed, took him, as now, in fact, it did, straight to the high French windows giving onto the garden, if in the watchful eyes of his "lost" companion, his swift unerring progress took on the familiar shape of flight, it was all, he was afterward to protest, without the vaguest shred of plan. He found himself, nonetheless, within full view of the way out and it was but natural that our poor friend should, before casting anchor and reefing sail, ask himself whatever in all the world checked his fair run into the green harbor and the wide free beckoning sea beyond. The answer was made for him in the sudden cry, the veritable "ahoy," of the lady who, tacking dangerously to port, was at this very moment bearing down upon our drifting gentleman, her signals all aflutter, her eyes shining with the bright, the triumphant, the unmistakable claim of "salvage." In the brief space, before she, in all truth, "boarded" him, and carried off her spoils to the, he somehow found eyes to see, precise corner of his preordained doom, he perceived that she wore—that she positively waved, as from the highest point of her top gallant mast—a dress which his friend, from wherever she might be viewing his unutterable extremity, must confess, in all her exquisite honesty, to be the very brownness of brownness.

He had made through it all, Miss Lighter from her corner in little glances over her shoulder amazedly observed, no smallest gesture on behalf of his embarrassment, waving away the proffered cup and glass, neglecting to light, as, in such a crisis, it was his invariable habit so to do, the protecting tip of a cigaret. He had, on the contrary—there could be no doubt of it—wonderfully listened; he had been, precisely, all ears, so that now, the party being at last over, she fixed him, as they walked together, with the sharpest of scrutinies. "She took you all," said Amy Lighter, "in. She perfectly held you." He fixed her, in his turn. "It was not," Grantham said, "a history of childish ills. It was not, moreover, the problem of transportation to and from school." His companion jumped quite over it. "She had then, she *has*," she cried, "a predicament." "Oh," he came all out with it, "the prettiest!"

He found, a few steps farther along, the proper preface. "I was not seized upon," her friend finally brought out, "as the detached, the dispassionate outsider. I was brought in—the lady's husband, let me say, is long since dead—I was fairly retained as the authority, the specialist." Miss Lighter made for him again one of her sudden jumps. "Your years, it could only be that," she said, "your years in Europe." He turned his full gaze upon her and taking her arm, since now they had arrived before her house, he guided her sharply away from the spot on which, he clearly sensed, she was firmly set to make the indicated, the all too simple final jump. "There is," he cut the ground out from under her, "no man—no man, at any rate, in the sense in which you have made it out—there is not, in fine, another man, spare the mark, for *her*." She gave it up, on this, releasing, as in pretty surrender, her arm, but he was not to escape so easily; he was not, as he had vainly hoped, to sleep on the matter, to refer it, for shaping and shading, to his own private contemplation, for taking now full possession of our poor sensitive friend, she quite dragged him up the steps of the house and into the parlor.

The figures in the crystal, which Grantham, at last, all eagerly, shined up for her, were five: the woman in brown, as they were secretly and forever sworn, and only so, to think of her; her two small children—he had been wonderfully right about them—a girl and a boy; and two others, for whose clearer definition he turned and turned his crystal to catch the searching sparkle of all possible light. They were the manservant in the house of the woman in brown, and the manservant's wife; they were butler and housekeeper; they were, and for this our narrator gave a special twist to his crystal, natives of some state or other—the woman in brown could not be sure—of Middle Europe. Their names, well, he had forgotten, but our two conspirators for the pleasant continuance of their so frivolous game, hit, all gaily, upon Peter Quint and Miss Jessel. "Oh, oh," this accomplished, Miss Lighter began, "I quite see it all— the figure in the tower, the figure across the pond." He caught her, as who should say, in midair. "My poor dear lady," he reproached her, "our play is set, I beg you to remember, in New," he dwelt upon it, "York. In West—" he added for special emphasis, "chester."

The proof of his having in some subtle sense given himself away stood out for her in the elaborate ritual he made of producing, first from one pocket and then from another, cigaret case and match box. She took a short turn, shrewdly watching, and then, suddenly, as the little fire of his match leaped up, she made her wildest, her sublimest jump of all. "You have tested it," she cried. "You have struck it suddenly with one fingernail, and now you turn a little away from it as if to say, 'Why, it has a hollow ring.' You have found, or you think you have found, the tiniest crack in the bell." He raised against her vehemence the hand that held his cigaret and with it made a little, it seemed to her evasive, symbol in the air. "You are bringing the curtain down, you know, before the last note of our overture has died away."

Miss Lighter sat down with a gesture of her own and faced him. "Well, then," she sighed, "trot out Peter Quint. I promise to attend with the utmost gravity. I shall even, if you insist, charmingly shudder." He made three little helpless wails, one for each stamp of his cigaret in the silver tray. "Hear me," he implored his friend, "out! Write your notice *after* the play. Quit ruffling," his voice actually rose, "your programme."

Upon the house of the woman in brown then (he began) had descended, on a properly wintry day, the manservant and his wife. For the longest while, or so his informant of the afternoon had chosen to believe, nothing beyond the general run of domestic events had happened, nothing, in any case, had, to the common view, taken place. She had been unable, his informant, to make a date, to find a name, for the first disturbing fact. She had become aware, for point of beginning, only of a sense that something, as she had put it (and put it again), was "up."

With this striking toss of her thumb, as it were, toward the faint pattern on the unlighted loom, a pattern which, nonetheless, held for her now attentive listener the high promise of a darkly rewarding intricacy, our lady of the afternoon had had all of a moment a little helpless drop. He had been able, however, in no time at all, our intuitive friend, to dive into the full depths of her silence and come up with what was—as Miss Lighter (he now slyly reminded her) would say—"eating" the lady. The lady was, in simple truth, trying, without success, to fit herself into the design she was striving to weave for him. What he should have guessed all along stood out, with the discovery, straight and bright for Charles Grantham: he was to be called upon to fit the lady into her own design, he was, in short, to work the pattern quite out for her. The lady had found the one, the perfect consultant in quandary, and he could only, holding at last in his very hand the fine clear distillation of his prefigured predicament, settle back in his chair and wave her on. "Incident! Incident!" he had softly cried, and when, at this, his poor bewildered confidant could only give back a halting "What?" he had found for his abject surrender a plainer form: "Dramatize! Dramatize!" he had then implored her.

He made out, all serenely now (for the enchanted Miss Lighter), what had, after an immense amount of "backing and filling," thereupon ensued, shaping the account here and there, she was not slow to see, with the refining touch of his exquisite sensibility. There had indeed been "incidents," the beauty of which, for both our friends, lay in the fact that there was nothing in a literal and vulgar sense that could be *proved*. The very frailest supports had sustained the lady's suspicion: the fleeting indiscreet lift of childish laughter in the dead of night, a quick silence covering but not concealing the scamper of small feet along an unlighted corridor, a corridor which, the distressed lady had leaned forward to confide, might well be a mere recurring avenue of dream. There had stood out, moreover (perhaps again in fancy), the signs and symbols of a far profounder mischief: coffee grounds (or were they?) in a silver porringer, the faintest lingering perfume—the lady could swear, and yet could not—in *purlieus* innocent and sacrosanct, which she had identified (God help her, she had wailed) as a cordial rich and green and French. What all might not, the lady upon this revelation had demanded, be going forward in the dark of the night, behind closed doors, by the light of a secret candle? To which her new found friend in his turn demanded to know what she had to show for "effect." "Upon," the lady had beautifully kept up with him, "the kids? Why, just," she had given it to him all at once, "just that they are definitely *theirs*."

He had moved quickly to squeeze from the arrived moment its farthest juices. "Measure it, measure it," he had cried, and when the lady could but blankly stare, he had wonderfully brought it out in—how the long diplomatic years had sealed them up—so many words. "Are the children pale, gloomy, jumpy?" he had asked her. "Do you see them as neurotic?" Her laughter had played all about him like the spray of a fountain. "Mercy, no!" when she had found space for words, she made answer. "They are utterly, they are absolutely, perfectly charming!"

And it was upon his recital of this wide, this breathtaking, turn of the "play" that Charles Grantham, gathering up hat and gloves, bowed to Miss Lighter, and, with a charming little cry of "Intermission, intermission," made, through her reiterated pleas of "Second Act," for the exit.

II

Amy Lighter made her friend, at an early hour on the following morning, an importunate sign, a sign which, he mournfully protested, was at least as wide as a church door; she knocked, in point of shameless fact, upon his portal. The next moment, it seemed to him, he was keeping pace with her along the pathway of a nearby park. "You are holding something back," she frankly charged him. "You fled from me to keep it to yourself." He gave her only the edge of his glance. "It is what," she, nose to the trail now, ended up triumphantly, "you advised her to *do*."

"Oh, to *do*," he marked it off for a closer look. "It was

134

what, on the contrary," he went on, after a dozen steps, "I advised her *not* to do."

This time she spied it plainly and she was after it in full cry. "You told her not," she snatched it up and fairly shook it in front of him, "to fire them!" She caught herself up, for her pride, a throb in advance of her companion's dolorous "ah," which, nonetheless, afflicted Amy Lighter with the sharpest sense of his having, as it were, shielded his eyes as for a closer view of one who, taken at casual glance for friend, turns out, on closer examination, to bear only the grossest illusion of resemblance. "What then *did* you tell her not to do?" the lady wailed.

"Not to claim my judgment," her friend, all gently, said. "I gave her the discreetest look of concern, I made her the politest of murmurs, and withdrew."

Miss Lighter pouted over it, with the expression of a child whose planned and promised pleasure the sudden coming on of rain has vastly diminished. "You walked out on it," she cried. "You have left us flat." It came to him, as he turned over her charming inclusive term, that he must figure, to her eager enterprise, as one who tears up a covenant in the very moment of its being signed, and he could but assure her that if he had, indeed, withdrawn, he had withdrawn, for the simple sake of the larger view, to the post of observation. "Oh, the larger view!" his friend's impatience flared out at him. "Watch a riot from too great a height and it becomes a charming native dance." This was a game at which, in long and expert play, he had a hundred times excelled, and leaning toward her smilingly, as from his old Legation chair, he made the sure, the easy, the almost flippant movement of the designated piece. "If you cannot see the dancing for the dancers," said Charles Grantham, "a ball is nothing more than a *bagarre*."

His companion took fifty paces in silence, during which— he had the touching proof of it in the clenching and unclenching of her fingers—she mightily tugged at the monstrous foundation of such an overwhelming axiomatic generalization as would have—she had but to loosen it from the imprisoning vines of her indignation—fairly squashed him where he stood. What she at long last came up with, abandoning the unequal struggle with the too formidable boulder, was a handful of the sharpest pebbles. "You should call on her. You should talk with the children. You should see for yourself what is going on." He scooped up and cast back at her a handful of his own. "Should I draw out the servants? Should I peek into pantries? Should I prowl about below stairs, upending, God save us all, mattresses, in search of Baudelaire and Benedictine?"

There followed for Grantham upon this singular, this unique, this indubitable "outburst" the shocked recognition of his having, in the very act of rejecting her strategy, fallen plump into the middle of her tactics. He had, moreover, his high preposterous note upon the troubled air condemned him to confess, exposed, as by the wild incautious waving of regimental colors, the precise and secret line of his retreat. She was upon him in a flash. "Ah," Miss Lighter groaned, "it is the *gentleman* who is afraid! Is it that you fear our lady of the afternoon might say 'Come in, Mr. Grantham, shake hands with Peter Quint'?" He could only now, smiling in but the smallest way, come out with it. "I am afraid of them all," said Charles Grantham, and as for further explanation he had no word, she strove to figure why, as she put it to herself, he had so cooled off overnight that now, his shoes removed, he was stealing quietly away from their predicament in his stockinged feet.

He had been brought, deviously and unaware, once again before her door, on the realization of which he performed, bowing over her hand, his little ritual of adieu, but grasping him figuratively by the nape of his neck, she guided him, taking no note of his decorous protests, firmly up the steps and into her parlor. She seemed to his disconsolate eye, as she took a turn the length of the room and back again, to pick up words and put them down, but in the end she could but show him, for all her pains, her two uplifted hands, as who should say, "Where were we?" "What," after a space Grantham put to her, "do you figure me as bringing to it? Should I come bearing, would you say, Tennyson and tea? And would that make everything 'as right as a trivet or an apple pie'?" She met this, as it were, at the door, with her merriest laugh, but he watched her—so it showed for him—set it in a chair for graver study, and he had, in the face of her long look at it, not the smallest of his squirmings. He was to come back to it, this moment; he was, long afterward, to bend above it, stirring its dust, lighting, so to say, matches over it, but it produced upon Grantham, as he sat there, no larger effect than the faint ticking of the other seconds which passed before Amy Lighter spoke. "I see you," she said, "as winning the children away from them. Surely the diplomatic ribbon is more enchanting than," she rose to it, "the *sommelier's* chain."

"Oh, oh," Charles Grantham closed swiftly in and turned it back on her. "And precisely who, dear lady, of all our little group, might find it so?"

His hostess held it for the longest while, turning it over and over. "Are you trying to tell me," she finally shrewdly cried, "that the woman in brown has made it all up, just to," she had a helpless gesture, "just to set you on her mantel-piece as an adornment?" Before he could make her any answer, she was in and out of a hundred doors, hitherto unguessed at, of his long low rambling apprehension. "Do you mean," she pitched it very high, "that she presented her children as charming and enchanted with this vulgar end in view? Do you mean there are perhaps no servants whatsoever of the kind, no dark passages and perils, no figure deep and secret?" There came to him, in the train of this, the realization that in some obscure desperation she had given up all her own striking turns of phrase, she had fallen in short, into his, as if she hoped, by getting quite inside of him, to ascertain what—thus yesterday she would have put it—made him "tick." "Oh, leave me out of it," implored Charles Grantham, "out of, at least, so utter and vast a dropping off. I'm not worth that for any lady's mantelpiece. I was only pulling at a thread to see what might unravel." She had a faint brave smile. "You left the lady, in pulling at your thread, stark, raving, as my mother used to say, naked," Amy Lighter said. He had his own small smile and word for this. "Oh, well, then clothe her, while I look the other way." His companion came at it through still another door. "Do you see the *children*, then, as making it all up? Perhaps the real and only villain is some story they have read." She had sat down but now she leaped from her chair. "Perhaps *the* story!" she fairly shouted.

He stared at her in frank discomfiture for by her new and sudden twists of the *donne*, her fresh and frantic glances, first from a point too high, and then a point too low, at their so fully walked about dilemma, she had made him wonder for a moment precisely who *she* was, precisely *where*, in or out of this so special interlude, he could fit her in and make her stick. But as, not knowing what in the world else to do or say, he moved a cautious hand toward hat and gloves, she quickly found to cry "Oh, no, you don't! I know perfectly well," she went on, "what you expect me to say next. You expect me to say that perhaps the servants are, in truth, agents of a special kind, assigned to keep a sharp eye on the children, who are in reality midgets, possessed of a police record as long as your arm." When, on this, he could but wildly gape, she continued, "Can't you see I'm making fun of you? Can't you see I'm showing you how easy and how utterly idiotic it is to kick the living daylights out of our poor little predicament?" She marked off a pause in which to bite her lower lip. "Can't you see," she plunged ahead, "that it is a predicament *within* a predicament—the predicament of you and me? What happens to us if I stand by while you proceed to rearrange the figures in our story to represent nothing more challenging, for peril faced and problem shared, than the inauguration of Benjamin Harrison?"

Not for long years had Charles Grantham been so turned upon, thrust at, and struck down; not, in fact—the precise instance came back to him in a rush—since the irascible plenipotentiary of a certain Balkan country, during a period of tender international relations, completely missing a negative and wrongly translating a salient verb, had risen from his chair to heap upon the speechless American diplomat coals of fire in five separate (one could scarcely have said distinct) languages. What stood out brightly for Grantham, what positively shone for him, was that the light which struck in, from wherever it struck in, played no longer upon the quintet in the crystal, but fairly bathed in fine cold brilliance the figures of Miss Lighter and himself, who, after making narrower and narrower circles about their mutual entanglement, stood suddenly motionless upon a tiny peak of time, uncertain, unhappy, un-, which afflicted our poor gentleman with the sharpest pain of all, comfortable.

"I was not," her friend heard himself remarkably saying, out of his profound embarrassment, "I was not even *presented* to the lady in brown." To which, Amy Lighter, a chilling quality in her small laugh, at once gave answer, "One is not presented to the victim of a street accident, but one does not," she made a struck gong of it, "just sit there." Upon which, her guest, immediately arising, hat and gloves in hand, could but make his most formal bow. "I should like," Charles Grantham said, "I should wonderfully like, to do some faint far justice to," he had a moment's groping for it, "our peril, but I have lost—ah, how clearly you have set it off for my reluctant heart—I have quite utterly and forever lost," he nobly, if all forlornly, came up to it, "the name of action."

The beauty of her next remark, and the fact of its appearing to him as beautiful, quite shimmered for our miserable gentleman, quite blinded him as with the radiant proof of his having somehow through it all still clutched the hem, so to speak, of her sustaining realism; the beauty of it, I say, lay in the plain truth that there was in it precisely no beauty, in the general sense of the term, whatsoever. "Nuts *alors!*" Amy Lighter quite simply said, and taking his hand a second in advance of his placing it upon the knob of her front door, she all sublimely brought out, "I will not let *anything* go!" He had, as he stepped out upon the porch, an italic of his own. "I leave it *all*," said Charles Grantham, "where it so wonderfully belongs—in, dear lady, your charming and capable hands."

III

It chanced, if chance it could be called, that Grantham was summoned, although we should perhaps not peer too closely into this, to Washington, in the mazes of which bewildering city he spent, one way and another, the ensuing fortnight, receiving no sign from Miss Lighter, making no sign of his own. If the days of our gentleman of the chancelleries were not too arduous, his nights, nonetheless, were visited by dreams of the most outlandish and terrifying nature. He was pursued, in recurring nightmares, by two small but dimly defined figures, whose clearest and, at the same time, awfullest characteristic was the presence, on their right hands, of two extra fingers covered with a sticky substance whose faint sweet aroma identified it, beyond doubt, as some kind of candy or other; but there was, nevertheless, to the sleeper's sense, in spite of this, the strongest and most dreadful suspicion that the stuff had undergone, in some monstrous manner, a dipping into, he found the word for it when he awoke, anisette. Through the perilous passageways of his dark haunted world, our dreamer, pursued and almost overtaken by his two small familiars, had more than once escaped the clutch of their horrid hands only by dint of running up a hundred stairs, and in the last and

140

nearest chase, he had been forced to climb that tall and vulgar pile of steel which affronts the Champs de Mars.

It was with the sharpest sense of relief, then, that Charles Grantham, at the end of his appointed time in our crowded capital, found himself again upon a train. On his arrival at his destination he gave but scant time to the refreshment of his spirits and his linen; changing into a clean collar, drinking off a cup of milk, he took his hat and gloves and made straightway for the home of Amy Lighter. Beautiful upon the stairs in something white and filmy (the maid having let him in), she poised for a long fine moment before, all joyfully, she swept down to claim both his hands for hers. Once again in her familiar, her, to him, only a little less than his recent dreams, haunted parlor, he sat in his accustomed chair and stared up at her.

"Something has happened," he said, all at once. "Oh, everything has happened," said Miss Lighter. "*You* have happened." "I mean," he took it straight up, "to our predicament—to *your* predicament." "Oh, to ours, to ours," cried his friend. He shook his head. "I gave it all to you," he said, "I quite plumped it in your lap." She gave it, he thought, too easy a wave. "Is it, then, all settled?" he asked. "It's all *everything*," she said. "It blew up, and it blew over." "On its side?" he incredulously wanted to know. "Away," she said, with another wave. He was on the very edge of his chair. "I am all ears," he almost wailed.

Thereupon Amy Lighter began with "I saw her at lunch, I saw her at tea, I was *there* to dinner." Grantham's "ah" had the effect on them both of a one-note chime dropping into the silence of a deserted house. He had another of his sharp senses, this time the sharp sense that the empty house in which his note sounded and lingered was theirs, and the fear rose in him that during their little pause she, too, all vainly, listened for the coming of footsteps and the opening of the door. She made it, when she went on, as simple and brief as could be, as if she feared, measuring stress and

141

strain, his fine sensitivity would not bear the weight of too oft-repeated squeals ("Then what do you suppose? Now, see if you can guess?") or of too many liftings of the narrative to high vertiginous peaks of insufferable suspense.

She had seen the servants: they were, the lady in white said, slight, fifty, deferential, Hungarian; they neither bowed too low nor smiled too often; she had, Miss Lighter said, liked them. The children, for their part, were, indeed, charming; they were all, she gave it a special shape for his delight, of a twinkling gravity. Grantham placed at the base of this a little garland of "ahs," but his hostess rushed on. It was, she pointed out, quite beautifully simple. The Quints (our two friends had the perfect smile for this)—the Quints had always wanted, had never had, no longer could hope for, children of their own. "I mean," began Miss Lighter, but he made with one finger a small up-beat, and she let it trail away. Oh, Miss Lighter rushed along, they had cast a spell on the children, all right, they had caught them in a bright enchantment, the dark prefigured secret of which our snooping lady had, in several visits to the house, searched for in vain.

Miss Lighter rose now for one of her turns about the room. "I found," she suddenly said to her guest, "positively and precisely *nothing!*" He gave her last word a hollow echo, through which she swiftly proceeded with "What, exactly, did we expect?" She charmingly brought him into it. "What strange sign, what curious symbol, what mark of what beast, what hint of huggermugger, what exchange of secret signals?"

"My poor dear lady," was all that Charles Grantham could find for this.

"An alembic under a bed?" she went on. "Verlaine beneath a tiny pillow? A stain on a lintel? A snatch of incantation? A dilated pupil? A rose turning black? There was, I repeat, precisely nothing." She walked up to his chair. "I even spent the night," said Amy Lighter.

"You spent the night?" he cried.

"I spent the night," she said again, and opening her hands, "Nothing," she slowly murmured. "A dripping faucet, a banging shutter, a board contracting and creaking in a cooling corridor." He gave, to this alliteration, a single bringing together of the palms of his hands. "Oh," she said, mistaking him, "our curtain has not come down. There remained for me an awesome task, the task, in short, of conveying to the woman in brown, once and for all, that there had been no obscene rites involving eye of newt and toe of frog, or scrapings from old consecrated bells, or counter-clockwise circlings of a moonlit church; I had to let her know, you see, that it had all been managed, the winning of her children's hearts, in broadest daylight, by the exercise of the most natural arts."

"Such as?" her friend gently breathed.

"Such as a bright eye, an attentive ear, a skilful hand," Miss Lighter came back at once. "The Quints, for I saw them at it, could, in their proper turn and time, be both audience and players." "And where, all the while," Grantham had to ask, "was our woman in brown?" "Oh, in a book," Miss Lighter cleared it up for him, "in a state, at a party yelling for help."

Her guest paid to this, the while his frown persisted, the solicited laugh. "But why in goodness' name," Grantham at length demanded, "didn't she, as you would have had me put it to her one day, 'fire' them?" That was easy enough for his companion. "Doubts are doubts," she said, "hopes are hopes, and above all, in this so special period, servants are servants."

Charles Grantham had a long admiring gaze at Amy Lighter before he settled further in his chair to say, "However did you, in the end, tell her?" She had her jolliest laugh of the afternoon before she—the music still in her tone—replied, "By virtue, can you ever forgive me, of three martinis—this at our final luncheon together in her home—

which had quite the opposite effect of sounding a clear bell for the poor dear lady. I should have attempted the business on my first. Instead of bringing the simple light of the matter in measured colors through my polished prism, I struck a confused and even blacker dread into her tortured heart." Grantham sat forward in his chair again. "I heard myself," pursued Miss Lighter, "attempting to describe in terms of two different sets of verse, a million glittering miles apart (at least they glittered for me then), how her children had walked in brightness, not in gloom, how they had come, in short, all clean and good and normal, out of our ghoul-haunted woodland—perhaps I should have stuck to Poe, or to the simple statement."

"But what you exactly said?" Grantham prompted her.

"What I exactly said," cried Amy Lighter, "was 'You can, my very, very dear friend, rest forever assured that whereas your darlings are blissfully aware that little lambs eat ivy, they do not entertain the slightest suspicion that it rains in their hearts as it rains on the town.' And I added, my hand on hers, 'Oh, never reproach their innocent hearts with *"Qu'a tu fait de ta jennesse?"* ' "

Grantham got up from his chair to take ten slow paces around his companion's remarkable revelation before he turned to her with, "And the effect upon your bewildered hostess of your altogether enchanting obliquity was precisely what?"

"Precisely the wildest imaginable," said Miss Lighter. "She gaped at me as if I had whispered to her ear the horrid proof that all her fears were true twice over. She rose and staggered to the cord to call the servants in. The scene that then ensued was indescribable, made up of pleas, and shouts, and tears, and gettings down on knees, and pointings toward the door. Not one of us could have grasped more than a third of it. I shouted out, I think in French, above the English and Hungarian; it will wake me shrieking, from my sleep, until the day I die."

144

Grantham had enormous difficulty in finding the tip of a cigaret with his lighted match, and his perturbation was not assuaged when, all of a sudden, Miss Lighter loudly laughed. "I can see you, you poor dear," she exclaimed, "standing there in the dreadful midst of it, holding your tray of *Idylls of the King* and orange pekoe!" It gave him such a drop as brought his companion to her feet for a gentle pat of his arm. "We could hear them, as we panted in our corners," Miss Lighter went back to it, "packing and sobbing, sobbing and packing; but they have gone, I may at once cheer you with it, to a distinguished, a tranquil, a less fearful household." He tucked this, with a sigh of relief and a gesture of finality, into its safe and ordered pigeonhole.

"The children," his narrator continued, "were at school. We awaited their coming in the highest apprehension, I tapping my fingers, my hostess cracking, it quite drove me mad, her knuckles."

"And when at long, I'm sure it must have seemed to you, last, they returned and were told?" quavered Grantham. "Why," she said, "they turned upon their mother, they screamed that they hated her and would always hate her, they said that she had sent away the people they, in the whole world, most loved. Thereupon they ran screaming from the house, and our poor stricken lady, still cracking her knuckles, dissolved in tears upon my bosom." Our diplomat covered his eyes with his hands, as if a glare too strong for him had searched him out.

"We sat there for hours," Amy Lighter took up her narrative again, "while she went over it and over it and over it and over it. There seemed to be, for the appeasement of her anguish, only the tiniest grain of consolation. This resided in the consideration that she would save, by their going— the servants, of course—three hundred dollars a month. It was upon one of her numberless reiterations of this vulgar fact, this saving shred of silver lining, that from the hallway in which they had been silently hiding, our two little eavesdroppers, who had crept all stealthily into the house by the back door, came into the room. Their eyes were dry and wide, their mouths quite open. 'Gee!' they cried, and 'Gee!' again. 'Do you mean you paid them three *hun*dred *dol*lars a *month?*' And when their mother said she had indeed, they brought out a long sequence of 'gees' and 'goshes' and 'by gollies.' You perceive, of course, they were figuring in terms of toys and candy and movies and pony rides, their share of the released booty."

Miss Lighter extracted from her friend's proffered silver case a cigaret with which, after leaning toward his flame, she drew a little line in the air. "I left them, all three of them," she finished up, "joyously blubbering and babbling and hugging and kissing. So endeth," she stabbed out her cigaret in a tray, "our dark tale, not with a whimper, but, I hope, my dear friend, a proper and satisfactory bang."

"Oh, the bang was all yours," said Charles Grantham nobly. "I quite stuck my fingers in my ears." He got up, crossed to the mantelpiece, picked up, studied, and set down, a bit of Staffordshire, and turned at last to her. " 'Madam Life's a piece in bloom,' " quoted Charles Grantham, " 'Death goes dogging everywhere; She's the tenant of the room. He's the ruffian on the stair.' I think your paraphrase of another poet came so easily to your lips to close out our tale, because you see in me the very type and sign of old J. Alfred Prufrock. Oh, I have paid my court from far across the room behind a chair, but I fully believe that if and when the ruffian breaks into the place, I will be able to wag my finger in his face and say (we come to still a greater poet), 'Shake then thy gory locks at me, and watch me if I tremble.' "

His hostess ran her sensitive fingers over what he had given her, but making nothing whatever out of it, she cried, "But there has been no such awful threat to any one of us!"

"Oh, oh, and that's just it," said Grantham. "If the dreadful object is presented so that I can plainly see it, why, who's afraid?" She sensed that one more step would bring him to his peroration, and, in silence, she let him take it. "If I should strike," he made his step, "at every rustling in the undergrowth, a high heroic stance, sword drawn from cane, and cry, 'Come out, come out!' and if there should advance in answer to my challenge, on veritable tippy-toe, the most comical of beasts, about its neck a pink and satiny ribbon tied in the fluffiest of bows, what, dear lady, in the name of Heaven, would become of me?"

Well, there it was, then, his beast in the dingle, out in the open at last, scampering about, and when she could find breath, Miss Lighter, merrily laughing, put a name to it. "A kitty cat," she cried, "a kitty cat for a tiger!"

"Oh," said Grantham, "for the matter of that, a bunny rabbit."

"But isn't that precisely what *I*, cocktail in hand, challenged from the bushes?" his friend gaily demanded.

"Oh, but you *challenged* it," he threw back at her, "while I watched, from a safe and sorry distance." He brought out, before she could prevent it, an epitaph. "Here lies one who tippy-toed away from it, away from you, away from *us*."

She cut, with a tired impatient gesture, straight through to the point around which, she had the strongest sensation, he was set to make one of his wide interminable circlings. "What are you trying to make out of it all?"

Oh, he had the answer for that; it was as if he had kept it, for the longest while, shined up and ready, in his most accessible pocket. "Nothing," Charles Grantham exquisitely wailed, "nothing," and in the deep silence that followed, a clock, somewhere, far away, sprinkled the disconsolate, the incomprehensible hour upon their bowed heads. There was for our lady—oh, for our gentleman, too—the feeling of a fine literature of living breaking into flame, flaring high, falling suddenly to ashes.

"I would marry you at the drop of a hat," she threw beautifully out for him.

147

He tenderly sank, almost up to his drooping shoulders, into the subjunctive. "Would *have*," he murmured, "had *I* but had—" He let it die away and arose, almost briskly, and took and held her hand. "They are sending me away," said Charles Grantham. She got up and took his other hand, applying the most affectionate pressure, meeting his eye with the deepest possible gaze, but they both felt it, I think, as a letting go and not a holding on. "Wherever in the world are you going?" she plaintively moaned.

"Ask me that again," he said sadly smiling, "at the door," and when, after turning the knob a moment later, he bent over her hand as they heard the faint, the unmistakable sound of the curtain rustling down, she asked him her question again.

"Why, here I go," cried Charles Grantham, with a little toss of his hand and his best, his most wonderful twinkle, "round the prickly pear," and he was off, shoulders squared, head erect, down the steps and up the street without a backward glance, leaving behind him, in the doorway, still staring, a bewildered lady in whose consciousness there was, forever after, to echo and echo again, a little broken fragment of question.

II
LESS ALARMING CREATURES

A New Natural History

A Trochee (left) encountering a Spondee.

The Hopeless Quandary.

CREATURES OF THE MEADOW

Left, the Aspic on a stalk of Visiting Fireman. Center, the Throttle. Right, a Ticket in a patch of Marry-in-Haste. Below, a 99-year lease working slowly toward the surface through the years.

A pair of Martinets.

*The Hoodwink on a spray of Raga-
muffin.*

The Bodkin (left) and the Chintz.

*Flowers (left to right): Baker's Dozen, Shepherd's Pie, Sailor's
Hornpipe, Stepmother's Kiss.
Butterflies (left to right): The Admirable Crichton, the Great
Gatsby, The Magnificent Ambersons (male and female), the Be-
loved Vagabond.*

The White-faced Rage (left) and the Blind Rage.

A GROUP OF MORE OR LESS PLEASANT BIRDS

Left to right: the Apothecary, the Night Watchman, the Scout-master, and the Barred Barrister.

The Goad.

The male Wed-
lock (left) cau-
tiously approach-
ing a clump of
Devil-May-Care;
at right, the fe-
male.

A female Shriek (right) rising out of the Verbiage to attack a female Swoon.

The Lapidary in a clump of Merry-Go-Round.

A Garble with an Utter in its claws.

157

The Dudgeon.

Two widely distributed rodents: the Barefaced Lie (left) and the White Lie.

The female Snarl (left) and the male Sulk.

An Upstart rising from a clump of Johnny-Come-Lately. The small rodent (right) is a Spouse.

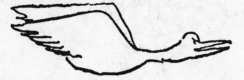

(Left to right) The Whited Sepulchre; the Misfit; the American Playboy, or Spendthrift, also sometimes called (southern U. S. A.) the Common Blackguard; a Stuffed Shirt; and (above) a Termagant.

The Femur (left) and the Metatarsal.

Top: Quench (left) and Arpeggio. Bottom: Therapy (left) and Scabbard.

The Living, or Spitting, Image
(left) and a Dead Ringer.

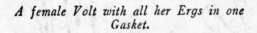

A female Volt with all her Ergs in one
Gasket.

The male and female Tryst.

The Early and the Late Riser.

A TRIO OF PREHISTORIC CREATURES

Left to right: the Thesaurus, the Stereopticon, and the Hexameter.
The tree is a Sacroiliac.

A Scone (left) and a Crumpet, peering out of the Tiffin.

The Tantamount.

A Serenade (left) about to engage in combat with a Victual.

THREE FRESH-WATER CREATURES

The Qualm *The Glib* *The Moot*

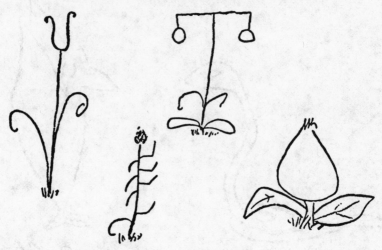

Left to right: Single Standard, False Witness, Double Jeopardy, Heartburn.

The Huff.   *A Gloat near a patch of I-Told-You-So.*

A Grope approaching, unaware, a Clinch in hiding.

The Peeve (or Pet
Peeve).

The Troth, Plighted (right) and
Unplighted.

The Common Carrier.

A GROUP OF DESTRUCTIVE INSECTS

The Coal Bin

The Door Latch

The Clock Tick (or Stop Watch)

The Tire Tool

The Window Ledge

The Ball Bat

168

Extinct Animals of Bermuda

IT HAS REMAINED for me, since nobody else apparently would bother, to look up in fossilized rocks and old Sunday newspapers the story of Bermuda's lost beasts, mammals, and other fauba, or "fauna," as it is sometimes correctly spelled. Nowadays, with only the horse and the rock-climbing gleeb still extant on the islands, people naturally do not photograph or trap as many species as they used to, and thus have time for the other activities for which the resort is famous: fan-tan, straight poker, five-card stud, and dealer's choice. Let us look at some of the more remarkable of Bermuda's extinct creatures.

Hackett's gorm, also known as the flying gouse (pl. gouses, not gice), was a tailless extravertebrate about whom only one fact has survived the centuries: he was discovered by Mr. and Mrs. W. L. Hackett and their daughter, Gloria (who married Benson Willetts). Coming unexpectedly upon a gorsey sort of furze place, the Hacketts went in and there was this gorm. It is also sometimes called Mrs. Hackett's gorm, Gloria's gorm, and Mrs. Willetts' gorm. The gorm was hunted for his skin for which, so far as I can find out, there was no conceivable use.

The waffle-crested bly, a bird with only two eyes, built his nest in hope chests with the works of dollar watches. He arrived in St. Georges each spring on the third of March at a quarter past two from Ecuador, bringing with him his mate or, failing that, somebody else's mate (for this reason he was sometimes called the mateless, or two-mated, bly). The female differed from the male in that she laid the eggs. You could cook a bly for seventeen hours and he still wouldn't be tender enough to eat.

Pritchard's olf, so called because he was first seen by a Herbert F. Pritchard, differs from other olfs, of which there were once thousands, in that he was the only one

Hackett's Gorm, the Waffle-Crested Bly, Pritchard's Olf, the Woan, or Larder Fox, the Common Thome.

Pritchard ever discovered. In his old age, Pritchard got the notion that he had not only discovered the olf, but *The New York Times*, and Allen's foot-ease. He died in 1764, protesting to the end that he was the author of Shakespeare's "Cymbeline." The olf had hoofs and two-ply, or reinforced, ears with which it was his custom to listen. In those days in Bermuda there was not a great deal to hear but it may be surmised that whatever there was, the olf heard. He was valued for his feet, out of which people made book ends, pin trays, cigarette boxes and clop-clops.

The woan, so called because he woaned, was frequently

seen, four or five hundred years ago, in larders and bureau drawers. Many people also saw him in their cups. Scarcely larger than a small blue cream pitcher, the woan had three buttons on the vest of his Sunday suit, and was given to fanning his paws at spindrift. He built his nest of gum wrappers and violin bows, which gave it roughly the shape of a gum-wrapped violin bow. The woan was capable of only one sound, a low, mournful *"goodle-goodle."* I miss him.

The common thome, so called because of his commonness—he cooled his soup with his hat and went to bed with his sox on—could only look in one direction, east. He fed on nubbins, grebe feathers, and the foxed pages of Ovid. In the winter he was cold but in the summer he was somewhat warmer. The thome's nest consisted of a moyst upended over a straband. He is either extinct or somebody took him.

I am sorry that I could not include a picture of Thompson's snab. But I couldn't. I can't do everything.

A Gallery of Real Creatures

The Gorilla.

173

The South American Eyra.

The Hoolock, or White-Browed Gibbon.

The Rock-Jumping Shrew.

The Awantibo.

The Northern Lynx.

The Lapp Owl.

The Duck-Billed Platypus.

The Tasmanian Devil.

The Gentle Lemur.

The Ethiopian Aardvark.

The Tarsier.

The Cynogale.

185

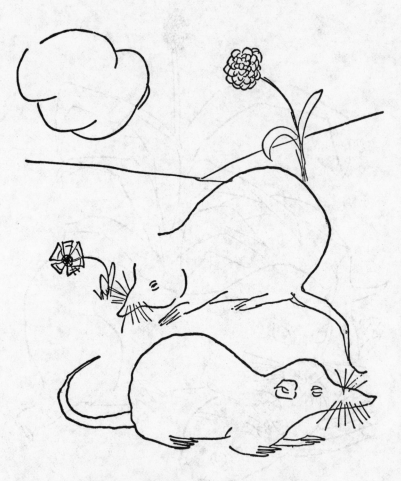

The Spider Muck-Shrew and Common Shrew.

Bosman's Potto.

The Cape-Maned Lion.

III
SOAPLAND

I—O Pioneers!

IN THE intolerable heat of last August, one Ezra Adams, of Clinton, Iowa, strode across his living room and smashed his radio with his fists, in the fond hope of silencing forever the plaintive and unendurable chatter of one of his wife's favorite afternoon programs. He was fined ten dollars for disturbing the peace, and Mrs. Adams later filed suit for divorce. I have no way of knowing how many similarly oppressed husbands may have clapped him on the back or sent him greetings and cigars, but I do know that his gesture was as futile as it was colorful. He had taken a puny sock at a tormentor of great strength, a deeply rooted American institution of towering proportions. Radio daytime serials, known to the irreverent as soap opera, dishpan drama, washboard weepers, and cliffhangers, have for years withstood an array of far more imposing attackers, headed by Dr. Louis I. Berg, a New York psychiatrist and soap opera's Enemy No. 1.

A soap opera is a kind of sandwich, whose recipe is simple enough, although it took years to compound. Between thick slices of advertising, spread twelve minutes of dialogue, add predicament, villainy, and female suffering in equal measure, throw in a dash of nobility, sprinkle with tears, season with organ music, cover with a rich announcer sauce, and serve five times a week. A soap opera may also contain a teaser ("Be sure to tune in next Monday for a special announcement"), a giveaway ("Send a box top and twenty-five cents for a gorgeous lovebird brooch"), a contest offer

("Complete this sentence and win a Bendix washer"), or a cowcatcher or hitchhike; that is, a brief commercial for another of the sponsor's products, such as a Kolynos plug on an Anacin program. It is the hope of every advertiser to habituate the housewife to an engrossing narrative whose optimum length is forever and at the same time to saturate all levels of her consciousness with the miracle of a given product, so that she will be aware of it all the days of her life and mutter its name in her sleep.

Beginning at ten-thirty in the morning and ending at six o'clock in the evening with the final organ strains of "Front Page Farrell," thirty-six soap operas are now being broadcast from New York stations Monday through Friday. Sixteen of N.B.C.'s run one after another, and C.B.S. has a procession of thirteen. Eight or ten other serials, without New York outlets, bring the nation's present total to around forty-five. The average is closer to fifty, and at one time before the war sixty-five such programs overburdened the air waves and the human ear. Soap opera has an estimated audience of twenty million listeners, mainly women in the home, for whose attention the serials' sponsors—Procter & Gamble, Lever Brothers, General Mills, General Foods, and other big manufacturers of household products—pay a total of nearly thirty-five million dollars a year. The average serial costs about eighteen thousand dollars a week, of which three thousand is for talent and fifteen thousand for network time. The latter figure includes basic time costs, plus a fifteen-per-cent cut for the advertising agency handling the show. Serials are variously owned, most of them by individuals or radio-production firms, some by sponsors, advertising agencies, networks, and local stations.

The headquarters of soap opera is now in New York and has been for a dozen years or so, but serials originated in Chicago. No other city has ever disputed Chicago's half-proud, half-sheepish claim to the invention of the story-coated advertising medium that either fascinates or distresses so many millions of people. Since soap opera is a form of merchandising rather than of art, the records of its beginnings are somewhat vague. It waited fifteen years for serious researchers, and it has had few competent critics. Almost none of the serial writers has saved his scripts. If the more than four thousand scripts (eight million words) of "Just Plain Bill," the oldest serial now on the air, had been saved, they would fill twenty trunks, and the entire wordage of soap opera to date, roughly two hundred and seventy-five million words, would fill a good-sized library.

The idea of a daytime radio program that would entertain the housewife and sell her a bill of goods at the same time was in the air in Chicago around 1928, "give or take a year," as one serial writer puts it. During the next four years, a dozen persons fiddled and tinkered with the ancient art of storytelling, trying to adapt it to the cramped limitations of radio, the young, obstreperous, and blind stepsister of entertainment. The principal figures in this experimentation were (not necessarily in the order of their appearance or importance) Mrs. Gertrude Berg, a matronly, warm-hearted woman, sincerely dedicated to the task of dramatizing Jewish family life; Mrs. Elaine Carrington, a magazine writer whose market had declined with the depression; Irna Phillips, a Dayton, Ohio, schoolteacher; Paul Rhymer, a young network executive; Frank Hummert, a smart advertising man; his young assistant, Mrs. Anne S. Ashenhurst; and Hummert's star writer, Robert D. Andrews, an able Chicago *Daily News* reporter who was destined before he quit, in 1942, to write thirty million words for radio (give or take three million). The progress of the serial pioneers was slow. There were major handicaps to overcome: the wariness of advertisers, mainly, and the thin resources of talent in the Middle West. But there was a smell of gold in Chicago, and the pioneers were indefatigable. In the field of radio narrative, continuous from day to day and week to week, they had one famous and successful nighttime model to study—"Amos 'n' Andy." It was a comedy program, of course, and the pioneers didn't want that; it had created, in George (King Fish) Stevens, a character worthy of a place in the fabulous line of rascals that extends from Sam Slick to Donald Duck, and the pioneers didn't want anything as difficult and wonderful as that; but it had proved that Americans like a continued story on the air, fifteen minutes a day, five days a week, and the pioneers did want that.

Mrs. Berg, a New York woman who did some of her early writing in Chicago, was one of the first of the pioneers to come up with a popular and durable soap opera, "The Goldbergs," which began as a nighttime show twenty years ago and took to the daytime air several years later. It ran until 1945, when Procter & Gamble, who had had it since 1937, dropped it. This incredibly long and loving saga of Molly Goldberg, her family, and her friends had become such an important part of Gertrude Berg's life that she was lost and bewildered when the serial ended its run. She herself had played Molly Goldberg and had come to identify herself completely with the character. For sixteen years, she had been known to her intimates as Molly. She found it impossible to give up the Goldbergs, and two years ago she set about putting them on the stage. In "Me and Molly," the old family reached Broadway last February, with Mrs. Berg in the leading role. She demonstrated, even to those critics who saw no art or significance in her play, why her beloved family had lasted for nearly two decades on the air. Mrs. Berg, as author and actress, had transferred to the stage the simplicity, honesty, and warm belief in common humanity that had distinguished her serial, for all its faults. "In her code of values," wrote Brooks Atkinson, "Mrs. Berg is more nearly right than Noel Coward, who is a more expert playwright; and her family makes better company than the overcivilized family J. B. Priestley introduced to us in 'The Linden Tree.'" Soap opera, last February, thus

194

won the applause, however mild, of gentlemen who up to that point had probably said of "The Goldbergs" no more than "Shut that damn thing off before I throw it out the window." Clarence L. Menser, later chief of program production for N.B.C. in Chicago, likes to feel that he had an influence on the early scripts of "The Goldbergs," but Mrs. Berg wrote them herself and the serial bore the lusty stamp of her own vitality. At about the same time, Paul Rhymer, a member of the N.B.C. staff in Chicago, began to turn out a serial called "Vic and Sade," which was eventually to become just as popular as "The Goldbergs." "Vic and Sade" began in June, 1932, and lasted more than thirteen years. A half-dozen old-timers fell by the wayside during the war years, along with "The Goldbergs" and "Vic and Sade," owing to retrenching by advertisers and other commercial factors. More than a score of the serials that were on the air in 1940 have since disappeared. "Vic and Sade," like another favorite, called "Myrt and Marge," differed from most serials in that it was basically humorous. Edgar Lee Masters, I am told, once said that the Rhymer serial presented the best American humor of its day.

Elaine Carrington, another of the pioneers, had sold many short stories to women's magazines in the nineteen-twenties. They dealt with the frustrations, heartbreaks, kindliness, nastiness, cruelties, and tragedies of the middle class. She created little men, cold women, and thankless children to the taste of various editors. Her dialogue was frequent and facile. She felt that radio might be more profitable than magazine writing in the depression years, and in 1932 she decided to take a crack at it. Her first program, "Red Adams," was put on by N.B.C., as a half-hour nighttime show, once a week. It was broadcast on a sustaining basis; that is, it had no sponsor and the network paid the production costs. Mrs. Carrington got seventy-five dollars a script. At the end of three months, the Beech-Nut Company decided to sponsor "Red Adams," as a daytime serial. They agreed to pay Mrs. Carrington a hundred dollars apiece for three scripts a week. They also wanted the title changed. Adams is the name of a Beech-Nut rival celebrated for the singing commercial that begins, "I like Chiclets candy-coated chewing gum." Mrs. Carrington changed the name to "Red Davis." In 1936, Procter & Gamble offered Mrs. Carrington twice as much money per script for five scripts a week. She accepted, and the name was changed again, this time to "Pepper Young's Family." Under the aegis of Procter & Gamble, Mrs. Carrington prospered and proliferated. "Pepper Young's Family" is still going, and she now is responsible for "Rosemary" and "When a Girl Marries," too.

Mrs. Carrington's original radio income of seventy-five dollars a week has grown to an estimated forty-five hundred. Unlike the majority of serial authors, who are merely hired to write soap operas and are known disparagingly as "dialoguers," Mrs. Carrington was wise and firm enough to retain the ownership of her literary properties. She leases broadcasting rights to the sponsors. Most dialoguers get credit on the air only once a week, but Mrs. Carrington's name is mentioned before and after each of her shows. Today she lives in a penthouse apartment in the West Fifties and a country place in Bridgehampton. Aided by only a few notes on a sheet of memo paper, she dictates her scripts into a dictaphone, usually standing. Her working hours are from 10 A.M. to 4 P.M., with time out for a long lunch. She never bothers about hearing a playback. Her secretary takes the record off the machine and transcribes the dialogue at her own office. Mrs. Carrington rarely listens to one of her soap operas—she prefers to call them daytime serials—and has never heard a broadcast of any of her colleagues' serials. She is known as the Member in Mink to the other members of the Radio Writers Guild, which she helped to found and on whose committees she has frequently served. When the Guild threatened to go out on strike in April, 1947, for recognition, reasonable rights, basic minimum pay, and a general "area of dignity," Mrs. Carrington agreed to walk out with her less prosperous co-workers. The networks finally consented to enter into negotiations with the Guild, and the strike was called off. The Guild won most of its demands from the networks but is now engaged in a grim battle with the American Association of Advertising Agencies.

No other woman writer of soap operas has written as many words as Irna Phillips, or made as much money. Miss Phillips, a brown-haired, blue-eyed native of Chicago now in her middle forties, became studio-struck after she graduated from the University of Illinois. She had originally decided to become a teacher, and after a year and a half at William Woods College, in Missouri, she was made an instructor at a normal school in Dayton, Ohio, where she specialized in storytelling and dramatics for children. In 1930, at the age of twenty-eight, she went back to Chicago on a visit and made a tour of its broadcasting studios, which still held a strong fascination for her. At WMAQ, she was mistaken for someone seeking an audition. A book was thrust into her hands and she was asked to read Eugene Field's "The Bow-Leg Boy." She was offered a job as an actress on the spot, but when she found out that she wouldn't be paid, she returned to her school in Dayton. In the days before the American Federation of Radio Artists and the Writers Guild were formed, the broadcasting industry took an easy and cynical advantage of actors and authors, many of whom, for the sake of a foothold, worked for nothing. On a later trip to Chicago, she was asked to write a script for a free half hour on one of the station's Memorial Day schedules. She did the job with considerable speed and also read it over the air. She was not paid for either her writing or her performance, but radio was now definitely in her blood and she came back to work for nothing throughout her summer vacation. She had her trunks packed for her return to Dayton in September when somebody at WGN asked her to write a family serial. When she discovered, to her surprise, that she would get fifty dollars a week for this, she unpacked and went to work. She spent the next seven months writing a serial called "Painted Dreams," and her salary rose to a hundred dollars a week. It wasn't long before the ambitious lady learned that the studio intended to peg her salary permanently at fifty-two hundred dollars a year. She instantly resigned and went to work for N.B.C. in Chicago, once again for no money at all but with the hope and determination to make a financial success of her writing and acting this time.

Miss Phillips began to write, and to act in, a serial called "Today's Children," which is still on the air. Once she got into the swing of things, she invented story lines with such facility that she could dictate six scripts a day. Soap operas involving family life were easy for her, since she was one of ten children. "Painted Dreams" had been ignored by the sponsors of soap operas for many months, but "Today's Children" was snapped up by a sponsor almost at once, and so were her subsequent ones—"Woman in White," "Right to Happiness," "The Guiding Light," "Road of Life," and "Lonely Women." All of them except "Lonely Women" are still being broadcast. Miss Phillips learned to dictate her scripts to a stenographer while sitting on the arm of a chair or pacing back and forth, acting out each part. In the beginning, she had typed her scripts, and then she sometimes ran so close to the broadcast deadline that pages were whipped out of her typewriter, mimeographed, and handed to the actors without editing. When she took up dictating, she could turn out sixty thousand words a week, or around three million a year. She learned a lesson in the tough field of radio when WGN and the Chicago *Tribune*, which owns that station, claimed the ownership of "Painted Dreams" and were sustained by the courts. She had copyrighted several of the scripts of this serial, but her claim that it was her property was disallowed, since it was held that she had been hired to write the serial and had not actually created it. This technical point has been a source of disagreement and litigation ever since soap operas began. Facing the hard commercial world, Miss Phillips developed a shrewd business personality. Her forthrightness used to frighten into numbed silence William Ramsey, of Procter & Gamble, perhaps the biggest sponsor's man in radio. They later became friends. Ramsey, some years ago, bought the rights to three of her serials—"Right to Happiness," for seventy-five thousand dollars, and "Road of Life" and "The Guiding Light," for fifty thousand dollars each, and the first two of these have since been written by others. The "Painted Dreams" case had taught Miss Phillips the art of establishing beyond legal doubt her rights to her own material. At the height of her production, in the middle nineteen-thirties, she is said to have made in some years as much as a quarter of a million dollars. The vast volume of scripts eventually became too much for her to handle by herself, and she hired a staff of assistants.

Miss Phillips' troubles were not over yet, however. In 1944, Emmons C. Carlson, promotion manager for N.B.C. in Chicago, filed suit against her for an accounting of her income on "The Guiding Light," asserting that he had helped originate the material. A lower court decided in favor of Miss Phillips, but a superior court, on appeal, reversed the decision, and Mr. Carlson received a large amount of money in a final settlement of the case. The sponsors of "The Guiding Light" at the time the suit was filed were General Mills, but they subsequently dropped the program. Ramsey grabbed the show for Procter & Gamble. In 1945, Miss Phillips returned to Northwestern, where she had studied for a year, to teach classes in the writing of radio serials on the side, and shortly afterward she moved to California. Her serials have been described as vehicles of evil and also as documents sincerely devoted to public welfare. Miss Phillips now writes only "The Guiding Light," for a thousand dollars a week.

In 1927, Frank Hummert, one of the most influential figures in the history of soap operas, became a vice-president of Blackett & Sample, a Chicago advertising agency. The Messrs. Blackett and Sample wanted to round out their firm with a topflight idea man. Hummert was one of the best-paid men in advertising. He had been chief copy writer for Lord & Thomas in New York since 1920 and was the white-haired boy of the company's president, Albert Lasker. Hummert is an extreme example of that variety of human being classified by Dr. William Herbert Sheldon as the cerebrotonic ectomorph—the thin, unmuscular type, thoughtful, sensitive, quiet to the point of shyness. He had been a reporter for a while in his younger days, but his recessive temperament was not suited to that aggressive calling. He liked to work at home, and during his seven years as a copy writer he rarely showed up at the office. He had hit on the idea of writing advertising as if it were feature news, and the idea was successful. The one thing he enjoys remembering from the old advertising days is the work he did on behalf of the Brunswick New Hall of Fame, which brought new voices to the operatic and concert stages. Blackett & Sample became Blackett-Sample-Hummert, though the new man was not a partner. The change was made because it was felt that his name would lend a certain prestige to the agency, and he began to build up a unit of his own in the company for the production of radio programs.

Sample introduced Hummert, one day, to a small, smartly dressed young woman named Anne S. Ashenhurst and later suggested to him that she might develop into a useful assistant. Hummert said he was skeptical, but he was persuaded to give the young woman a trial. Mrs. Ashenhurst was a graduate of Goucher and had been a reporter for the Baltimore *Sun* and the Paris *Herald*. She was the wife of

John Ashenhurst, a reporter she had met on the *Herald*. Her lack of radio and advertising experience was offset by what proved to be a sound understanding of how to catch and hold the ear of the woman radio listener. Like Hummert, she had an inventive mind and could make up a story line and write nimble dialogue. Hummert and Mrs. Ashenhurst figured that the largely fallow daytime air of twenty years ago could be transformed into valuable advertising time.

Things moved slowly at first. Advertisers favored evening hours, because they were convinced that radio entertainment would not be popular during the day. Most men and many women, they pointed out, worked from eight or nine in the morning until five in the afternoon. They admitted that the millions of American housewives acted as purchasing agents for the home, but they did not see how this peripatetic mass of busy women could be made into an attentive audience. The housewife was notoriously all over the place, upstairs and down, indoors and out, feeding the children, cleaning the house, hanging up clothes in the yard, talking on the phone. Hummert and his assistant decided to invent a daytime program first and then try to adjust it to the ambulant nature of the housewife. What they needed to begin with was a young writer with an indestructible typewriter, strong wrists, a story sense, and the knack of stringing out words. They came up finally with a young man beyond their dreams of stamina and fluency, who was eventually to become one of radio's legendary figures, Charles Robert Douglas Hardy Andrews.

Andrews was a reporter on the Chicago *Daily News* and editor of its *Midweek* magazine. If Hummert was a perfect ectomorph, Andrews was a superb example of what Dr. Sheldon has called the mesomorph—big, strong, sanguine, energetic, and inclined more to activity than to contemplation. He was almost six feet tall, weighed two hundred pounds, and boasted a chest measurement of forty-six inches. He dressed better than most reporters, liked to wear rings, and always carried a cane. He was once described in the now defunct *Chicagoan* as "a pen-and-ink illustration of a college-graduated heavyweight champion in a love story in a slick-paper magazine." The cathedral calm of the sound-proof office had no allure for Andrews. He could pound a typewriter in a room with a dozen other people pounding typewriters, and he could write in his bedroom while the neighbors' children bawled and radios blared. The attention of Hummert and Mrs. Ashenhurst had been called to a serial story in the *Daily News* entitled "Three Girls Lost" and signed Robert D. Andrews. Andrews had, on a bet, batted out "Three Girls Lost" in seven days, writing about fifteen thousand words every night. The friend who didn't think he could do it must have been unaware that Andrews had once won a typing contest sponsored by the Royal Type-writer Company. Andrews was later to turn out a hundred thousand words a week over a period of years, without losing a pound or whitening a hair.

The Hummert office phoned Andrews one day at the *News* and asked him to come up for a conference. Andrews' first serial for Hummert was "The Stolen Husband," and it was read over the air by an actor impersonating the au-thor, a device that was not successful, in spite of the fact that, in passages of dialogue, the actor changed his tone and accent for the various characters, in an effort to build the interest up. The audience response was not enthusiastic, so the final chapters were done with several actors. Meanwhile, Grosset & Dunlap had decided to publish "Three Girls Lost" as a novel, and the Fox Film Corporation had bought the movie rights for a new young actress named Loretta Young. Andrews' breakneck writing speed was mentioned with a trace of awe by a columnist or two. A gossip journal-ist, digging into the past of the demon writer, revealed that at the age of sixteen he had rattled off, for a hundred and fifty dollars, a hundred-thousand-word serial story for a newspaper-contest promoter and that he had been city editor of the Minneapolis *Journal* before he was twenty-one. When Andrews hit his stride and began to turn out five radio scripts a day, the author of a book called "How to Write for Radio" declared that he was not one man but three or four. "Charles Robert Douglas Hardy Andrews," said the author, "is a syndicate."

Hummert's second radio venture, "Bill the Barber," is still on the air, under the title of "Just Plain Bill." The story of the barber, his daughter, and his son-in-law and their mixups with the good people and the bad was written by Andrews for its first ten years. He was next set to writing "Ma Perkins," which *Variety* held to be "Just Plain Bill" in skirts. Bill was a widower, Ma was a widow. Each was a kindly and respected figure in a small town, and both could hold their own, in the end, with a series of spiteful women, deceitful men, powerful bankers, and tough gangsters. "Ma" was another enduring hit. Hummert and Mrs. Ashenhurst had found a formula that worked.

Hummert now proposed to General Mills that they sponsor daytime serials for children. General Mills boldly agreed to give the idea a try. Andrews wrote two of them, "Terry and Mary" and then "Skippy," the latter based on the famous cartoon character created by Percy Crosby, who was paid a thousand dollars a week for the radio rights. The kiddies loved "Skippy," and Wheaties became a household word. Andrews formed a secret society of the air for the young followers of Skippy, got up a code book based on the old "Gold Bug" cryptogram, and drew a diagram of a secret grip that he had stolen from a national fraternity. You could get this paraphernalia by sending in box tops, or facsimiles, and a signed statement from your mother that you ate Wheaties twice a day. A popular but somewhat unfortunate contest was staged, and the young winner, who got a free trip to Chicago and a week of entertainment, turned out to be a difficult brat who hated Wheaties and whose many brothers and sisters had helped him send in more facsimiles of the Wheaties box top than any other contestant.

Not all listeners were as enchanted as the children and General Mills. A Scarsdale woman told a meeting of her Parent-Teacher Association that "Skippy" was a dangerous and degrading form of entertainment, and newspapers everywhere printed her charges. A panel of psychologists hired by Hummert pooh-poohed the Scarsdale lady's fears and said that the loud and rambunctious adventure serial was a good thing for America's over-cloistered young. A kidnapping sequence in the story aroused criticism. Although it was written long after the Lindbergh case, indignant ministers and editorial writers denounced it as an attempt to profit by exploiting a tragedy. A new story line was instantly devised, and Andrews wrote twenty-five scripts in five days to catch up. Percy Crosby, who had been moaning and wringing his hands over his mild little character's lost innocence, breathed easier. But "Skippy" was not to last much longer. General Mills were disturbed when they heard that Andrews was not only a newspaperman but a writer of books; the chances were they had a drinking fellow and a bohemian on their hands, and this might get to the listening women and distress them. To forestall old wives' tales and young mothers' fears, Andrews had himself photographed eating Wheaties and sliced bananas with the child actors of "Skippy." He swears today that these actors once gave him a cocktail shaker and two bottles of Scotch for Christmas. The excitement over "Skippy" didn't last long, but it at least had the effect of diverting the public's mind from serials for adults.

By the middle thirties, most of the pioneers had set up shop in New York. Clarence L. Menser came along a little later, and a year ago he became famous as the vice-president of N.B.C. who cut Fred Allen off the air, a gesture as foolhardy as an attempt by your nephew to strike out Ted Williams. Chicago was no longer the center of daytime radio serials but just another outlet. Hummert and Mrs. Ashenhurst formed a production company of their own in New York. In 1935, they were married. They have prospered and are now the producers of thirteen soap operas and six half-hour shows, five of them musicals and the sixth a mystery, "Mr. Keen, Tracer of Lost Persons," for which Mrs. Hummert selected a beautifully apt theme song, Noel Coward's "Some Day I'll Find You." The Hummert firm is the largest and most successful concern of its kind. The Hummerts choose the casts for all their shows. Men known as supervisors or script editors act as liaison officers between the Hummerts and their staff of writers, who are occasionally shifted from one serial to another when they show signs of running dry or muttering to themselves after too long a stretch with the same group of characters. One writer, Marie Baumer, has worked on eight serials in the last ten years, and another, Helen Walpole, has dialogued six since 1939.

The Hummerts have employed two hundred serial writers since they went into radio. They have fourteen on the staff now, and they can call on a reservoir of thirty others. The Hummerts think up their own ideas for serials. When they do, Mrs. Hummert writes an outline of the plot, suggesting incidents for the first three months or so and indicating key dialogue. Copies of this are given to five writers, and the one whose sample script seems to hit it off best is picked to do the serial. He is given an opportunity to write at least five scripts in advance, and from then on is supposed to stay that far ahead. When Ned Calmer, now a news commentator, was writing a Hummert serial, "Back Stage Wife," he built up a backlog of nineteen scripts so that he could take a trip to Mexico. When the story line was suddenly changed, for some reason or other, he had to cancel his vacation and start all over again. For the last year, Mrs. Hummert has delegated some of her work, but before that she personally kept the story lines of all the serials going by turning out synopses for her writers.

Let us now turn back to Robert Andrews and see what became of him, in order to complete this survey of pioneers' progress. Until 1932, when he came to New York, Andrews wrote radio scripts at night and worked on the Chicago *Daily News* during the day, and he somehow found time to turn out a novel, "Windfall," which was made into the movie called "If I Had a Million." When he got to New York, he wrote radio scripts in a penthouse on Central Park West, typing from noon to midnight seven days a week. He smoked as many as five packs of cigarettes a day and drank forty cups of coffee. For a long period, he kept seven radio shows going, and he rarely had fewer than five, most of them soap operas. He has had a hand in more than twenty-five programs during his radio career. He averaged well over a hundred thousand words a week for years, and his sprint record was thirty-two thousand in twenty hours. In 1935, he decided he needed an outside interest, and he began an intensive research into various periods of history, with the idea of writing a dozen or so novels. One dealing with Daniel Defoe was published in 1945 and one dealing with the era of Alexander Hamilton will be out next year. One morning in April, 1936, Andrews decided to have a fling at writing for the movies, and the next day he was on a train for Hollywood and Warner Brothers. He wrote twenty-seven radio scripts on the train. For a while, he continued to do six serials, and he did four for several years after he got to Hollywood, now working at the studio during the day and batting out the radio scripts at night. He kept at "Bill" until October, 1942. This was his last radio stint. He has written, alone or in collaboration, forty-five movies in the last twelve years, including "Bataan," "The Cross of Lorraine," and "Salute to the Marines." It will come as no surprise to you that he has recently found time to write a novel about his old occupation, soap opera.

Andrews answered a brief telegraphic query of mine some weeks ago with a letter, no doubt written between teatime and the cocktail hour, that ran to eight thousand words. In it, he advanced an astounding explanation for giving up the writing of radio scripts. "I just got tired," he said. Why, Charles Robert Douglas Hardy Andrews!

II—Ivorytown, Rinsoville, Anacinburg, and Crisco Corners

THE LAST time I checked up on the locales of the thirty-six radio daytime serials, better known as soap operas, that are broadcast from New York five days a week to a mass audience of twenty million listeners, the score was Small Towns 24, Big Cities 12. I say "score" advisedly, for the heavy predominance of small towns in Soapland is a contrived and often-emphasized victory for good, clean little communities over cold, cruel metropolitan centers. Thus, daytime radio perpetuates the ancient American myth of the small town, idealized in novels, comedies, and melodramas at the turn of the century and before, supported by Thornton Wilder in "Our Town," and undisturbed by the scandalous revelations of such irreverent gossips as Sherwood Anderson and Edgar Lee Masters. Soapland shares with the United States at least five actual cities—New York, Chicago, Boston, Washington, and Los Angeles—but its small towns are as misty and unreal as Brigadoon. They have such names as Hartville, Dickston, Simpsonville, Three Oaks, Great Falls, Beauregard, Elmwood, Oakdale, Rushville Center, and Homeville. "Our Gal Sunday" is set in Virginia, but no states are mentioned for the towns in the other serials.

The differences between small-town people and big-city people are exaggerated and oversimplified by most serial writers in the black-and-white tradition of Horatio Alger. It seems to be a basic concept of soap-opera authors that, for the benefit of the listening housewives, distinctions between good and evil can be most easily made in the old-fashioned terms of the moral town and the immoral city. Small-town Soaplanders occasionally visit, or flee to, one of the big cities, particularly New York, out of some desperation or other, and they are usually warned against this foolhardy venture by a sounder and stabler character in tones that remind me of such dramas of a simpler era as "York State Folks" and "The County Chairman." A few months ago, Starr, a young, selfish, and restless wife who ornamented "Ma Perkins" with her frets and tears, ran away to New York. She promptly met two typical Soapland New Yorkers, a young woman who talked like Miss Duffy in "Duffy's Tavern" and an underworld gent with a rough exterior and a heart of gold. This type of semi-gangster threads his way in and out of various serials, using such expressions as "on the up-and-up," "baby doll," and "lovey-dovey stuff," and, thanks to some of the women writers, the fellow has become a kind of extension of Editha's burglar. In "Rosemary," a conniving chap named Lefty actually conceived a fond and pure devotion for a little girl. But the Soaplanders do not have to come to New York, as we shall see, to become entangled with the Misses Duffy and the Lefties and all the rest.

A soap opera deals with the plights and problems brought about in the lives of its permanent principal characters by the advent and interference of one group of individuals after another. Thus, a soap opera is an endless sequence of narratives whose only cohesive element is the eternal presence of its bedeviled and beleaguered principal characters. A narrative, or story sequence, may run from eight weeks to several months. The ending of one plot is always hooked up with the beginning of the next, but the connection is unimportant and soon forgotten. Almost all the villains in the small-town daytime serials are émigrés from the cities—gangsters, white-collar criminals, designing women, unnatural mothers, cold wives, and selfish, ruthless, and just plain cussed rich men. They always come up against a shrewdness that outwits them or destroys them, or a kindness that wins them over to the good way of life.

The fact that there are only two or three citizens for the villains to get entangled with reduces the small town to a wood-and-canvas set with painted doors and windows. Many a soap town appears to have no policemen, mailmen, milkmen, storekeepers, lawyers, ministers, or even neighbors. The people live their continuously troubled lives within a socio-economic structure that only faintly resembles our own. Since the problems of the characters are predominantly personal, emotional, and private, affecting the activities of only five or six persons at a time, the basic setting of soap opera is the living room. But even the living room lacks the pulse of life; rarely are heard the ticking of clocks, the tinkling of glasses, the squeaking of chairs, or the creaking of floor boards. Now and then, the listener does hear *about* a hospital, a courtroom, a confectionery, a drugstore, a bank, or a hotel in the town, or a roadhouse or a large, gloomy estate outside the town limits, but in most small-town serials there are no signs or sounds of community life—no footsteps of passers-by, no traffic noises, no shouting of children, no barking of dogs, no calling of friend to friend, no newsboys to plump the evening papers against front doors. A few writers try from time to time to animate the streets of these silent towns, but in general Ivorytown and Rinsoville and Anacinburg are dead. This isolation of soap-opera characters was brought about by the interminability of daytime serials, some of which began as authentic stories of small-town life. The inventiveness of writers flagged under the strain of devising long plot sequences, one after another, year after year, involving a given family with the neighbors and other townsfolk. Furthermore, the producers and sponsors of soap opera and the alert advertising agencies set up a clamor for bigger and wider action and excitement. The original soap-opera characters are now often nothing more than shadowy and unnecessary *ficelles*, awkwardly held on to as confidants or advisers of the principal figures in the melodramas that come and go in chaotic regularity. Even "Mrs. Wiggs of the Cabbage Patch" followed the formula and degenerated into radio melodrama after six months. Its heroine spent her time dodging the bullets of gangsters and the tricks and traps of other scoundrels from the city.

If the towns in Soapland are not developed as realistic communities, neither are the characters—except in rare instances—developed as authentic human beings. The reason for this is that the listening housewives are believed to be interested only in problems similar to their own, and it is one of the basic tenets of soap opera that the women characters who solve these problems must be flawless projections of the housewife's ideal woman. It is assumed that the housewife identifies herself with the characters who are most put-upon, most noble, most righteous, and hence most dehumanized. Proceeding on this theory, serial producers oppose the creation of any three-dimensional character who shows signs of rising above this strange standard. Advertising agencies claim—and the record would appear to sustain them—that a realistically written leading woman would cause the audience rating of the show to drop. The housewife is also believed to be against humor in the daytime— in spite of the long success of the truly funny "Vic and Sade"—on the ground that comedy would interfere with her desire to lose herself in the trials and tribulations, the emotional agonies and soul searchings, of the good women in the serials. The only serial that deliberately goes in for comedy now is "Lorenzo Jones," whose narrator describes it as "a story with more smiles than tears." The lack of humor in most of the others is so complete as to reach the proportions of a miracle of craftsmanship.

The principal complaint of audience mail in the early days of the serials was that they moved so swiftly they were hard to follow. Surveys showed that the housewife listens, on an average, to not more than half the broadcasts of any given serial. Plot recapitulation, familiarly called "recap," was devised to slow down the progress of serials. "We told them what was going to happen, we told them it was happening, and we told them it had happened," says Robert D. Andrews. The listeners continued to complain, and action was retarded still further, with the result that time in a soap opera is now an amazing technique of slow motion. Compared to the swift flow of time in the real world, it is a glacier movement. It took one male character in a soap opera three days to get an answer to the simple question "Where have you been?" If, in "When a Girl Marries," you missed an automobile accident that occurred on a Monday broadcast, you could pick it up the following Thursday and find the leading woman character still unconscious and her husband still moaning over her beside the wrecked car. In one sequence of "Just Plain Bill," the barber of Hartville said, "It doesn't seem possible to me that Ralph Wilde arrived here only yesterday." It didn't seem possible to me, either, since Ralph Wilde had arrived, as mortal time goes, thirteen days before. Bill recently required four days to shave a man in the living room of the man's house. A basin of hot water Bill had placed on a table Monday (our time) was still hot on Thursday, when his customer stopped talking and the barber went to work.

Soap-opera time, by an easy miracle, always manages to coincide with mortal time in the case of holidays. Memorial Day in Hartville, for example, is Memorial Day in New York. Every year, on that day, Bill Davidson, Hartville's leading citizen, makes the Memorial Day address, a simple, cagey arrangement of words in praise of God and the Republic. One serial writer tells me that the word "republic" has been slyly suggested as preferable to "democracy," apparently because "democracy" has become a provocative, flaming torch of a word in our time. For Soapland, you see, is a peaceful world, a political and economic Utopia, free of international unrest, the menace of fission, the threat of inflation, depression, general unemployment, the infiltration of Communists, and the problems of racism. Except for a maid or two, there are no colored people in the World of Soap. Papa David, in "Life Can Be Beautiful," is the only Jew I have run into on the daytime air since "The Goldbergs" was discontinued. (Procter & Gamble sponsored "The Goldbergs" for many years, and the race question did not enter into its termination.) Lynn Stone and Addy Richton, who have written several serials, were once told by a sponsor's representative to eliminate a Jewish woman from one of their shows. "We don't want to antagonize the anti-Semites," the gentleman casually explained. They had to take out the character.

Proponents of soap opera are given to protesting, a little vehemently, that serials have always promoted in their dialogue an understanding of public welfare, child psychology, and modern psychiatric knowledge in general, and that this kind of writing is supervised by experts in the various fields. There was an effective lecture on the dangers of reckless driving in "The Guiding Light" one day, and I have heard a few shreds of psychiatric talk in a dozen serials, but I have found no instances of sustained instruction and uplift in soap opera. During the war, it is true, at the behest of government agencies, many writers worked into their serials incidents and dialogue of a worthy sociological 'nature. Charles Jackson, the author of "The Lost Weekend," who wrote a serial called "Sweet River" for more than two years, brought to his mythical town factory workers from the outside and presented the case for tolerance and good will. Social consciousness practically disappeared from serials with the war's end, and Soapland is back to normalcy. Three weeks after Charles Luckman's food-conservation committee had begun its campaign, Ma Perkins invited a young man who had not been satisfied by a heavy breakfast to "fill up on toast and jam." It was just a slip. The script had been written before the committee started work. But, after all, there is plenty of bread in Soapland, which never has scarcity of production.

A study of the social stratification of Soapland, if I may use so elegant a term, reveals about half a dozen highly specialized groups. There are the important homely philosophers, male and female. This stratum runs through "Just Plain Bill," "Ma Perkins," "David Harum," "Life Can Be Beautiful," and "Editor's Daughter," a soap opera not heard in the East but extremely popular in the Middle West, whose male protagonist enunciates a gem of friendly wisdom at the end of every program. ("Life Can Be Beautiful," by the way, is known to the trade as "Elsie Beebe." You figure it out. I had to.) Then, there are the Cinderellas, the beautiful or talented young women of lowly estate who have married or are about to marry into social circles far above those of their hard-working and usually illiterate mothers. (Their fathers, as a rule, are happily dead.) On this wide level are Nana, daughter of Hamburger Katie; Laurel, daughter of Stella Dallas; and my special pet, Sunday, of "Our Gal Sunday," who started life as a foundling dumped in the laps of two old Western miners and is now the proud and badgered wife of Lord Henry Brinthrop, "England's wealthiest and handsomest young nobleman." Christopher Morley's famous Cinderella, Kitty Foyle, also lived in Soapland for some years. Mr. Morley was charmed by the actors and actresses who played in "Kitty," but he says that he never quite gathered what the radio prolongation of the story was about. Kitty eventually packed up and moved out of Soapland. The late Laurette Taylor received many offers for the serial rights to "Peg o' My Heart," which was written by her husband, J. Hartley Manners, but it is said that she rejected them all with the agonized cry "Oh, God, no! Not that!" On a special and very broad social stratum of Soapland live scores of doctors and nurses. You find scarcely anyone else in "Woman in White," "Road of Life," and "Joyce Jordan, M.D." The heroes of "Young Dr. Malone," "Big Sister," and "Young Widder Brown" are doctors, and medical men flit in and out of all other serials. The predominance of doctors may be accounted for by the fact that radio surveys have frequently disclosed that the practice of medicine is at the top of the list of professions popular with the American housewife.

A fourth and highly important group, since it dominates large areas of Soapland, consists of young women, single, widowed, or divorced, whose purpose in life seems to be to avoid marriage by straight-arming their suitors year after year on one pretext or another. Among the most distinguished members of this group are Joyce Jordan, who is a doctor when she gets around to it; Helen Trent, a dress designer; Ellen Brown, who runs a tearoom; Ruth Wayne, a nurse; and a number of actresses and secretaries. For some years, Portia, the woman lawyer of "Portia Faces Life," belonged to this class, but several years ago she married Walter Manning, a journalist, and became an eminent figure in perhaps the most important group of all, the devoted and long-suffering wives whose marriages have, every hour of their lives, the immediacy of a toothache and the urgency of a telegram. The husbands of these women spend most of their time trying in vain to keep their brave, high-minded wives out of one plot entanglement after another.

All men in Soapland must be able to drop whatever they are doing and hurry to this living room or that at the plaint or command of a feminine voice on the phone. Bill Davidson's one-chair barbershop has not had a dozen customers in a dozen years, since the exigencies of his life keep him out of the shop most of every day. In eight months, by my official count, Kerry Donovan visited his law office only three times. He has no partners or assistants, but, like Bill, he somehow prospers. The rich men, bad and good, who descend on the small town for plot's sake never define the industries they leave behind them in New York or Chicago for months at a time. Their businesses miraculously run without the exertion of control or the need for contact. Now and then, a newspaper publisher, a factory owner, or a superintendent of schools, usually up to no good, appears briefly on the Soapland scene, but mayors, governors, and the like are almost never heard of. "The Story of Mary Marlin," just to be different, had a President of the United States, but, just to be the same, he was made heavily dependent on the intuitive political vision of his aged mother, who, in 1943, remained alive to baffle the doctors and preserve, by guiding her son's policies, the security of the Republic.

The people of Soapland, as Rudolf Arnheim, professor of psychology at Sarah Lawrence, has pointed out, consist of three moral types: the good, the bad, and the weak. Good women dominate most soap operas. They are conventional figures, turned out of a simple mold. Their invariably strong character, high fortitude, and unfailing capability must have been originally intended to present them as women of a warm, dedicated selflessness, but they emerge, instead, as ladies of frigid aggressiveness. The writers are not to blame for this metamorphosis, for they are hampered by several formidable inhibitions, including what is officially called "daytime morality," the strangest phenomenon in a world of phenomena. The good people, both men and women, cannot smoke cigarettes or touch alcoholic beverages, even beer or sherry. In a moment of tragedy or emotional tension, the good people turn to tea or coffee, iced or hot. It has been estimated that the three chief characters of "Just Plain Bill" have consumed several hundred gallons of iced tea since this program began, in 1932. Furthermore, the good women must float like maiden schoolteachers above what

216

Evangeline Adams used to call "the slime"; that is, the passionate expression of sexual love. The ban against spirituous and amorous indulgence came into sharp focus once in "Just Plain Bill" when the plot called for one Graham Steele to be caught in a posture of apparent intimacy with the virtuous Nancy Donovan. He had carelessly upset a glass of iced tea into the lady's lap and was kneeling and dabbing at her dress with his handkerchief—a compromising situation indeed in Soapland—when her jealous husband arrived and suspected the worst.

The paternalistic Procter & Gamble, famous for their managerial policy of "We're just one big family of good, clean folks," do not permit the smoking of cigarettes at their plants during working hours except in the case of executives with private offices. This may have brought about the anti-cigarette phase of daytime morality, but I can adduce no evidence to support the theory. The supervision of Procter & Gamble's eleven soap operas is in the tolerant hands of the quiet, amiable William Ramsey, who smokes Marlboros. In daytime radio, the cigarette has come to be a sign and stigma of evil that ranks with the mark of the cloven hoof, the scarlet letter, and the brand of the fleur-de-lis. The married woman who smokes a cigarette proclaims herself a bad wife or an unnatural mother or an adventuress. The male cigarette smoker is either a gangster or a cold, calculating white-collar criminal. The good men may smoke pipes or cigars. A man who called on the hero of "Young Dr. Malone" brought him some excellent pipe tobacco and announced that he himself would smoke a fine cigar. As if to take the edge off this suggestion of wanton sensual abandon, a good woman hastily said to the caller, "Don't you want a nice, cold glass of ice water?" "Splendid!" cried the gentleman. "How many cubes?" she asked. "Two, thank you," said the visitor, and the virtue of the household was reëstablished.

Clean-living, letter-writing busybodies are unquestionably to blame for prohibition in Soapland. When Mrs. Elaine Carrington, the author of "Pepper Young's Family," had somebody serve beer on that serial one hot afternoon, she received twenty indignant complaints. It wasn't many, when you consider that "Pepper" has six million listeners, but it was enough. The latest violation of radio's liquor law I know of occurred in "Ma Perkins," when a bad woman was given a double Scotch-and-soda to loosen her tongue. Letters of protest flooded in. The bad people and the weak people are known to drink and to smoke cigarettes, but their vices in this regard are almost always just talked about, with proper disapproval, and not often actually depicted.

As for the sexual aspect of daytime morality, a man who had a lot to do with serials in the nineteen-thirties assures me that at that time there were "hot clinches" burning up and down the daytime dial. If this is so, there has been a profound cooling off, for my persistent eavesdropping has detected nothing but coy and impregnable chastity in the good women, nobly abetted by a kind of Freudian censor who knocks on doors or rings phones at crucial moments. Young Widder Brown has kept a doctor dangling for years without benefit of her embraces, on the ground that it would upset her children if she married again. Helen Trent, who found that she could recapture romance after the age of thirty-five, has been tantalizing a series of suitors since 1933. (She would be going on fifty if she were a mortal, but, owing to the molasses flow of soap-opera time, she is not yet forty.) Helen is soap opera's No. 1 tormentor of men, all in the virtuous name of indecision, provoked and prolonged by plot device. One suitor said to her, "After all, you have never been in my arms"—as daring an advance as any of her dejected swains has ever made in my presence. Helen thereupon went into a frosty routine about marriage being a working partnership, mental stimulation, and, last and least, "emotional understanding." "Emotional understanding," a term I have heard on serials several times, seems to be the official circumlocution for the awful word "sex." The chill Miss Trent has her men frustrated to a point at which a mortal male would smack her little mouth, so smooth, so firm, so free of nicotine, alcohol, and emotion. Suitors in Soapland are usually weak, and Helen's frustration of them is aimed to gratify the listening housewives, brought up in the great American tradition of female domination. Snivelled one of the cold lady's suitors, "I'm not strong, incorruptible, stalwart. I'm weak." Helen purred that she would help him find himself. The weak men continually confess their weakness to the good women, who usually manage to turn them into stable citizens by some vague and soapy magic. The weak men and the good men often confess to one another their dependence on the good women. In one serial, a weak man said to a good man, "My strength is in Irma now." To which the good man replied, "As mine is in Joan, Steve." As this exchange indicates, it is not always easy to tell the weak from the good, but on the whole the weak men are sadder but less stuffy than the good men. The bad men, God save us all, are likely to be the most endurable of the males in Soapland.

The people of Soapland are subject to a set of special ills. Temporary blindness, preceded by dizzy spells and headaches, is a common affliction of Soapland people. The condition usually clears up in six or eight weeks, but once in a while it develops into brain tumor and the patient dies. One script writer, apparently forgetting that General Mills was the sponsor of his serial, had one of his women characters go temporarily blind because of an allergy to chocolate cake. There was hell to pay, and the writer had to make the doctor in charge of the patient hastily change his diagnosis. Amnesia strikes almost as often in Soapland as the common cold in our world. There have been as many as eight or nine amnesia cases on the air at one time. The hero of "Rosemary" stumbled around in a daze for months last year. When he regained his memory, he found that in his wanderings he had been lucky enough to marry a true-blue sweetie. The third major disease is paralysis of the legs. This scourge usually attacks the good males. Like mysterious blindness, loss of the use of the legs may be either temporary or permanent. The hero of "Life Can Be Beautiful" was confined to a wheel chair until his death last March, but young Dr. Malone, who was stricken with paralysis a year ago, is up and around again. I came upon only one crippled villain in 1947: Spencer Hart rolled through a three-month sequence of "Just Plain Bill" in a wheel chair. When their men are stricken, the good women become nobler than ever. A disabled hero is likely to lament his fate and indulge in self-pity now and then, but his wife or sweetheart never complains. She is capable of twice as much work, sacrifice, fortitude, endurance, ingenuity, and love as before. Joyce Jordan, M.D., had no interest in a certain male until he lost the use of both legs and took to a wheel chair. Then love began to bloom in her heart. The man in the wheel chair has come to be the standard Soapland symbol of the American male's subordination to the female and his dependence on her greater strength of heart and soul.

The children of the soap towns are subject to pneumonia and strange fevers, during which their temperatures run to 105 or 106. Several youngsters are killed every year in automobile accidents or die of mysterious illnesses. Infantile paralysis and cancer are never mentioned in serials, but Starr, the fretful and errant wife in "Ma Perkins," died of tuberculosis in March as punishment for her sins. There are a number of Soapland ailments that are never named or are vaguely identified by the doctors as "island fever" or "mountain rash." A variety of special maladies affect the glands in curious ways. At least three Ivorytown and Rinsoville doctors are baffled for several months every year by strange seizures and unique symptoms.

Next to physical ills, the commonest misfortune in the

world of soap is false accusation of murder. At least two-thirds of the good male characters have been indicted and tried for murder since soap opera began. Last year, the heroes of "Lone Journey," "Our Gal Sunday," and "Young Dr. Malone" all went through this ordeal. They were acquitted, as the good men always are. There were also murder trials involving subsidiary characters in "Portia Faces Life," "Right to Happiness," and "Life Can Be Beautiful." I had not listened to "Happiness" for several months when I tuned in one day just in time to hear one character say, "Do you know Mrs. Cramer?", and another reply, "Yes, we met on the day of the shooting." Dr. Jerry Malone, by the way, won my True Christian Martyr Award for 1947 by being tried for murder and confined to a wheel chair at the same time. In March of this year, the poor fellow came full Soapland circle by suffering an attack of amnesia.

The most awkward cog in the machinery of serial technique is the solemn, glib narrator. The more ingenious writers cut his intrusions down to a minimum, but the less skillful craftsmen lean upon him heavily. Most soap-opera broadcasts begin with the narrator's "lead-in," or summary of what has gone before, and end with his brief résumé of the situation and a few speculations on what may happen the following day. The voice of the narrator also breaks in from time to time to tell the listeners what the actors are doing, where they are going, where they have been, what they are thinking or planning, and, on the worst programs, what manner of men and women they are: "So the restless, intolerant, unneighborly Norma, left alone by the friendly, forgiving, but puzzled Joseph . . ."

Another clumsy expedient of soap opera is the soliloquy. The people of Soapland are constantly talking to themselves. I timed one lady's chat with herself in "Woman in White" at five minutes. The soap people also think aloud a great deal of the time, and this usually is distinguished from straight soliloquy by being spoken into a filter, a device that lends a hollow, resonant tone to the mental voice of the thinker.

In many soap operas, a permanent question is either implied or actually posed every day by the serial narrators. These questions are usually expressed in terms of doubt, indecision, or inner struggle. Which is more important, a woman's heart or a mother's duty? Could a woman be happy with a man fifteen years older than herself? Should a mother tell her daughter that the father of the rich man she loves ruined the fortunes of the daughter's father? Should a mother tell her son that his father, long believed dead, is alive, well, and a criminal? Can a good, clean Iowa girl find happiness as the wife of New York's most famous matinée idol? Can a beautiful young stepmother, can a widow with two children, can a restless woman married to a preoccupied doctor, can a mountain girl in love with a millionaire, can a woman married to a hopeless cripple, can a girl who married an amnesia case—can they find soap-opera happiness and the good, soap-opera way of life? No, they can't—not, at least, in your time and mine. The characters in Soapland and their unsolvable perplexities will be marking time on the air long after you and I are gone, for we must grow old and die, whereas the people of Soapland have a magic immunity to age, like Peter Pan and the Katzenjammer Kids. When you and I are in Heaven with the angels, the troubled people of Ivorytown, Rinsoville, Anacinburg, and Crisco Corners, forever young or forever middle-aged, will still be up to their ears in inner struggle, soul searching, and everlasting frustration.

III—Sculptors in Ivory

SINCE 1942, when that Paul Bunyan of prose, Charles Robert Douglas Hardy Andrews, quit writing "Just Plain Bill," after batting out twenty-six hundred scripts in ten years, or enough words to fill sixty long novels, seven women and two men have taken turns at "dialoguing" this oldest of the thirty-six daytime serials now on the New York air. "Bill," as it is known to its friends—radio wags and cynics call it "Just Plain Bull"—celebrated its sixteenth anniversary in September, 1948, and it is still rolling steadily along, with no end in sight. The durability of this grandfather of soap opera warrants our listening for a while to the ticking of its ancient mechanism.

A phrase of James Russell Lowell's could be twisted to apply to the writing that goes into "Bill" and most other serials: "the frank prose of undissembling noon." We will come later on to a handful of writers who have tried to throw an evening light over Soapland, but its sun is usually directly overhead, casting a steady and monotonous glare, unrelieved by the subtlety of shadows. Examples of the text of "Bill" would be, as the critics say, unrewarding. Its nature can be indicated well enough by a description of its three principal characters, who have been in perpetual motion since 1932, and by a summary of one plot sequence they were involved in.

"Just Plain Bill" is a typical soap opera except for one major point—its protagonist is a man. Bill is a barber in a town called Hartville. The serial has, however, a perma-

223

nent heroine in Nancy, his daughter, whose happy but frantic marriage is Bill's chief interest in life and the target of nearly all the serial's menaces. Most of the time, Bill is merely sword and shield in defense of his daughter's happiness, and the constancy of his concern and the nature of his solicitude are more like a mother's than a father's. Nancy's husband, Kerry Donovan, serves to thicken the plots with his obstinacy, jealousy, and suspicion, but at the end of every episode he invariably perceives, with Bill's guidance, the virtue and loyalty of his wife and the purity of her usually cloudy motives.

I happened to tune in on "Bill" one afternoon, quite a long while ago, just in time to catch the last episode, or chapter, of a story sequence involving a villainous old lady named Henrietta Blackstone, who had apparently been leading a wicked and spidery existence in a gloomy mansion just outside the town of Hartville. I gathered from the final broadcast of this particular plot that for two months or more Henrietta had been the central figure in a dark pattern of double-dealing and gunfire during which one or two people had been killed and a detective had been severely wounded. The evil Mrs. Blackstone had obviously tormented Bill not only beyond that patient man's endurance but also beyond the endurance of the writer of the serial, for her end was sudden, unexpected, and contrived. Henrietta sat holding a revolver. "I should have pulled the trigger and let Bill Davidson have it," she muttered aloud. "Like this!" Bang! So much for Henrietta Blackstone. She had let herself have it, through the heart.

The new story line that began the day after Mrs. Blackstone's demise lasted three months, and I listened to all but two or three of the broadcasts. This sequence got under way with the arrival in Hartville of one Graham Steele, a wealthy Chicago man who wanted to find out how his brother-in-law, the wounded detective, was getting along. Mr. Steele is accompanied by his eighteen-year-old daughter.

Nora. (It will be easier if we shift into the historical present at this point.) The injured detective recovers, vanishes from the scene, and is never heard of again. As soon as he arrives in town, Graham Steele reports to Bill at his barbershop. Everybody who comes to Hartville reports straight to the barbershop, since Bill is the town's leading citizen.

Graham Steele is enchanted by Bill's goodness, Nancy's sweetness, gentleness, and beauty, and Hartville and Blackstone Manor. He rents the Manor and moves in, to the dismay of his daughter, who hates Bill, Nancy, Hartville, and the Manor. This is because Nora wants to be in Chicago with a young actor, named Ralph Wilde, of whom her father disapproves. She suspects that her father, a widower, has a pale, Soapland fancy for Nancy, and she knows it when he hires Nancy, at fifty dollars a week, to tutor her in sweetness, gentleness, and light. Nancy takes the job to get money to buy Kerry a birthday present.

Good, clean, devoted Nancy tries to keep the deal a secret, but Kerry finds out about the salary checks. For the ninety-third time in the fifteen years of "Just Plain Bill," he moons around in a brooding mood of jealousy. Nora, wanting to make trouble, figures that he is ripe for the lure of a pretty, extramarital face, and she brings a friend in from Chicago, Margot Marner. Margot is the beautiful and worldly, hence baddish, secretary of a famous Chicago judge named Henshaw, whom Donovan, who is a lawyer, vastly admires. Steele takes over the abandoned Apple Orchard Theatre for the stage-struck Nora to prance around in. He fails to stipulate that Ralph shall not be a member of the summer-stock company, and Margot brings Ralph with her. A child when it comes to illicit admiration, Nancy is innocently unaware of Graham Steele's interest in her charms—and small wonder, since his ardor has all the drive of an impassioned Kewpie. It took me seven weeks to realize he was in love, and I am usually quick about those things. I thought that one of the major afflictions of Soapland had seized him.

I figured he was going blind or was about to lose the use of both legs.

Margot's plans to alienate Kerry's affections are aborted by her growing recognition of Nancy's fineness, and she begins to desert the cause of the conniving Nora, not, however, before Margot and Kerry enter the empty Orchard Theatre to escape a storm. (Thunderstorms rage through Soapland all summer long.) They are in the theatre only a few minutes, but it took several days to act out this incident. It was well written and acted, and the sound of spectral hands applauding in the dark auditorium was effective. Kerry and Margot fall through a rotten board on the stage to this applause. Margot gets back home somehow, but Kerry wanders around in a stupor for several days—about two weeks, our time. Who should pick him up on the highway and put him to bed in a trailer but Judge Henshaw, trailing in from Chicago on vacation! Judge Henshaw, you see, is to be the hookup for the next plot sequence, now that this one is soon to come to a close.

A messenger Kerry sends to phone Nancy gets Nora by mistake, and that young lady, posing as Nancy, says she never wants to see Kerry again. Her deception is finally revealed and Kerry and Nancy get together. Nora, who has wavered between childish nastiness and adult villainy throughout, puzzling, with her uneven character, the actress who played her, the director, and me, abruptly becomes all hugs and kisses, a penitent child enchanted and saved, like Margot, by the goodness of Nancy and the kindliness of Bill. Graham Steele, just as abruptly, forgives the weak Ralph Wilde and blesses his coming union with Nora, although Ralph has threatened the life of his father-in-law-to-be with a straight razor, Wednesday through Friday, the week before. Graham (the barber has called him by his first name from the start, observing one of radio's strongest conventions) prettily announces, before all, his misguided but pure love for the astonished Nancy (Bill has been on to it all the time), and the Steeles and Wilde and Margot go back to Chicago. The aggression of Nora and Ralph has been changed to goodness by a process of eroticization created and copyrighted by the producers of soap opera. If they had been truly bad, they would have been eliminated by a fortuitous automobile accident or window fall, but since they were just weak, they were eroticized. Presto! Chango! Magico!

In the history of soap opera, only a few writers have seriously tried to improve the quality of daytime serials. One of these was Charles Jackson. In 1942 he was asked to write a serial called "Sweet River," and he took it on to tide him over the twelve months that he planned to spend writing a novel about an alcoholic. To begin with, he got fifty dollars a script, but before long he was paid two hundred, or a thousand a week. Jackson developed a certain guilt sense about the novel because it wasn't winning bread for the family, and for a long time he kept this reckless indulgence in purely speculative prose a secret from his wife. He would stuff the early chapters of the now famous book in a desk drawer whenever his wife came into his study, and go back to tapping out the dialogue of his serial, like a good husband. "Sweet River" was about a minister whose wife had died, leaving him with the task of bringing up their two young sons. The plot was concerned with the minister, his sons, his neighbors, and his mild and prolonged love affair with a schoolteacher whose cheek he never patted and whose hand he never held, for ministers and schoolteachers in Soapland are permitted only the faintest intimations of affection. Once he got going, Jackson wrote the serial carefully and seriously, and he is still proud of the way he handled the problems faced by his four principals. This serial, like "Portia Faces Life" and a dozen others, was thought up by an advertising agency, and Jackson was handed a description of the central characters and a detailed outline of plot sequence for the first eight months. He worked in New

York, but every six weeks he went to Chicago to confer with the experienced Max Wylie, who had created the show and was in charge of it. Jackson finished "The Lost Weekend" within a year, as planned, and went to Hollywood, where he continued to write the serial for a year and a half. After he gave it up, two or three other writers took flings at it, but its audience steadily declined and it was shortly taken off the air.

The experiences of Addy Richton and Lynn Stone form an interesting chapter in the history of those authors who have tried to raise the standards of soap opera. In 1936 they became tied up with the fortunes of one Edward Wolf, of Wolf Associates, Inc., a New York "package" firm; that is, an organization that thinks up ideas for serials, hires writers, actors, directors, and the other figures essential to their production, and turns over the "package" to an advertising agency, which then leases it to a sponsor. The interest of a sponsor's representative, incidentally, may be variously engaged—by the submission of a few scripts, together with an extended plot outline, by recordings of actors playing a few scenes, and, on rare occasions, by "live auditions," in which the actors play out scenes for the sponsor's man. One sponsor's man was won over when the agency salesman simply showed him enormous cardboard panels on which were pasted, in sequence, three months' clippings of "Joe Jinks," a comic strip. "A serial goes like that," the agency man explained. Wolf had an idea for a serial to be called "Hilltop House"—the story of the woman superintendent of an orphanage. Miss Richton and Miss Stone wrote a lot of scripts under the name of Adelaide Marstone, a nom de plume that was Wolf's idea. For a year, no agency could capture the fancy of any sponsor with "Hilltop House." During this time, Wolf paid the two writers twenty-five dollars a week and then fifty dollars. He intended to star Selena Royle in the serial, but it was finally taken by Palmolive, who wanted it as a vehicle for a high-paid radio actress named Bess Johnson. On another Palmolive program, she had made that firm's Lady Esther famous.

"Hilltop House" ran for four years and was steadily rated among the first ten soap operas in popularity. There were sixty-five of them throughout the country during that period. The authors tried to keep the story true to life and to let Miss Johnson, as the superintendent of the orphanage, solve the problems of the children without the facile help of old D. E. Machina. Wolf told the ladies to "keep it down in the cellar," which means, I suppose, not to lift it over the heads of the housewives, but the authors say that the cellar was clean and that they discovered artistic integrity and a certain altruism in Wolf. He let them deal frankly with the real problems to be found in orphanages and delve into child psychology. He staunchly defended them at agency conferences. ("The girls know what they are doing, the girls are right.") Serial writers are lucky if they have a champion to stand up for them in such conferences. Budget-watching, profit-conscious, high-pressure agency men are often inclined to oppose the serial writer who has something different to offer or something serious to say. Their motto is, quite simply, "A soap opera sells merchandise. If it doesn't sell merchandise, something is wrong with the story."

Wolf fancied himself a connoisseur of dramatic effects and plot gimmicks, and that did not make things too easy for the girls. He liked episodes to open with a rock crashing through a window. There is a message tied to the rock, of course. Bang! You got something. He insisted on one long sequence that involved the kidnapping by gypsies of a foundling who turned out to be an heiress. The girls were also plagued by Wolf's flair for promotion projects. On "David Harum," a horse was being given away each week to the winner of a contest. An agency man, struck by an inspiration from heaven, suggested that "Hilltop House" give away a baby each week as a prize—a swell tieup with the kidnapping of the infant heiress, see? Wolf was entranced, but shocked officials in charge of adoptions in New York and other states put their collective foot down with a resounding thump.

In 1941, Palmolive shifted agencies, and the new advertising firm insisted on a lower talent budget. Wolf refused to take a cut and removed "Hilltop House" from the air. The agency replaced it with a serial called "The Story of Bess Johnson," which didn't last long. Miss Richton and Miss Stone then wrote a program of their own, "This Life Is Mine," a superior serial, from all accounts, that ran for more than two years as a sustaining program over C.B.S., under the sympathetic supervision of Robert J. Landry, then that network's chief of program writing. A former *Variety* editor, a long-time severe but honest critic of radio, the author of a first-rate survey of the industry, from Marconi to Gabriel Heatter, Landry is a man who bothers to understand the problems of writers, to encourage their experiments, and to defend their interests. He allowed the girls to develop the story in their own way, using more actors than usual and, when they wanted to, an orchestra instead of the eternally boring Hammond organ, or "God box," which fills the daytime air with its depressing strains. "This Life" attracted attention, but it never got a sponsor, probably because it was set up on a talent budget of around thirty-five hundred dollars a week, or about a thousand dollars more than the average at that time. "Hilltop House" came back to the air just a few months ago. The Misses Richton and Stone are again writing the serial, which now stars Grace Mathews in the leading role.

Perhaps the most interesting figures in the field of radio serial writing are two sisters and a brother—Sandra, Gerda, and Peter Michael, natives of Denmark. They came to America with their parents shortly after the First World War, spent their childhood on a farm in Montana, and then moved East. Their headquarters today is near Greenwich, where Sandra lives with her husband, John Gibbs, who is a radio agent, and, at the last count, eight cats. Peter and Sandra, with the occasional assistance of Gerda, have had two superior serials on the air, "Against the Storm" and "Lone Journey." The Michaels' "Lone Journey" was abandoned by its sponsor last fall, and "Against the Storm" has been gone for many a year. Peter and Sandra, in trying to bring their special kind of literary quality to the daytime air, have fought an unequal struggle against the powers that insist on conformity to the pattern. They yielded to this pressure last summer and dragged the familiar murder trial into "Lone Journey," which up to that point had told the simple story of life on a Western ranch. They wrote it well, but the clammy hand of convention was on them and on their serial and they were glad to give up a program they no longer considered their own.

Sandra began writing "Against the Storm" in 1939. Its prose, often sensitive, occasionally poetic, was a startling change from the general run of factory-made wordage. So was its aware, realistic, and outspoken story. It was concerned with a college professor alive to the dangers of Fascism and plagued by the complacency and opposition of his colleagues. It also dealt with the situation of a family in Europe, where many of its scenes were laid. Mr. Gibbs took the first batch of scripts to William Ramsey, chief of the far-flung radio activities of Procter & Gamble, who own four soap operas, lease seven others, and sponsor, all told, nineteen daytime and nighttime programs.

A brief sketch of Ramsey may explain why Gibbs gave him first chance at this new departure in radio serials. As a child, Ramsey displayed a precocious aptitude for the piano, and he was marked for a concert career. Since it is not easy to step straight from Yale onto the concert stage, he got a job with Francis H. Leggett & Co., and later went to work for P. & G. He married and had three children, and the great musical career was out. Procter & Gamble approached radio gingerly in the early years. The firm contented itself with a couple of cooking programs, one of them Ida Bailey Allen's. Since P. & G. regarded these as arc, and Ramsey was known to be up on music and interested in the drama, he was put in charge of radio for P. & G., and he has been in charge for twenty years. He and six assistants read all P. & G. scripts before they are broadcast. Their soap-opera scripts alone run to nearly three thousand a year, or about six million words. Ramsey is a quiet man, frequently overcome by fits of shyness, but he is nonetheless a redoubtable trouble shooter. He comes to New York once a month from Cincinnati to call on his writers and on the account men in the six advertising agencies that divide up the handling of P. & G. programs. He is a tactful liaison officer between the agencies and the writers, and he listens to complaints, makes suggestions, and irons out problems or lets them ride until tempers cool and reason prevails. Experienced P. & G. writers get as much as a thousand dollars a week, as against the two hundred and fifty paid the average serial "dialoguer."

Ramsey had shown a certain daring in getting P. & G. to sponsor the Jewish "The Goldbergs"; the Irish "The O'Neills"; "The Guiding Light," which treads the touchy precincts of religion; "Right to Happiness," a favorite target of soap-opera critics; and "Vic and Sade," which brought comedy to the humorless daytime air. Ramsey had taken up three of these serials when they were dropped by their original sponsors. He decided to put on "Against the Storm," but he was uncertain about Sandra Michael's ability to keep a serial going. It chanced that Mrs. Jane Crusinberry, the author of "Mary Marlin," wanted to take a vacation. Ramsey persuaded her to let Sandra Michael write the program during her absence. Miss Michael handled "The Story of Mary Marlin" adroitly and was then commissioned to write "Against the Storm." Its success was immediate and, for a soap opera, phenomenal. It became the only daytime serial ever to win one of the George Foster Peabody awards for radio excellence, given annually by the University of Georgia. "Against the Storm" was dropped in December, 1942, after a three-year run. The reason for its closing is still a controversial issue. The Michaels insist that pressure was brought to bear by the agency to make it more like a typical daytime show, and that Sandra asked that her contract be terminated. The agency contends that the plot ran its course in the first two years and that the serial then deteriorated into a series of charming vignettes peopled by interesting and worthy personalities, with just no story line left. At any rate, the large number of listeners this program had originally attracted began to decrease steadily, according to the figures of the Crossley system of audience research subscribed to at that time by the sponsor of the show.

The Crossley company gave up the program-rating business last year, but there are still two systems of audience measurement by means of which the popularity of radio programs is indicated. The highly publicized Hooperatings are better known to the layman than the ratings of the A. C. Nielsen Company, and we will glance at the Hooper method first. C. E. Hooper, the head of the organization that does the measuring, has more than fifteen hundred checkers, all of them women, in thirty-six large cities. These checkers measure the audience of a given serial by phoning as many persons as they can reach while it is being broadcast. A checker makes contact with, on the average, sixteen persons during a fifteen-minute program. If a serial has an outlet in each of the thirty-six cities, the checkers working on that serial make contact with about 3,675 homes. During the past five years, the checkers have discovered that radios are actually turned on during the daytime in only about one out of every six houses they call. Now, if fifteen per cent of all the people called are listening to their radios, and thirty-seven per cent of these are listening to the serial in question, this particular rating would turn out to be 5.5. Surveys have shown that there are sixty-six million radio sets in thirty-seven million American homes, and Hooper cross-sections have been criticized as incomplete, since they take in only the listeners in large cities. Hooper has just perfected a new system of audience research to supplement his original ratings. The new method covers all population areas and is not confined to homes with telephones. Now that the listeners in rural regions and small towns have been checked along with the residents of the thirty-six large cities, the rating of "Just Plain Bill" has gone up. The report of the so-called "U. S. Hooperatings" for January and February puts "Bill" in tenth place, or much higher than he is usually rated in the cities. The A. C. Nielsen Company's ratings are also based on cross-sections of listeners in cities, towns, and rural areas, and this organization has developed the so-called audimeter, a device that can be attached to a radio set in such a way that it automatically registers hours of listening and keeps track of the various programs that are tuned in. There are now fourteen hundred audimeters in use. The Nielsen method has increased in popularity among sponsors and agencies during the past year.

Hooper checkers have found that the average rating of all daytime serials is about 5.5. This "average" rating indicates that a serial has a healthy temperature; the danger point seems to be about 3.5, below which a soap opera must not fall, at least for a protracted period. Our old friend "Just Plain Bill" has had its comparatively low moments, but it invariably makes a strong recovery. If you will strike a light, we will have a look at the record of "Bill" for the past two years. In May, 1946, it was rated 4.2; by the following January, it had shot up to 6.5; four months later, it was down to 5.9; eight months after that, in January, 1948, it had a rating of 6; in May, it was up to 6.6. The ratings of all serials fluctuate constantly, and it would be futile to try to keep track of them. "Big Sister," for example, began 1948 as the No. 1 serial, with a rating of 7.9; in February it had sunk to thirteenth place, but a month later

234

it was rated No. 2. So it goes with the best of them. I have no doubt that many a higher-ranking program would gladly exchange ratings with "Bill" if, by so doing, it could master the secret of that old plodder's durability.

Let us now drop in at the broadcasting studios to see how the actors and actresses are bearing up. Since the strange business of soap opera began, all the players put together have read, counting rehearsals and broadcasts, a total of at least 1,100,000,000 words. You would probably like to know how the heroes and heroines of the daytime microphones have managed to preserve their sanity in the face of this Niagara of prose. So would I.

IV—The Invisible People

IN THE early days of radio, before the American talent for organization had taken hold, the noisy young industry was something like the deck of a sinking ship. Reminiscences of old-timers sound curiously like tales told by survivors of disasters. "Norman Brokenshire was the first announcer to get Douglas Fairbanks and Mary Pickford on the air," one of these old-timers said recently. "First question he asked Pickford, she slid to the floor in a dead faint. I guess you could say she invented mike fright. People began to drop to studio floors after that like flies in December. Once Jefferson De Angelis suddenly dropped his script and began tugging at the microphone, trying to pull the wires out of the wall. Another time, an old Shakespearean actor from the Mississippi Valley got mike fright and couldn't read the lines 'I am Sioux. I make no peace with Chippewa.' Another actor yelled at him, 'You're Sioux, you big goddam ham, you make no peace with goddam Chippewa.' They cut 'em off the air. Probably the maddest moment of all was the day Brokenshire's script ran short. He ad-libbed as long as he could and then he said, 'Ladies and gentlemen, the sounds of New York,' and stuck the microphone out the window."

Mr. Brokenshire, one of the first announcers, claims that he planted the seed of radio daytime serials more than a quarter of a century ago, in another of those moments of confusion and desperation typical of the broadcasting business in the early nineteen-twenties. It seems that he was ordered, one day, on a few hours' notice, to get an act together for a free half hour on the evening schedule—if you could call it schedule—of a metropolitan station. He phoned some performers and asked them to stir up something, but they did not show up on time, and Brokenshire was stuck after his opening announcement. He ad-libbed for five minutes or more and then spotted a book lying on a table in the studio. He grabbed it, found that it was a collection of short stories, and began to read one of them aloud. He had got through only a couple of pages when his performers arrived. They filled out the rest of the time with some kind of offhand monkeydoodle. In the next few days, hundreds of letters came in asking that the story be finished over the air. Brokenshire contends that he had discovered the vanguard of that audience of twenty million listeners now addicted to soap opera. I solemnly enter the Brokenshire claim in the record, noting in the margin that nothing much was done about the potential serial audience for nearly ten years and pointing out to the veteran announcer that among those who might not be eager to contribute toward the erection of a monument to the planter of the seed are the invisible people, the actors and actresses who in the last twenty years have suffered and struggled in some two hundred daytime serials, thirty-six of which are now being broadcast from New York stations.

In the beginning, a player was lucky to get ten dollars a broadcast in New York, five dollars in Chicago, and two dollars and a half in Los Angeles. Many performers actually worked a year or longer for nothing, in order to get a foothold in the new medium. Until late in the nineteen-thirties, a vicious practice of kickbacks took as much as thirty-five per cent of the weekly income of most players. When one actor collapsed from hunger some fifteen years ago and was taken to a hospital, it was discovered that five separate cuts had been taken off his weekly pay of a hundred and twenty-five dollars. A distinguished American actor's widow, who was supposed to be paid a hundred and fifty dollars a week, always ended up with less than a hundred. It wasn't until the American Federation of Radio Artists was founded, in 1937, that the abused actors and actresses could count on receiving what was owed them. Even N.B.C. and C.B.S., shame on them, used to take a percentage off the wages of certain players appearing in shows produced by the networks themselves. A.F.R.A. put a stop to that. Also thanks to A.F.R.A. rules, a player may not be paid less than $30.50 for a fifteen-minute broadcast and an hour of rehearsal, or $152.50 for a five-day-a-week show. Many leads and featured players in soap opera work for this minimum basic pay, but a favored few—big names and individuals deemed indispensable to programs—get from three hundred to seven hundred dollars a week. Bess Johnson, who not only played the lead in "Hilltop House" but read the commercials, too, enchanting her sponsor, got sixteen hundred dollars a week, the highest salary in soap-opera history. With forty serials on the New York air in an average year, about a hundred and fifty of the twenty-six hundred members of A.F.R.A. in the city have permanent parts, and around eighteen hundred other members play part-time roles. About half of all the members make less than two thousand dollars a year. In 1947, the thirteen serials put on by Frank and Anne Hummert alone employed eight hundred and fifty actors and actresses.

In the cradle years of daytime serials, in Chicago, the herculean script writer Robert D. Andrews sometimes had as many as six of them going at a time, and a young actor named Don Ameche often played the lead in four of them every morning except Saturday and Sunday, running from studio to studio and floor to floor, rarely having more than a minute, and at times only twenty seconds, to get from microphone to microphone. With a few celebrated exceptions, radio actors were anonymous in the pioneer days, and Chicagoans who could tell you the names of network vice-presidents did not know that the vibrant voice of their favorite serial hero belonged to Ameche or that Robert Walker played, as Andrews puts it, "all the sad young men who lost all the bright young girls in all the old serials." Once, a couple of acrobats made Andrews a proposition. They said they would play shouts and murmurs, street cries, and crowd voices in his serials for seventy-five dollars a week and kick back twenty-five dollars to him. He wasn't in charge of casting and he did not go in for kickbacks; besides, a couple named James and Marian Jordan were playing miscellaneous voices in the Andrews serials for a combined salary of fifty a week. As Fibber McGee and Molly, they are now among the best-known and most highly paid comedians on the air. Today, A.F.R.A. will permit a radio actor to play two parts on one program, but no more unless he gets additional salary. An A.F.R.A. rule abolished multiple characterization years ago, putting an end to some mighty ingenious vocal virtuosity. J. Scott Smart used to have a dozen radio voices, and often played several parts on one show, but now, for appearing as the single-tongued star of "The Fat Man," a mystery series, he makes ten times as much money as he did in the good old days. A.F.R.A. has done quite a lot about credits for actors, too, since the days when radio accomplished a little miracle of anonymity by presenting "The Shadow" week after week without going to the trouble to announce that its title role was played by a Mr. Orson Welles.

An hour or so before a serial is to be broadcast, the actors and director assemble in the studio assigned to them. Most studios look as if they had been hastily abandoned by frightened people. There is a long, bare table, which seems to have been shoved around a lot, a scattering of collapsible aluminum chairs, a Hammond organ in one corner, the contraptions of the sound-effects man in another. "The walls are faintly pock-marked as part of the acoustical treatment," Robert J. Landry, once in charge of programs for C.B.S., writes in "This Fascinating Radio Business." "Indirect lighting plays upon shy grays, muddy whites, disappearing blues. The entire décor achieves a calculated neutrality so that the place never intrudes upon the event. It is primarily a colorless cavern, largely characterless, windowless save for the plate-glass barrier between the cast and the production trio of director, assistant director, and engineer. There is a vague tendency to claustrophobia and an odd feeling of being sealed off from the nearby New York side street even while united with millions of American parlors by the strange intimacy of the hookup." The glassed-in control room at the far end of the studio is generally empty until after the actors have assembled, but presently an engineer appears and begins to monkey around inside. The actors sit down at the table and read their parts aloud while the director and the assistant director follow the script. Everybody seems bored or contemptuous or indifferent, and the first reading is usually kidded, the players going in for falsetto voices, comically paraphrased speeches, and adverse criticisms of the script. "My God, it's sure corn syrup today," the leading man will wail. "Look, Harry, do I have to say this goo here? Listen—'I'll give you the world to wear like a locket on the golden chain of my love.' For God's sake, Harry, can't we cut that?" All the other players loudly sympathize, except one old actor, who says, without interest, "What the hell! It's just radio." He yawns. The director (Harry) has to make up his mind about cutting that line. If the script is running long, as scripts often do, he can cut the gooey line with impunity, but if length is not a factor, he has to consider the temperament of the author; maybe she's one of those writers who never listen to broadcasts of their stuff and don't care what is done to it, but then again she may be dialogue-proud, like Mrs. Elaine Carrington, and her prose must be treated with respect.

A few months ago, Mrs. Carrington attended the opening broadcast, over WCBS, of a new serial, "Marriage for Two." As soap-opera broadcasts go, this was a gala occasion.

There was a great deal of hugging and kissing on the part of the ladies involved in the big event. The actors got red carnations and the actresses got gardenias. The script was rehearsed five times, as against the three readings of an average script. Mrs. Carrington, whose dialogue is usually inviolable, allowed the cast to vote on whether the word "gorgeousest" should be retained. The players voted unanimously for "most gorgeous." They couldn't, however, get rid of the latest of Mrs. Carrington's I'll-give-you-the-world lines, of which she is extremely fond in moments of high romance. Staats Cotsworth, the leading man and one of the ablest actors in daytime radio, was forced to say, "I want you to have the whole world for a bauble to swing at your wrist." Since the opening episode dealt with the moony conversation of a young couple in love, the sound of kissing had to be imitated. Cotsworth gallantly relieved the embarrassed sound man of his customary task and did the kisses himself by bussing the back of his own wrist in each of the rehearsals. Mrs. Carrington gaily warned him and the young actress who played his fiancée not to fall in love and reminded them that her romantic dialogue had been too much for the two leads in "Rosemary," another of her serials, and that they had been married not long before. The serial took to the air promptly at 2:30 P.M. For this première performance, the part of a seamstress had been especially written in for an actress named Marion Barney, who plays the mother in Mrs. Carrington's "Pepper Young's Family" and "Rosemary" and the mother-in-law in the prodigious author's "When a Girl Marries." Miss Barney has appeared on the first broadcast of every serial Mrs. Carrington has written. She is regarded as a mascot who brings luck to the Carrington ventures.

Now let's get back to an ordinary broadcast on an average day. During a rehearsal hour, the first reading of a script is done sitting down. The next two readings are given in front of the microphone. During the first stand-up rehearsal, the organist drifts in and takes his place and the sound man begins to putter among his paraphernalia, checking through the script for opening and closing doors, pistol shots, thunderstorms, and so on. The organist and the sound man seem oblivious of the actors and what they are saying. In the stand-up rehearsals, the director makes his final cuts and changes with an eye on the studio clock. With five or six seconds to go before the show hits the air, he saunters into the control room. The engineer says, "O.K.," and the director says, "Let's go," and points through the glass at the announcer. The director can no longer be heard by the actors, but he guides them through the script, like an orchestra conductor, with a dozen hand signals—cutting his throat with an index finger, stretching an imaginary elastic, and so on.

The serial player, standing there with one eye on his script and the other on the director, is not one of the happiest members of the acting profession. By the time he has dropped the last page of his script quietly to the floor at the end of the broadcast, he will have been on his feet for three-quarters of an hour. The actors and actresses have the advantage of being permitted to dress any way they want to, inasmuch as they are not on exhibition, but even this slight consolation failed one leading man a few years ago. He happened to be playing opposite an actress who had read her part for so many years that she had completely identified herself with the role. When, during the final rehearsal of her great moment in one sequence, her wedding to the leading man, she noticed that he was wearing his hat, she sobbed at the director, "Look at him—he's wearing his hat at a time like this." The actor-bridegroom announced plaintively that his head was cold, but the director, fearing that the scene might blow up on the air, made the unhappy fellow take off his hat. Actresses who identify themselves with the parts they play form an irritating handicap to the director and to the other members of the cast. One lady took her role so seriously that she carried the characterization over into her private life, to the annoyance and bewilderment of the friends, acquaintances, and even strangers whom she was constantly offering to help out of the predicaments she was sure they were in. The imitation of emotion comes more easily to these dedicated performers than to the others. Now and then, an emotionally detached actor and actress, supposed to be caught in an amorous mood but aware that they are in reality just reading words from pieces of paper, will clasp each other's free hand in an effort to pump into the scene some feeling of warmth. The hand-holding helps a little, since an emotional scene is likely to die of malnutrition when the panting performers come to the point where their final embrace is simulated by the sound man, kissing the back of his own hand. They know, too, that the sound man sometimes misses his cues and that there may not even be this little vicarious sign of their mutual affection.

Most actors dread the periodical appearance in soap-opera scripts of a singularly syrupy kind of dialogue written in by reluctant authors in support of a commercial device known as a premium offer, or giveaway, or deal. For a period of several weeks once or twice a year on most soap-opera programs, a piece of costume jewelry is mailed to the listeners who send in a quarter and a box top for a forget-me-not pin, a lovebird brooch, or an orchid clip. In most instances, the pieces of jewelry are credited in the script to the leading woman of the serial, who, it turns out, is something of a genius at designing the stuff. She is often forced to tell her listeners, at the end of a program, that they, too, can own a gorgeous, beautiful, resplendent, and scintillatingly decorative gadget exactly like her own. To make things gooier, the dialogue in the opera itself during this sales period is used to plug the jewelry. In one studio the other day, a young actress new to radio encountered her first giveaway dialogue during rehearsal. The reading of the script, with interpolations, went something like this:

YOUNG ACTRESS: I am happy to meet you, Mrs. Nelson, and where in the world did you get that perfectly stunning orchid clip? Why, it gleams like virgin gold, and just look at those gorgeous colors—exactly like a rainbow and sunset coming together in a resplendent display of almost unimaginable beauty. . . . For heaven's sake, do I have to read this glop?

MRS. NELSON: I'm glad you like it. I designed it myself. . . . I'm afraid you're going to have to read it, dear.

DIRECTOR: Look, darling, this is what we call a giveaway and I couldn't cut it out without cutting myself out of a job. Just get hold of yourself and be brave.

One pair of lovers in a soap opera were made to drag some reference to a gorgeous and resplendent forget-me-not pin into their courtship conversation. "I will always think of this as our forget-me-not-pin day, George," quavered the young actress. "I'll remember it every year forever, darling," said the actor. "Our forget-me-not-pin day." My favorite line of giveaway prose, however, ran as follows: "A perfect lapel pin . . . particularly with that gleaming gold-flashed bowknot pin that the heart-shaped enclosure with the real four-leaf clover in it is suspended from." The giveaway business began, as far as I can find out, about fifteen years ago, when Frank Hummert decided to offer a photograph of the leading actress in "Ma Perkins," to get some idea of how many listeners the program had. A gloomy skeptic had told him that the program was probably not heard by more than a million housewives. "If you have a million listeners," Norman Corwin once said, "you are practically talking to yourself." As it turned out, a million one hundred thousand persons sent in for photographs. This was not a precise method of measurement, either, since there is no way of figuring what percentage of an audience is likely to send in for premium offers, but the giveaway became popular as a device to stir up interest in a program, and to check on how it's going, from time to time.

Many an actor and actress famous on Broadway or in Hollywood was once an anonymous voice in one soap opera or another, but no serial has had a more interesting roster of names than "The Goldbergs," which began on the night-time air in 1929, became a daytime serial in 1932, and, except for a gap of eight months, when Mrs. Gertrude Berg, its author and leading lady, was in Hollywood, ran until 1945. Alfred Ryder was the original Sammy Goldberg, and when he gave it up to join Eva Le Gallienne's company, in 1932, Everett Sloane, later an Orson Welles associate and now one of the most versatile actors on the evening air, took over. You could have heard the voice of Van Heflin on "The Goldbergs" in 1936 and that of Joseph Cotten the following year. Each of them played a romantic lead in one of the scores of plot sequences devised by Mrs. Berg. Joan Tetzel, who was later to remember Mama so effectively on Broadway, was a Goldberger for all of 1938. Marjorie Main played in the serial for three years, and George Tobias for seven. If you listened to Mrs. Berg's show in 1936, you may have heard the piping tones of a three-year-old neighbor child. That was Garson Kanin, aged twenty-four, doing one of his best imitations. Philip Loeb was on the program in 1943 and not long ago played opposite Mrs. Berg in "Me and Molly," the recent Broadway play about the Goldbergs. Minerva Pious, the celebrated Mrs. Nussbaum of the Fred Allen show, won her "G" in 1944, and Keenan Wynn was on the show for one day in 1936. Fourteen years ago, the lucky listener would have heard the voice of Mme. Schumann-Heink on three occasions. She played a social worker, and gave the serial a radiance to remember when, one day, she sang Brahms' lullaby. And Jan Peerce, the celebrated star of the Metropolitan, sang for ten years on every Yom Kippur and Passover program of "The Goldbergs." Other serials have had their famous names, among them Helen Menken, Selena Royle, Betty Garde, Paul McGrath, Claudia Morgan, Myron Mc-

Cormick, Raymond Edward Johnson, House Jameson, Alan Bunce, Thomas Chalmers, and Francis X. Bushman, but no other soap opera has touched Mrs. Berg's record.

It would take a patient accountant to compute just how many radio performances Mrs. Berg gave in the role of Molly, but the final figures would show that she is surpassed by Arthur Hughes, who has played the title role of "Just Plain Bill" since September, 1932, and seems likely to go on in this ancient vehicle as long as he is able to stand up in front of a microphone. Bill Davidson, the barber and first citizen of Hartville, has become nothing less than the alter ego of Arthur Hughes. More of his mail is addressed to Bill Davidson than to Arthur Hughes. He conscientiously studies his scripts before, and even after, rehearsals and broadcasts, often going over them at night. His interest in his alter ego is serious, and he plays Bill with sincerity and dignity. Through the years, hard-bitten directors have been impressed by Hughes' skill in transcending the material with which he often has to cope. Since a serial runs to a half-million words a year, the writing, naturally, is sometimes trite and tired or careless and awkward, but this never confounds Arthur William Hughes-Davidson. He can even transmute into simple honesty the bathos and mawkishness that occasionally creep into the scripts. In the last six years, he has had to adjust himself to the various writing styles of nine serialists. Most remarkable of all, Mr. Hughes-Davidson somehow takes the curse off the almost inevitably comic effect of disaster following disaster, year after year.

For more than fifteen years, Ruth Russell has played Bill's daughter in the serial, and James Meighan has been her husband, Kerry Donovan. The talent and long experience of Miss Russell and Mr. Meighan give a further air of authenticity to the family of Bill Davidson, in spite of the imposing odds of plot and incident and a tendency in the scripts to present their happy marriage as one that preserves forever the glow of courtship. For more than a decade, Miss

246

Russell and Mr. Meighan have been known to the personnel of a restaurant in the R.C.A. Building as Mr. and Mrs. Donovan of Hartville. The waitresses fondly call them Nancy and Kerry, and most of them do not know their real names. They do know, however, that the Donovans lost their first child, Nellie, in an automobile accident in 1938 and that their son, Wiki, is seven years old. The waitresses may not know, incidentally, that Wiki is played by a young woman. Fifteen boys tried out for the part, but those with voices of the right pitch and tone were too young to read smoothly enough.

Most serial writers drop in to hear a broadcast of one of their scripts only at long intervals, and some of them have never seen the actors who play the roles they create. Martha Alexander, who for six months last year wrote one of the most intelligent and skillful serials on the air, "The Second Mrs. Burton," is an exception to this rule. In the best tradition of soap opera, she got her start in Chicago, where she directed plays for a children's theatre and also occasionally coached semi-professional actors. She brought to serial writing the conviction that the author should know intimately the talents and temperaments of the players. She was often on hand for rehearsals and broadcasts of "The Second Mrs. Burton." One day, she tried a daring expedient in a medium governed by a set of stern rules officially known as daytime morality. Her script had the leading male character ask his serial wife three times to say "Ah," and when the puzzled lady's lips were finally shaped to his satisfaction, he was supposed to kiss her, remarking, "All the other men ask their wives to say 'Prunes.'" It wasn't until the last rehearsal that the actress playing the wife got the idea. She protested that this kind of amatory goings on was not in character for the good soap-opera wife she was trying to create. In striving to bring realism to daytime radio, Miss Alexander often came up against all the old, formidable taboos, even though, in the case of the "ah" kiss, it is probable that not more than one-tenth of one per cent of the listeners would have had any idea what the shameless husband was up to.

"The Second Mrs. Burton," in Miss Alexander's hands, became an honest story of the problems of a second wife who has to deal with a stubbornly righteous husband, his adolescent son, and his difficult first spouse. In trying to bring her characters to life, the author sometimes made them a little too real for the comfort of either the sponsor or the advertising agency. In one sequence, a young artist, named Ted Miller, expressed an affection for the second Mrs. Burton that was fairly warm for the frightened old conventions of daytime programs, though Miss Alexander told her story with taste, subtlety, and, most startling of all, frequent touches of quiet humor. One day, the bold author had her heroine say to the young artist, "Some part of me wants you to fall in love with me." That did it. Disapproving letters from listeners poured in, and ninety per cent of the women correspondents demanded that Ted Miller be banished from the serial and that Mrs. Burton remember she was a good, clean American wife. The character of the artist was not the only cause of the disagreement that developed between Miss Alexander and her agency. Last December, she asked to be relieved of her contract, and "The Second Mrs. Burton" has since become a soap opera indistinguishable from the run-of-the-mill product. It turned into a real cliffhanger, as melodramatic serials are called in the trade, when the second Mrs. Burton went over a cliff with her stepson while they were trying to slide downhill on a sled. Thirteen days (our time, not theirs) after the accident, Mrs. Burton and the boy were still marooned in a cave below the edge of the cliff, where I cheerfully abandoned them forever.

A soap-opera director not only has to deal with temperament and tantrum; he is often up against plight and predicament. Some years ago, on "Mary Marlin," a young actress walked casually out of the studio, took the elevator down to the street, and went home. She had somehow got the idea that the third reading, called the dress rehearsal, was the actual live broadcast for that day. The director had signalled to the announcer to begin his commercial before he realized the young lady had disappeared. Fortunately, there was a minute or so before the missing player's first cue was reached in the script. The assistant director went into frantic action and managed to dig up somebody to take over the part. This is not too difficult in a building full of actresses coming and going, but they say that the gentleman who directed "Mary Marlin" that day tenses up and begins to breathe rapidly whenever the case of the vanishing actress is mentioned.

Perhaps the most agonizing quarter hour in the history of soap opera befell the director and cast of "Just Plain Bill" some years ago as the result of a plane wreck. Robert Andrews was then writing the serial in Hollywood and sending his scripts in by air mail. In the accident, a whole week's supply of scripts was lost, and Andrews had no copies. He got on the long-distance phone shortly before the next "Bill" was to go on the air and began dictating a new script to a stenographer at C.B.S., where "Bill" was then playing as a morning program. She made five copies, and as each page was finished, it was torn from her typewriter and carried into the studio. The cast actually began the program with only the first page of that day's script, and they never had more than a single sheet in their hands during the entire broadcast. The actors were pale and tense, and they were occasionally forced to slow their reading down so far that the listeners must have believed they were all falling asleep. Page 5 was brought to them just as James Meighan had finished reading the last sentence on Page 4. The program ended on schedule, and the shaken actors and actresses went home to lie down.

In addition to scripts ad-libbed over the long-distance phone, vanishing actresses, and the like, there is a long calendar of minor problems with which the soap-opera director is confronted every day. Take the sound effects, for example. It is up to the director to pass on their accuracy and authenticity. A few summers ago, on "Just Plain Bill," its director was dissatisfied with the tinkling sound made by what was supposed to be a pitcher of iced tea. What the sound man really held was a pitcher of water containing five or six lumps of coal. (Coal is always used for ice, because it doesn't melt.) "It isn't quite right," said the director, frowning and cocking his head like an attentive spaniel. "Shake it again." The bored sound man jiggled the pitcher. The director shook his head sorrowfully. "It still sounds like water," he said.

Let us glance at the curious quandary of one soap-opera actor. This fellow came back to New York from Hollywood and was given the same leading role in a soap opera that he had played nine years before. He began to have the sensation that he was being followed, and he would glance continually over his shoulder on his way to and from the studio. He was even bothered by a singular tendency to change taxicabs, as if it were necessary to elude a mysterious pursuer. He finally figured out what was the matter. He was reading, day after day, the identical lines he had read nine years before. It was his past that had come up to haunt him.

V—The Listening Women

DURING the nineteen-thirties, radio daytime serials were occasionally sniped at by press and pulpit, and now and then women's clubs adopted halfhearted resolutions, usually unimplemented by research, disapproving of the "menace of soap opera." Husbands and fathers, exacerbated by what they regarded as meaningless yammering, raised their voices against the programs, and some of them, pushed too far, smashed their sets with their fists, like Mr. Ezra Adams, in Clinton, Iowa. But it wasn't until 1942 that the opponents of the daytime monster discovered in their midst a forceful and articulate crusader to lead the assault on the demon of the kilocycles. He was Dr. Louis I. Berg, of New York, psychiatrist and physician, author, and, according to *Who's Who*, medico-legal expert. In a report published in March, 1942, and widely quoted in the press, Dr. Berg confessed that he had been unaware of the menace of the radio serial until late in 1941. His examination of several female patients undergoing change of life had convinced him that radio serials were a main cause of relapses in the women. He thereupon made a three-week study of two of the aggravations, "Woman in White" and "Right to Happiness." He found these serials guilty of purposefully inducing anxiety, dangerous emotional release, and almost everything else calculated to afflict the middle-aged woman, the adolescent, and the neurotic. "Pandering to perversity and playing out destructive conflicts," Dr. Berg wrote, "these serials furnish the same release for the emotionally distorted that is supplied to those who derive satisfaction from a lynching bee, who lick their lips at the salacious scandals of a *crime passionnel*, who in the unregretted past cried out in ecstasy at a witch burning." Hitting his stride, Dr. Berg referred to "the unwitting sadism of suppurating serials." The Doctor then admitted, "There are several excellent ones," and added, somewhat to my bewilderment, since he had set himself up as a critic, "Naturally, an analysis of them has no place in a study of this kind." In a later report, Dr. Berg set down such a list of serial-induced ailments, physiological and psychological, as would frighten the strongest listener away from the daytime air. It began with tachycardia and arrhythmia and ended with emotional instability and vertigo.

Dr. Berg's onslaught was not unlike the cry of "Fire!" in a crowded theatre, and a comparable pandemonium resulted. The uneasy radio industry decided to call in experts to make a study of the entire field. Professors, doctors, psychologists, research statisticians, and network executives were all put to work on the problem. In the last five years, their findings have run to at least half a million words. This vast body of research covers all types of programs, and an explorer could wander for weeks just in the section devoted to soap opera. Among the outstanding investigators are Dr. Paul S. Lazarsfeld, of Columbia University, whose Bureau of Applied Social Research has the dignified backing of the Rockefeller Foundation, and Dr. Rudolf Arnheim, professor of psychology at Sarah Lawrence College, who, for *his* three-week study of serials, had the fascinated assistance of forty-seven students at Columbia University. C.B.S. appointed Mrs. Frances Farmer Wilder, a former public-relations director in radio, as program consultant with special reference to the investigation of daytime serials. Both N.B.C. and C.B.S., the only national networks that broadcast soap opera, appointed research committees, and were cheered up by their reports, which admitted that soap opera could be greatly improved, but decided that its effect on the listening woman was more likely to be benign than malignant. The cry of "whitewash" went up from the enemy camp, but the networks were able to prove that the data of their specialists agreed in general with studies made by independent researchers in the field. It is not always easy to distinguish between independent investigators and the ladies and gentlemen whose work is stimulated by the networks, and I am not even going to try.

In 1945, Mrs. Wilder summarized the findings of the C.B.S. experts in a pamphlet called "Radio's Daytime Serial." If you have been worried about America's womanhood left home alone at the mercy of the daytime dial, you will be relieved to know that forty-six out of every hundred housewives did not listen to soap opera at all. This figure was approximately confirmed a year later by checkers working for the United States Department of Agriculture, which had presumably become worried about the effect the serials were having on the women in small towns and rural areas of the country. Estimates differ as to how many serials the average addict listens to each day. Mrs. Wilder puts the figure at 5.8. She also points out that a housewife listens to a given serial only about half the time, or five programs out of every ten. On the other hand, a survey by an advertising agency indicates that the ladies listen to only three broadcasts out of every ten.

There have been all kinds of measurements of the social stratification of the listening women, and all kinds of results. There is a popular notion that only ladies of a fairly low grade of intelligence tune in soap operas, but some of the surveys would have us believe that as many as forty per cent of the women in the upper middle class, or the higher cultural level, listen to soap opera. The most interesting specimen that the scientists have examined in their laboratories is the habitual listener who has come to identify herself with the heroine of her favorite serial. Many examples of this bemused female have been tracked down by Dr. Arnheim and other workers, and a comprehensive analysis of the type was completed last year by Professor W. Lloyd Warner and Research Associate William E. Henry, both of the University of Chicago, at the instigation of the Columbia Broadcasting System. They made a study of a group of listeners to "Big Sister," using as subjects mostly women of the lower middle class, and found that almost all of them were "identifiers," if I may coin a pretty word. Let us take a look at the summary of their conclusions about the nature of the serial and its impact on its audience. "The 'Big Sister' program arouses normal and adaptive anxiety in the women who listen," wrote Warner and Henry. "The 'Big Sister' program directly and indirectly condemns neurotic and non-adaptive anxiety and thereby functions to curb such feelings in its audience. This program provides moral beliefs, values, and techniques for solving emotional and interpersonal problems for its audience and makes them feel they are learning while they listen (thus: 'I find the program is educational'). It directs the private reveries and fantasies of the listeners into socially approved channels of action. The 'Big Sister' program increases the women's sense of security in a world they feel is often threatening, by re-affirming the basic security of the marriage ties (John's and Ruth's); by accentuating the basic security of the position of the husband (Dr. John Wayne is a successful physician); by 'demonstrating' that those who behave properly and stay away from wrong-doing exercise moral control over those who do not; and by showing that wrong behavior is punished. The 'Big Sister' program, in dramatizing the significance of the wife's role in basic human affairs, increases the woman's feeling of importance by showing that the family is of the highest importance and that she has control over the vicissitudes of family life. It thereby decreases their feeling of futility and makes them feel essential and wanted. The women aspire to, and measure themselves by, identification with Ruth, the heroine; however, the identification is not with Ruth alone, but with the whole program and the other characters in the plot. This permits sublimated impulse satisfaction by the listeners', first, unconsciously identifying with the bad woman and, later, consciously punishing her through the action of the plot. Unregulated impulse life is condemned, since it is always connected with characters who are condemned and never related to those who are approved."

"Big Sister" is written by two men, Robert Newman and Julian Funt, and they have made it one of the most popular of all serials. For more than two years it has dealt with a moony triangle made up of Ruth Wayne, the big sister of the title, her estranged husband, Dr. John Wayne, and another doctor named Reed Bannister. The authors, I am told, plan to tinker with the popular old central situation, but they are aware that they must proceed with caution. The identifiers are strongly attached to the status quo of plot situation, and to what psychologists call the "symbols" in soap opera—serial authors call them "gimmicks"—and they do not want them tampered with. Thus, the soap-opera males who go blind or lose the use of both legs or wander around in amnesia are, as the psychologists put it, symbols that the listening women demand. As long as the symbols are kept in the proper balance and the woman is in charge and the man is under her control, it does not seem to make a great deal of difference to the female listeners whether the story is good or not.

We come next to that disturbing fringe of the soap-opera audience made up of listeners who confuse the actors with the characters they play. These naïve folk believe that Bill Davidson, the kindly Hartville barber of "Just Plain Bill," is an actual person (he is, of course, an actor, named Arthur Hughes), and they deluge him with letters in the fond belief that he can solve their problems as successfully as he does those of the people in the serial. James Meighan and

Ruth Russell, who play the husband and wife in "Just Plain Bill," have had to lead a curious extra-studio life as Mr. and Mrs. Kerry Donovan. When it became apparent to the listening audience, some thirteen years ago, that Mrs. Donovan was going to have her first child, the network and local stations received hundreds of gifts from the devoted admirers of the young couple—bonnets, dresses, bootees, porringers, and even complete layettes were sent by express to the mythical expectant mother—and when, several years later, the child was killed in an automobile accident, thousands of messages of sympathy came in. Such things as this had happened before, and they still happen, to the bewilderment and embarrassment of network executives. In 1940, when Dr. John Wayne married the heroine of "Big Sister," truckloads of wedding presents were received at the C.B.S. Building on Madison Avenue. This flux of silver, cut glass, and odds and ends presented the exasperated broadcasting system with a considerable problem. Gifts for babies had always been disposed of by sending them to children's hospitals and orphanages, but the wedding gifts were another matter. Since network men are a little sheepish about the entire business, they are inclined to change the subject when the question of the misguided largess of listeners is brought up.

The quandary is enlarged when, in addition to gifts for the nursery, parlor, and dining room, checks, paper money, and even coins arrive for this serial hero or that who has let it out over the air that he is in financial difficulties. The money, like the presents, cannot very well be returned to the senders, for fear of breaking their naïve hearts, and the sponsors have adopted the policy of giving it to the Red Cross and other charities. In addition to the newly married, the pregnant, and the broke, soap-opera characters who are single and in the best of health and circumstances receive tokens of esteem, in a constant, if somewhat more moderate, stream. One young actress who plays in a Procter & Gamble serial estimates that she is sent about three hundred pounds of soap every year, much of it the product of her sponsor's rivals. The year 1947 was the Big Year for live turtles and alligators, and radio listeners from all over the country bombarded the studios with gifts of hundreds of these inconvenient creatures.

Mrs. Carrington's "Pepper Young's Family" used to have a recurring scene in which a man and his wife were heard talking in bed—twin beds, naturally. When the man playing the husband quit and was replaced by another actor, indignant ladies wrote in, protesting against these immoral goings on. Equally outraged was the woman who detected that Kerry Donovan, the husband in "Just Plain Bill," and Larry Noble, the husband in "Backstage Wife," were one and the same man. This pixilated listener wrote Kerry Donovan a sharp letter revealing that she was on to his double life and threatening to expose the whole nasty mess unless the bigamous gentleman gave up one of his wives. The key to this particular scandal is simple. One actor, James Meighan, plays both husbands. A woman in the Middle West once wrote to N.B.C. asserting that the wrong man was suspected of murder in her favorite serial. She said she was tuned in the day the murder took place and she knew who the real culprit was. She offered to come to New York and testify in court if the network would pay her expenses.

Even the listening women who are shrewd enough, God bless them, to realize that serial characters are not real people but are played by actors and actresses expect superhuman miracles of their idols. They never want them to take vacations, but usually the weary players manage to get away for a few weeks in the summer. Sometimes they are replaced by other performers, but often the characters they play are "written out" of the script for the periods of their absence. Thus, the housewives who love Mary Noble, the heroine of "Backstage Wife," are not told that Claire Niesen, who plays that role, is taking her annual vacation.

Instead, the script arranges for Mary Noble to visit her sick mother in San Diego for a while or travel to Bangkok to consult a swami who has the secret of the only known cure for that plaguy summer rash of hers. Now and then, a serial audience hears one of its favorite characters complain of a severe headache. This is almost always a symptom of brain tumor. It means that the part is going to be written out of the soap opera forever, perhaps because the player wants to go to Hollywood, or the author is bored with the character, or the producer has to cut the budget. In any case, the listeners become slowly adjusted to the inevitable, and when the character finally dies, many of them write letters of condolence, often bordered in black.

The gravest real crisis in years came a few months ago when Lucille Wall, who plays Portia in "Portia Faces Life," was critically hurt in a fall in her Sutton Place apartment. Until her accident, Miss Wall had taken only one vacation in eight years, and her devoted audience was alarmed when her replacement, Anne Seymour, went on playing Portia week after week. The news that Miss Wall was in the hospital in a serious condition spread swiftly among her followers, and letters, telegrams, flowers, and gifts poured in. Because of this evidence of her popularity, Miss Wall improved rapidly, to the amazement and delight of her doctors, who had told her that she could not go back to work for a year. When she got home from the hospital, Miss Wall spoke to her listeners at the end of a "Portia" broadcast one day over a special hookup at her bedside, thanking them for their kindness and promising to be back soon. She repeated this message on the Thursday before Mother's Day, and again, some time later, while she was still recuperating. On June 14th, after being away less than four months, she began to play Portia again.

This reporter is too tired, after more than a year of travel in Soapland, and too cautious in matters of prophecy, to make any predictions about the future of soap opera. One thing, though, seems certain. The audience of twenty million women has taken over control of the daytime serial. The producers must give them what they want and demand. The formula has been fixed. The few serious writers who have tried to improve on it are gradually giving up the unequal struggle. It is probable that superior serials, like "Against the Storm," winner of a Peabody Award for excellence, are gone from the air forever, and that only the old familiar symbols and tired plots will survive.

Your guess is as good as mine about the effect that television will have on the daytime serial. The creeping apparition called video has already made several experiments with continuous narratives. Two of them have been dropped, but one called "The Laytons," the story of a family, though off the air at the moment, will be back next month. It differs from soap opera in that it is a half-hour nighttime show once a week, but the agent I sent to watch a performance at the WABD studio at Wanamaker's reports that it has the basic stuff of the daytime serials, even if the producer is horrified at the mention of such a thing. Just how television could manage to put on a fifteen-minute program five times a week, I have no idea, but from what I know of American technological skill, I wouldn't bet that it can't be done. There is a problem, however, that the wizards of television may find insurmountable if they attempt to transpose any of the current radio serials to the screen. The researchers have discovered that the listening women have a strong tendency to visualize the serial heroine and her family. Some of them even go so far as to describe to their interviewers what the different women characters wear. If their favorites did not come out to their satisfaction on television (imagine their dismay if they find that the tall, handsome hero of their daydreams is really a mild little fellow, five feet four), the ladies might desert the video versions by the million. The way around that, of course, would be to invent entirely new soap operas for telecasting, and "The Laytons" may well be the first lasting adventure in this field.

It is hard for one who has understood the tight hold of "Just Plain Bill," "Big Sister," and some of the others to believe that their intense and far-flung audience would ever give them up easily. If soap opera did disappear from the air (and I see no signs of it), the wailing of the housewives would be heard in the land. I doubt that it could be drowned out even by the cheers and laughter of the househusbands dancing in the streets.

I took the train from Hartville one day last week, waving good-bye to Bill Davidson and his family, and vowing—I hope they will forgive me—to put my radio away in the attic and give myself up to the activities and apprehensions of the so-called real world. I have also put away the books and pamphlets dealing with the discoveries of the serial researchers. In closing, though, I think you ought to know that Benton & Bowles, an advertising agency, recently employed a system invented by Dr. Rudolph Flesch, of New York University, to determine mathematically the comparative understandability, clarity, and simplicity of various kinds of prose and poetry. The agency wanted to find out just how easy it was to understand that old and popular serial of Elaine Carrington's called "When a Girl Marries." The results of Dr. Flesch's formula showed that this soap opera is as easy to understand as the Twenty-third Psalm and a great deal clearer than what Abraham Lincoln was trying to say in the Gettysburg Address. I don't know about you, but when the final delirium descends upon my mind, it is my fervent hope that I will not trouble the loved ones gathered at my bedside by an endless and incoherent recital of the plot of "When a Girl Marries." It will be better for everyone if my consciousness selects that other clear and famous piece of English prose, and I babble of green fields.

IV
A SHEAF OF DRAWINGS

The Patient

1. Pulse and Temperature.

2. *A fit of temper.*

3. *His nurse tells him the plot of "Miracle of the Bells."*

4. *Lunch time again.*

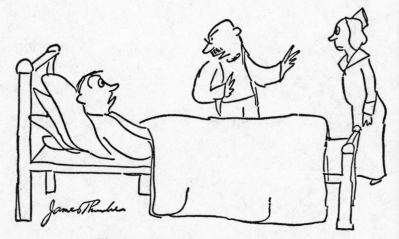

5. *The doctor describes a streptococcus case.*

6. *The Linked Puzzle.*

7. *Momentary Content: The Sports Page.*

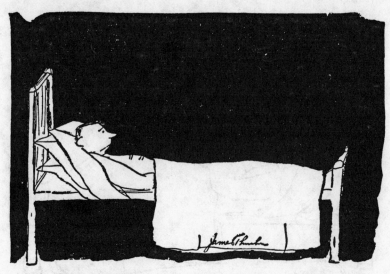

8. Black Doubt: Is his wife out with an Old Beau?

9. The jolly visitors.

A MISCELLANY

"I'm getting tired of you throwing your weight around."

"Mush!"

"Let me take your hat, Mr. Williams."

"*Sunday Morning.*"

"*I wear it for luck.*"

Death comes for the dowager.

272

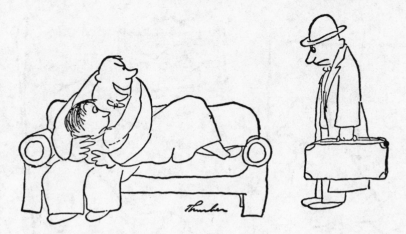

"*The eternal feminine, Mr. Blake, the eternal feminine!*"

"*No, I won't apologize—and neither will your father.*"

"I can't find any serenity in contemplation because I keep thinking of this one girl."

"Well, sir, he was the most astonished magician you ever saw in your life."

"*I wouldn't even let Cary Grant lounge around my house in the afternoon.*"

"Sometimes the news from Washington forces me to the conclusion
that your mother and brother Ed are in charge."

American Folk Dance.

"Don't you want to greet the rosy-fingered dawn?"

"I'm the Times man. Did they have pistol permits?"

"Where did you get those big brown eyes and that tiny mind?"

"Comb the woods!"

"We had to hang it sideways, unfortunately."

"*I couldn't make* any *man happy. I'm a femme fatale.*"

THE OLDEN TIME

The Dragon.

The Voice of the Questing Beast.

The Giant.

Falconry.

The Joust.

The Long Bow.

The Boar Hunt.

Supper.

V

TIME EXPOSURES

From the files of the
"NEW YORKER'S" TALK OF THE TOWN

THE NEW Reptile Hall was officially opened a few days
ago in the Museum of Natural History and we visited it
amidst a group of youngsters who kept crying "Good
night!" and their mothers who kept murmuring "Mercy!"
The place is like that. It might be called the Conan Doyle
Hall, with certain exhibits marked: "Strong Influence of
Lewis Carroll." Things out of the dead worlds of Sir Arthur's writings and Mr. Carroll's "Looking Glass" are here
but you have to accept the word of eminent scientists that
they once lived. Place of honor goes to the dragon lizards
which, brought from the Dutch West Indies, lived disconsolately for a while at the Bronx Zoo. They look like dinosaurs reduced nine-tenths and, in fact, were spotted for
dinosaurs by excited travellers who saw them rear up on
their hind legs at a distance and gave the Sunday papers an
annual feature story for ten years until the Museum went
down and caught a few. The largest is nine feet long.

Even taking into account the grimly handsome Sphleno-
don, which looks exactly like William Boyd in the last act
of "What Price Glory," we like most the group of fat Bra-
zilian horned frogs which have soft velvety black and green
heads and must have been cronies of Tweedledum and his
brother. Some of the exhibits tie up neatly with literature,
such as the Russell's Viper, which has the title rôle in the

Sherlock Holmes story, "The Speckled Band," and the tiny mongoose which is the Rikki-tikki-tavi of Kipling's tales. The mongoose is shown snapping its fingers at a King Cobra, which mongooses devote their life to chivvying about and killing, thus becoming, in our opinion, the world's bravest animal.

In one case reposes the world's largest frog and although right next door is a tiny reptile whose sex life and fighting skill are described minutely, the sign by the world's largest frog frankly says, "Nothing is known of its habits," thus giving us an example of the oddities of scientific research to ponder about the rest of our life. All the snakes are here, including one with no card telling what it is, and the Green Mamba, which is as lovely as a jade necklace and as poisonous as the devil. The snake that interested us most, though, is the Pine Snake, for this is the one the lady snake charmers play with, and it is described as harmless and of very gentle disposition, the worst it ever does being to make a noise like a hot iron plunged into water.

We never go to the Museum but we look up two favorite exhibits of ours. One is the incredible raccoon bear, a cross between those two animals and, we like to believe, a sheer figment of the craftsmanship of the whimsical doctor who said he found one in Tibet. The other is the thirty-six-ton siderite which Peary brought back from Greenland after two vain tries. The sign tells of the immensity of the task and relates that the mammoth hunk of almost pure iron was finally brought here and given to the Museum. But how this was done is left to our imagination, which never fails to be both interested and baffled.

Where Time Has Stopped   FEBRUARY 25, 1928

THERE IS no more absorbing afternoon's walk, we think, than one which properly begins near Chatham Square in the Bowery. Go a little way down Oliver Street—not too fast or you'll miss it—and you come upon the oldest cemetery in the town. Two hundred and fifty years ago this was a great peaceful burial ground far from city noise. Once its trees masked a battery of guns stationed there by George Washington. The ground was granted by Peter Stuyvesant to the first Jews in North America, who came here from Brazil in 1654. Now all that is left is a meagre patch of earth with a few tottery tombstones. The bare little quadrangle is a convenient place for the tenement people on two sides of it to hang out their wash.

Continuing up the Bowery to the region of Second Street, swing over to Second Avenue and, if you look close, you will find a narrow passageway to a great hidden field hemmed in by the buildings of Second Avenue, the Bowery, Second Street, and Third Street. There are no headstones here but there are several hundred marble vaults underground. A wall of pure marble surrounds this ancient cemetery and holds the burial tablets of the dead. Here Peter Lorillard was buried for a time, and the tablets bear such famous names as Beekman and Spring, Ogilvie, Scribner, De Forest, and Oliphant. The oldest vault is that of Peter Nichols, who was a farmer and owned this land a hundred years ago. This is called the New York Marble Cemetery and a block away, open to the view of the passerby, is another known by the same name, the most tranquil cemetery in town to look upon, probably. The two are separate institutions, however, being owned by different corporations of vault owners. This one is on Second Street, east of Second Avenue. It has two hundred vaults and also many tombstones and monuments, lovely—as we once saw them—in the snow. The caretaker, who has been its guardian for thirty years, told us a year or two ago that several burials are still made here annually. The law requires the use of hermetically sealed caskets placed in marble vaults equipped with brass locks.

This is the most notable of these small burial places. The

291

ground is hallowed by greatness. James Monroe was buried here until 1858, when his remains were taken to Richmond, and John Ericsson, inventor of the ironclad, until 1880, when an American gunboat carried him home to Sweden after one of the most notable military processions the city had ever seen. Still lying here are Colonel Robert Anderson, hero of Fort Sumter; Stephen Allen, an early mayor of the city; Adam and Noah Brown, who built Oliver Hazard Perry's ships; Mittens Willett, a famous actress of Augustin Daly's era; and members of such families as the Kips, Blennerhassets, Hazards, Ogdens, Mortons, Stantons, and Griswolds.

There remain two cemeteries to visit, built by descendants of the first Portuguese Jews. One of these is the tiny triangle with twenty headstones familiar to Greenwich Villagers, on Eleventh Street, east of Sixth Avenue. The cemetery of those who died of plagues, particularly the dread yellow fever of 1798, it once covered many acres. The second, on Twenty-first Street, west of Sixth, has perhaps a hundred and fifty tombstones. Burials were made here as late as 1851, although it was against the law then, and several of the bereaved families had to pay a fine of two hundred and fifty dollars. The Portuguese Jews formed the Congregation Shearith Israel whose present congregation—their synagogue is at 99 Central Park West—has repeatedly rejected offers of hundreds of thousands for the Twenty-first Street site. Once a department store wanted to arch a building over the cemetery, leaving it undisturbed, but that plan was rejected, too.

Bagdad-on-the-Subway   MARCH 31, 1928

THE TRAIL of O. Henry is growing dim, we found, in conscientiously picking it out the other day through the streets and squares in which he lived and about which he wrote so many stories. His favorite region, out of which he rarely adventured (it is recorded that the farthest north he ever walked was the corner of Seventy-second Street and the Drive, where he said to a companion, "Haven't we passed Peekskill yet?") was that bounded roughly by Gramercy Park, Madison and Union Squares and Third Avenue. It seems a little strange that some society of sentimentalists has not invaded this district with its memorials and plaques, but the fact is there is nothing to protect any of the O. Henry haunts from the careless pickaxe of improvement. Nothing, unless you count an unlabelled portrait of him in the lobby of the Hotel Caledonia in West Twenty-sixth Street. This is the place where eighteen years ago in June he was stricken with the illness that caused his death.

Unlike even the house in Washington Square where the minor poet, Alan Seeger, lived, the house most commonly associated with the minstrel of the Big Town of Razzle Dazzle bears no tangible remembrance of him. It is at 55 Irving Place, and the two rooms he had are now occupied by the Medical Department of the Workmen's Circle. The curator of the O. Henry tradition here seemed to be a blonde young lady busied with papers and petitions of sad-eyed workmen sitting on benches outside a railing. She had heard that O. Henry once lived here—sightseers drop in occasionally—but that was all.

Our experience was likewise ironical at what is now the Van Clede Hotel, a dark building with a sign reading "A Good Place to Eat," in East Fifteenth Street. Until eight years ago it was the Hotel America. This was the setting for the story "The Gold That Glittered," and O. Henry adorned the place with the tradition that here many a South and Central American revolution was conceived. It is no longer the headquarters of "generalissimos and imperators" but the present manager remembered the legend. He was obviously puzzled, however, when we asked about O.

Henry, and finally suggested that perhaps we meant Henry George, who once lived at a hotel a few doors away.

Next we visited the ancient beer hall which O. Henry called "Old Munich" and where his famous story "The Halberdier of the Little Rheinschloss" was laid. It used to ramble from an ornate Third Avenue entrance around to another entrance on East Seventeenth Street, a dusky hall heavy with rafters and studded with tankards and steins. The Third Avenue entrance we found has been abandoned, quite recently, and through dim windows we gazed at two melancholy faucets dripping water slowly in a bare room. The old restaurant remains, however, and you go in the curious Seventeenth Street entrance to find the rafters and the tankards intact. Here the tradition is preserved in the recollection of the son of the man who ran the place in the writer's day. He pointed out to us a little table for two set before a great fireplace. "O. Henry used to sit there," he said. "His favorite drink," he added solemnly, "was the Scotch highball."

Our adventure ended there. There are other places, but somehow we didn't have the heart to be met by strange stares and vague replies. We do not advocate making a museum of the district, but some society might at least give out souvenir blotters, that one might remember the addresses.

The Caledonia   APRIL 28, 1928

WE HAVE Mr. F. P. A. to thank for a pleasant sequel to some notes we made here a few weeks ago about places where O. Henry used to live. Mr. Adams politely announced in the *World* that we were in error when we said O. Henry had lived last at the Caledonia. He avowed it was the Chelsea. We were prepared to bow to this, but one spring morning we happened into the Caledonia again and became convinced that we were unquestionably right after all. We found, too, that it is all a pretty serious matter with the people there.

When we first strolled into the Caledonia we couldn't find anyone: the desk and switchboard were deserted. It was like twilight inside the old lobby, even though the April sun was bright outside. It would have been easy to make off with the photograph of O. Henry tilted against the wall on the mantelpiece. We rang a lot of bells and after due time an elevator boy came from somewhere below stairs, and he turned out to be full of a fiery defence of the Caledonia's claim to being the last residence of O. Henry. He went into his elevator and got us a book about Mr. Porter and showed us where Mr. Arthur W. Page—he said the name importantly—wrote that it was the Caledonia. He said *that* name as if it were a shrine. Then he hunted up Mrs. Burget for us. She is the very kindly lady who manages the hotel and she led us into a mellow old sitting-room (the manager's office) and showed us her O. Henry things, books and clippings and odds and ends. Then she took us to Room 21. "He did move away sometimes but he always came back," she said. "The last time, his room had been rented so he stayed in 28 until 21 was vacant again and then moved in here." When we had looked about and seen "the very bed" he slept in, she knocked on the door of the room next to 21. There was no answer. "Captain Pitman is out," she said. "He lived in that room when O. Henry was here and he knew him and has got autographed books and lots of clippings. He will tell you that O. Henry lived there until they took him to the hospital."

Then she told us about Mr. Miller. He was the manager in O. Henry's time, and just a few days before our recent call he had been in to revisit the Caledonia and had told her then how he had been one of the last to say good-bye when the author made his final departure. "They were just starting to drive away with O. Henry," said Mrs. Burget. "Mr. Miller went out and told him he would be back in a day or two, he was certain. But O. Henry smiled and said you could never be certain about things like that."

It was just two days later that O. Henry, at the Polyclinic Hospital, uttered his last phrase: something about opening the blinds and letting in the light. An interesting fact is that the hospital has no record of him. This is because the government took over the hospital in 1918 and lost all the records. There is one official record, of course—in the city's vital statistics archives—and we looked it up, not because it means a great deal to us, or to Mr. Adams, but because it is so important to the elevator boy and Mrs. Burget. The record gives, as his final residence, 28 West Twenty-sixth Street—the Caledonia.

Last Call   MAY 19, 1928

OLDER RESIDENTS around Gramercy Park were astonished to find one night in April no lights in Allaire's. A padlock hung on the hospitable doors of the famous old *bierhalle*. Sentimental inquirers learned finally that the night before a few silent gentlemen had eaten the last dinner ever served in the place. Its passing was not generally known, however, until proclamation was made that there would be an auction of its equipment last week.

Allaire's Scheffel Hall has brooded for fifty years in Seventeenth Street, a few steps from Gramercy Park, the Washington Irving house, and the O. Henry house. Twenty-five years ago it was a favorite sanctuary of musicians and artists and literary men. Visitors went there to have a look at William Sydney Porter and Richard Harding Davis and Stephen Crane sitting about over pipes and beer. Fourteen kinds of domestic and imported beer were on tap, the steaks were celebrated, and some days as many as three hundred orders of pigs' knuckles and sauerkraut were served. A musty tone of tranquillity was given by high shelves holding old steins, smoky rafters veining the ceiling, and faded scenes of duellists and rollicking monks and burgomasters painted on the walls. It had been copied in a fashion after a hall in Munich (hence O. Henry's name for it, Old Munich) and "seemed atmospherically correct," said that writer, "when viewed through the bottom of a glass." When such a view was pleasantly legal the hall flourished, and even after prohibition it held on somehow for ten years more. Slowly the old patrons drifted away. No one came any longer at ten in the morning to sit over cheese and wine late into the twilight. Some nights there was no one there at all but the waiters, whispering and melancholy.

We attended the auction Wednesday. Drab proprietors of little Third Avenue restaurants shuffled about looking for bargains in dishes. Morbid fellows out of work idled in, drawn by the drooping flag of the auctioneer. The floor was dustily littered and the room was heavy with stogie smoke. The auctioneer, wearing a bright gray hat, sat in a chair on a bare table-top and chanted prices. There was a stepladder before the great fireplace. Somebody had climbed up to hang a numbered tag on the huge dark-wood clock above it. Its every wheel was made by hand in Germany and it had chimed the hours away for fifty years. There were fingermarks, too, on the dust of the powder horn above the clock, inviolate for decades. On tables around the walls were ranged chinaware and kitchen utensils and, in close formation like prisoners, two hundred pewter-lidded steins. The auctioneer chanted the fine old virtues of the steins. An elderly Teutonic gentleman picked one up, sighed, and put it down. Nobody, while we were there, broke the spell of his fascination and bid for them. Finally a man bought ten platters and seventy-five plates. This proceeding was recorded by the auctioneer's assistant, who stood behind the old cigar case and pushed down the surprised restaurant cat when it jumped up and rubbed against his arm. The breaking of the glass in that cigar case one day twenty years ago formed the starting point for O. Henry's story, "The

Halberdier of the Little Rheinschloss." The small disaster caught his fancy and he wrote of it, "I did not like things to happen in Old Munich. Nothing had ever happened there before." The stogie smoke at length got into our eyes and so we left.

Childs in Paramount   JUNE 9, 1928

ALTHOUGH EXPLORERS had often told us that one must see the new Childs restaurant under the Paramount Theatre, which combines the best features of the two, we had never, until yesterday, visited it. There are two lovely entrances. One is on Forty-third Street and the other on Broadway next to the National Shirt Shop. The latter entrance is prominently marked "Restaurant," but you must look sharp to find the familiar script name under that.

Entering the place, you begin a research magnificent. Beautiful winding Paramount stairs lead down to where a lady in blue stands at the approach to a long Childs corridor and murmurs, with fine Paramount courtesy, "Please keep on going."

At length you come upon a great field of tables and chairs and may discern, far to the west, the shining food counters. This is the largest Childs on Manhattan. Its quality blends with the quality of Paramount as a rainbow with the sunset. In the gigantic hook-up, Childs tables are lit by the soft glow of many finely wrought Paramount lanterns hanging from the groined ceiling. Once, we had heard, a Paramount usher used to stand at the entrance to the dining-room and say, "Trays straight ahead, please, Publix Service." He is no longer there. We asked a pretty Childs lady about him. "Oh," she said, "he went back to Paramount." Such little pronouncements have a portentous ring in these vast halls.

Adventurously we made the rounds with a bright tray. Even the careless vegetable salad is sculptured with great care where Childs and Paramount meet. There is a shape of grandeur about the meatless meat things. We sat alone at a remote table. Behind us a hundred whispering diners seemed lost in the dreamy expanse of Service. We shouted at our waitress (you feel you must raise your voice, as on a prairie where a wind is blowing), "Has this place ever been filled?" "No," she said, "everybody doesn't know about it yet." Everybody should, somehow. As sheer spectacle, as something romantic in Mergers, it is worth seeing. One sits and weaves dreams about a narrow gold staircase at the back. It is not an exit. It just winds mysteriously into darkness. One expects to hear a deep musical thunder round about. All is quiet, however, until a spoon drops with the clatter of a shield falling in a castle. It would be a wonderful place for a weekend, or to learn to play the xylophone.

One Wonderful Hour
AUGUST 18, 1928

THE BYRD-HOPS-OFF HOUR, given through the courtesy of the Tidewater Oil Company, was in some respects the high-water mark of our summer. Having been about a great deal, we have the vanity to believe we can outguess any entertainment and know what is going to happen. This was a night of surprises. We were surprised when Mayor Walker got up to speak. Not one of the two hundred persons in the gray and gold room of the National Broadcasting Company forgot himself and applauded. This definitely establishes a broadcasting room as more awesome than a church even, for Mr. Walker was applauded in a church the time Governor Smith's daughter was married. The mayor boggled his broadcasting and that was surprising. He kept turning, with his little grimaces, to his visible audience, which was behind him, and thus many of his words were lost on the twelve million persons who were, figuratively, in front of him. A nervous, tip-toeing radio man touched the mayor's back and pushed him nearer the microphone. The mayor ventured a wisecrack about this, and fumbled it. That was surprising.

If the awe-struck audience's immobility unsettled the mayor, the whole soft-shoe procedure unsettled the sturdy members of Byrd's crew, his chief cook, his steward, his mechanic, all stiff and uneasy in front-row seats. Big and strong fellows, they were cowed by fussy gentlemen who directed them, by little gestures, to stand up, to say something, to shut up, to sit down. Each man bravely spoke a tremulous, albeit well-rehearsed, line over the radio and resumed his seat, frightened. The ordeal was painful. The audience stirred restlessly. It was a triumph for something. Byrd himself read his speech in calm, easy cadences, thanking those who have aided him, thanking especially, in a neatly turned phrase, the Tidewater Oil Company, makers of Veedol.

The attempt to give, in a soft-toned gray and gold room, the lusty, bustling effect of a crew of muscular adventurers loading their ship did not exactly come off. A tall man in a dinner jacket kept solemnly dropping a heavy iron chain onto the floor, picking it up and dropping it again. Another man blew a deep-toned whistle. The members of the orchestra growled and murmured and said, "Gangway." A fat second-violin stomped both feet. This imitation of the loading of the Byrd ship at the Jersey docks accompanied the announcement over the radio of the inventory of the ship's cargo, including Veedol oil. The racket was suspended at intervals for musical numbers, and for the reading of breathless telegrams of Godspeed from Assistant Secretary of the Navy Robinson, Gene Tunney, Vice-President Shea of the Tidewater Oil Company, Clarence Chamberlin, and Lady Astor, whose cable, "If men must fly, women must pray," was received without a sound one way or the other.

The climax came when a colored youth in a white jacket read a speech for Matt Hansen, the Negro hero who is the only survivor of Peary's dash to the pole. The colored youth was superb. Heckled every few paragraphs by the wild gesturing of the orchestra leader, he paused each time at the right place. This gave Grieg's "In the Hall of the Mountain King" a break. That piece accompanied the youth throughout his fifteen-minute talk except when he told, or tried to tell, about the April day when Peary planted the American flag in the ice of the North Pole. At this point hell broke loose. The man with the chain dropped it rapidly, the man with the whistle blew it loudly, a canvas wind machine was set going, a motor was turned on which flapped four strips of leather against a table leg in imitation of an airplane engine, and two trumpeters, a trombonist, and two French-horn players leaped to their feet and blared "The Stars and Stripes Forever." No pigeons were let loose.

Afterwards, on the way down in the elevator, a clerkish chap, who didn't appear strong enough to do it, said he was going to get off at the thirteenth floor for the Palmolive hour, and did. Personally, we were at home, tired but happy, by 9:30.

Discoveries West   OCTOBER 13, 1928

WE WENT adventuring into the brawling avenues along the North River, got lost immediately, and stumbled into Little W. 12 St., as the street signs describe it. This thoroughfare is but two blocks long, given over to ducks, celery, and calves for sale, and it leads you to the rim of DeLamater Square, where it expires. DeLamater Square is at the confluence of Tenth and Eleventh Avenues, and is really an esplanade for the three Cunard piers. Probably nobody knows it has so fine a name. It is just called the docks by most people, yet it is almost as broad as the Place de la Concorde. Trucks pound by with cargoes of dressed meats, fittings and valves, Uneeda biscuits, tile, salad dressing, doors and sashes, and coal. This is the playground of the ten-ton truck. Tenth and Eleventh Avenues surge toward a lonely little island in the middle of the vast square, divide against a tawdry hotel called the Strand (a fountain ought to be here) and go their separate ways.

We followed Eleventh Avenue up past the Red Star and the White Star lines to City Plaza which, in case you have never caught the name, is the ugly square between Twenty-second and Twenty-third Streets in front of the Jersey ferries. Wide concrete walks provide easy access to the ferries but ruin the grass. Farther north we discovered Thirteenth Avenue. As in the case of DeLamater Square, it is practically unknown. It is the farthest west and the dreariest of these *boulevards exterieurs*, and to be arithmetically correct, should be called Twelfth Avenue, because it is but one block west of Eleventh. The pier houses are small and dismal, their ships sail for points which are not important. Across the streets are gloomy places that were once saloons —four or five in a row. Several are restaurants now. Through the cobwebby windows of the others the old bars may be seen.

Thirteenth Avenue staggers north and dies, by drowning, at Twenty-eighth Street. At any rate, for some reason it is flooded here with a foot or more of water. To one side, an old abandoned taxi sat in the flood. Probably an old chauffeur was sprawled over its wheel. We didn't investigate. North of here the avenue becomes a pathway slinking around warehouses and piles of stone until (we found out on a map later) it comes out finally in the Forties as Twelfth Avenue, which it should have been called all the time.

Hot Dog OCTOBER 27, 1928

THE COMING of the Zeppelin should have some simple, if belated, memorial as the biggest hot-dog event of the year. From Atlantic City and Coney the camp followers of sensation hurried to Lakehurst—the hot-dog men, the hawkers of novelties, the balloon sellers. Their stands lined the dusty road leading to the edge of the landing field. Later comers opened their suitcases on the ground and boldly accosted the sightseers. A tall colored man, who wore a silk hat and sold peanuts, also dispensed jollity like merchandise. We gathered that he followed disaster around the country because the prospect of disaster whets the appetites of people. On this occasion the prospect was an overdue airship, with a hole in one of its stabilizers. The hawkers jollied the crowds. "Well-l-l, a loaf of bread and a pound of meat and all the mustard you can eat." The people were, as the banter of the wise vendors indicated, a gay, ornery, unmanageable crowd, not come soberly to gaze at a new Columbus sailing out of Europe, but to see what would happen when a wounded ship landed.

When the ship appeared over the field a captain of marines pleaded for silence. "The landing crew cannot hear the commands," he shouted. The people in machines tooted their horns in response to this. Noise and confusion added a spice to danger. "Throw away your cigarettes," cried the captain. The crowd went right on smoking. The officer cupped his hands and bellowed: "Put out your cigarettes, pipes, cigars—" The crowd took it up. "Peanuts, popcorn, Coca-Cola." A captain of marines isn't used to that.

Against the marine's protests that someone might be killed, the crowds broke over the guards and rushed for the Zeppelin, as it nosed down, and dust hid the ship from view. There were struggles as the guards fought back. A man with a banana in one hand and a small American flag in the other was shoved by a marine and fell down. He kept his hold on the banana. A truck careened across the field, driving into the ranks of people, scattering them, forcing them back. The people were thrilled and made guttural sounds.

In the end, order was restored, without serious accident, and a discontented mob scurried off the field. There was a rush for trains and buses and automobiles. The professional vendors had departed, aware that you can't sell to disgruntled sensation seekers, but a few townspeople, left with homemade sandwiches on their hands, shouted their wares futilely at the crowds. There was a fight for seats in the sightseeing buses. Persons with return tickets were crowded out by interlopers waving five-dollar bills. The most hardboiled survived. The scene of struggle was lighted by a glow from a small refreshment stand near by. The stand's sign bore an American flag draped over the legend "Hot Franks, Soft Drinks."

Big Boy   MAY 4, 1929

THE TALL, somewhat paunchy, but still erect figure of Jack Johnson may be seen about Broadway these days. He walks proudly. He never forgets his gloves. His step is a little less springy, and his face no longer gleams in the ebony and gold splendor which admiring Londoners compared to a "starry night" almost twenty years ago when he was the rage over there. He might pass for thirty-five. He was fifty-one on his last birthday. People turn to look at him as he walks majestically about the town, but most of them probably do not recognize the man many experts call the greatest heavyweight of them all. It is different from the day in 1911 when he sailed into New York on the Kronprinzessin Cecilie with a white valet, a white secretary, a limousine, a touring car, and two racers, boasting of the prodigious amounts of his weekly hotel bills abroad. Crowds followed him around in the years of his glory, but the once famous champion and notorious *bon vivant* has fallen on less glamorous days. He is not broke, but he is not affluent. Wealth he never hoarded. The fifty-one hundred dollars he got for boxing Philadelphia Jack O'Brien before the war, for instance, he spent in four days, on dinners, a ring, and an automobile. Now he is eager to sell stories of his life for money. Unlike the ordinary celebrity, he has not one but three autobiographies in mind: the story of his fights, the story of his loves, and the story of his travels. If you are interested in buying these works, you can get the lot for one hundred thousand dollars.

Jack Johnson lives in Harlem, gets around to the prize-fights, and takes in the shows, some of which he sternly criticizes as immoral. We called on the old champion at the offices of his agents in a building way over in the West Forties. He sat in a swivel chair behind a desk, gesturing now and then with a big banded cigar, closing his eyes to listen, opening them wide when he talked. His plans are uncertain, but he may go into a vaudeville act, as he did some years back, or he may fight some more obscure fights, as he has been doing off and on for several years, for small profits, in the West and Southwest. He won a match in 1926, but was knocked out the following year by an unknown colored boxer named Bearcat Wright of Omaha, tasting the bitter cup that he himself handed to Fitzsimmons in 1907 and the groggy Jeffries in 1910. He still thinks he could lick Tunney, and that Dempsey would be easy. ("Dempsey is one o' dem slashin' boys, and de slashin' boys is mah meat.") Corbett is the only white heavyweight for whom he has any real respect, and the only one he calls "Mistah." It saddens him to recall that Mistah Corbett picked Jeffries to win on that fourth of July nearly twenty years ago.

Some people have the notion that Johnson is still legally banned from America. He gave himself up in 1920, however, and served ten months in Leavenworth for violation of the Mann Act, after evading sentence for seven years, living abroad. He is free to come and go. The churches and the women's clubs, which made his heyday miserable, have forgotten. The death of his first white wife, and his subsequent marriage to another white woman, are vague memories. Proof of this was given, not long ago, when Johnson was cheered by the clergy at a general conference of the Methodist Church in Kansas City at which he denounced liquor, saying, "To serve God, you must train the mind as well as the soul." His Café de Champion in Chicago was padlocked some years ago.

Johnson enjoys recalling the old times. He loves to talk of his favorite city, Budapest, and of the time at the start of the war when the Germans did not molest several trunks containing his wife's sables. During the war, he says, he did secret-service work in Spain, at the request of a Major Lang, U.S.A. Of his "deeper life" he is proud and sensitive. "Ah am," he says, "a very tendah man." He likes to display his hands and face to show how unscarred they are by battle. There is no mark on his head. His skull was X-rayed in San Francisco eighteen years ago. It took five and a half minutes to get the rays through, as against the customary five to fifteen seconds. The bone was found to be from a half to three-quarters of an inch thick, which is thicker than the skull of an ox. Surgeons said that a blow which would fell a steer would simply jar Mr. Johnson.

We were going to ask him about the time Ketchell knocked him down, but thought better of it. Anyway, the old boy probably remembers only that a few seconds later he knocked the gallant middleweight into the next county. We inquired about Mr. Johnson's literary tastes, and he said that he enjoys the books of Richard Harding Davis. Apparently he has never heard Paul Robeson sing. At any rate, he told us he had never met him. We found ourselves on dangerous ground when we brought up the name of Bill Robinson. Jack's eyes had been closed, but they opened quickly and shone like the headlights of a Pierce Arrow. "Nevah mention Bill Robinson in the same breath with Jack Johnson," he warned us. "When he takes off his dancin' shoes he is through, whehas Ah am a deep an' culluful personality."

Jack Johnson is living up on 148th Street now, no longer

in the magnificent style of the years of his grandeur. He once had an apartment in New York that you reached by walking over an expensive, deep, and colorful crimson plush carpet. Legend has it that the day Johnson took up residence there, the carpet was stretched all the way out to the curb. But those were the great days of the dimming past, the days when Lil Ahthuh owned a white Mercedes racing car, hired white people to serve him, and was feared by every white heavyweight prize fighter in the world.

Last Day   MAY 11, 1929

AT NOON of the Waldorf-Astoria's last day, the famous tables in the windows of the main dining room were taken up largely by women. Luncheon cost five dollars. There was no chance to brood peacefully, however, for the restlessness of dissolution was all about. At tea time, the air of disintegration was intense. The low murmuring tranquillity of the Rose Room was gone. Waitresses and patrons had the quick, flurried reactions of those who hear the pickaxe at the walls. "Where can we check our coat?" we asked a tight-lipped waitress. "Better keep hold of your coat if you want to take it away with you," she snapped, angrily. We sat on our coat. It turned out that we should have kept hold of our teapot too. A headwaitress came over and took it away and sold it to a woman at the next table for two dollars and a half. The woman liked ours better than her own because the top fitted more snugly. Tea thus being over, we wandered about the corridors.

It was mostly women, hundreds of them, who were weeping the old hotel away. The Rubinstein Club, the first woman's organization to make the Waldorf its headquarters, was holding its last meeting. The women were dressed in frilly white garden frocks, with floppy hats, although it was gloomy and rainy outside. Some of them were quite old and had to be helped about, but they wore light things gaily too, like doomed inhabitants of a siege town, resolved to go out bravely. Many of them carried potted plants under their arms, last souvenirs. This seemed to inspire in others that curious desire, which sometimes gets the best of even the nicest people, to make off with everything that isn't nailed down. Everyone moved about in a twitchy and furtive way. Our own companion, a lady of exemplary habits, was white and silent for ten blocks after we left, not, it came out, because of grief at the passing of old traditions, but because, as she nervously revealed at last, she had gotten away with ten small ashtrays.

We dropped in for the last time at midnight. People in evening dress were quietly slipping out. The music of a waltz drew us to the Jade Room, where people were dancing soberly, as on a sinking ship. It was all quite sad, but our tears were spared by the last memory of all—a small talk we had with an aged elevator man. "Do you dread leaving the old Waldorf?" we asked, perversely, knowing full well his sobs would break our heart. "Not me, brother" he said, loudly, "I got plenty Waldorf."

Mob Scene

OCTOBER 26, 1929

THERE'S A BROKEN plate-glass window for every sale in Fourteenth Street. If you like riots and accidents and take a sardonic pleasure in watching women revert to type, go down to Fourteenth Street on a Bargain Day. Blue and white flags are hung out, as for a holiday, in front of the store which is having the sale—although this bit of information may be misleading, for usually the stores on both sides hang out flags too, thus catching the overflow and saving the cost of a half-page newspaper ad. On the morning of the sale, six or eight police, assigned to this special duty, arrive early, but the women are there before them, surging up from subways, flowing down from the "L." By a quarter of nine, grim, chattering, they have been formed into line, four abreast, and begin to surge against the grilled gates which the storekeepers long ago found necessary to avoid being stormed before everything is ready. Wooden frameworks are put up the night before to protect the windows but, as intimated above, they frequently don't work.

At the R. Smith sale, near Sixth Avenue last week, they didn't work. We were there when they broke, and a window with them. The gates were opened at a signal from within, the police bawled for order. Unheeding them, the ladies began to push. Animal squeals went up all along the line. They rose to a shriek, and the big drive was on. A railing around a window gave way, the glass broke, and a great piece fell like the blade of a guillotine. Two children were injured. The police bawled threats, but momentum was fed the column from half a block away, and there was no breasting it. It was many minutes before the victims could be removed.

When the first thousand or so women got inside, there to shout insults and grab things, the outer gates, two in number, were finally forced shut by main, blue-coated strength. A two-hundred-pound officer guarded one; the other, which was before the broken window, was locked for the day. This left a bottleneck—and with the bargain hunters still scurrying in from Jersey and Queens. The officer was instructed to let a few women in at a time, but as soon as he got the door slightly ajar they ganged him and he went down like a set-upon football tackle. Three or four policemen came to his rescue, but by the time they got him on his feet and restored the line of blue, two or three hundred women and a few men had got in the store. Some men accompany their wives, as a sort of interference, get the women inside, and depart—if they can.

S. Klein's, in Union Square, is the Gettysburg of the war against cops for dollar-ninety-eight dresses. Here, when they have a sale, the sidewalk is roped off to keep the ladies from raging out into traffic and knocking down innocent trucks. Klein's once worked out a scheme to keep order with-

in their store. They arranged rope aisles in serpentine fashion, putting in several corners that the shoppers had to turn,
and thus avoided a long straightaway down which the attacking column could storm thousands strong. The system
didn't work, though. The ladies just tore the ropes down.

Psychographs   MARCH 1, 1930

ROBERT H. DAVIS, of the *Sun*, has been taking pictures of
prominent people for years and years, with a small folding
camera that you can stick in your pocket. A couple of hundred of them, enlarged from the small negatives, have just
been shown at the Amerian Art Association, Anderson Gal-
leries. The afternoon we were there, the man in charge was
showing a physician, a specialist, around and they stopped
in front of the portrait of Vance Thompson. "That man is
seriously sick," said the doctor. "He is dead," corrected the
guide. Thompson died five days after the picture was taken.

Davis doesn't make a point of taking photographs of
people when they are feeling fine, or even when they are
looking pleasant. He wants the truth. The negatives are
untouched, and every mark and scar and wrinkle on the
face shows in his pictures. One of the earliest displayed is
of the late Frank A. Munsey playing with a squirrel. It was
taken sixteen years ago with the same camera that took the
most recent sitter, Gene Tunney. Tunney's face looks
touched up, but isn't, the fact being that the former prize-
fighter has one of the smoothest complexions you'll find
among prominent gentlemen, excepting maybe among actors. Davis took a second picture of Tunney, but is still
debating whether to put it on the walls. It shows the former champion in one of his notable tempers—hair standing
up, eyes glaring. Davis had twitted him about his interest
in Shakespeare just before he pressed the bulb.

This amateur photographer's method is to get a man
talking about something he is deeply interested in, and take

one picture, and then get him angry, or depressed, or thoughtful, by changing the subject, and take another. Thus he has made many successful "double-studies." One pair is of Robeson, whose temper changes as fast as Tunney's. The first shows him bright-eyed, laughing; the other intense and sombre. On the second photograph Robeson has written "Nobody knows de trouble I see." Davis had got him on the subject of "The Emperor Jones" when he took this one.

Davis has made some excellent studies of bankers, explorers, and whatnot. Rear Admiral Byrd is shown in an esthetic pose; Casey Jones, the aviator, peers intensely at you; General Harbord was caught looking high-powered; and there are interesting pictures of Edison's protégé, Wilber Huston; John McBride, the ticket-agency man; Earl Carroll, with all his freckles showing; Dr. Robert Norwood, rector of St. Bartholomew's; Paavo Nurmi; Jack Powers, a colored man who was once cook for Theodore Roosevelt; David Sarnoff, of the Radio Corporation; Bill Tilden; and Reginald Turner, the man in whose arms Oscar Wilde died.

Davis is going to will his collection to a museum. He never sells any prints and rarely gives any away, even to his subjects.

Humanists and Others   MAY 17, 1930

THE PERSONALITIES, rather than the intellects, of the men who took part in the big Humanism debate in Carnegie Hall last week won the interest of the young lady who accompanied us there. Her attention kept drifting from what Mr. Irving Babbitt, the great Humanist leader, was saying to the way he wore his evening clothes and the way he peered over his glasses. Because she was not attracted to the gentleman personally, she began, in her naïve, childish way, to grow cold toward his theories and beliefs. "Mr. Babbitt," we told her, sternly, "believes in decorum, continence, and all the other admirable virtues—he's not a man like Ernest Hemingway, for instance." "I know he isn't," said our lady. We kept hoping that Mr. Henry Seidel Canby, who was the next speaker and who is also a Humanist, might win our companion over to a better way of life. We tried to concentrate on his arguments, which were considerably less profound than Mr. Babbitt's. Our companion, however, closed her eyes and began to go quietly to sleep. We nudged her. "I don't want to listen," she said, irritably. "I'm sure he wears overshoes." This angered us. We, too, were conscious of a slightly disturbing conviction that Mr. Canby probably does wear overshoes when the weather is dampish, but what kind of argument is that against a man's philosophy of life? We told our companion that we deplored the physical basis of her judgment in intellectual matters. "I bet he catches cold easily," she said, and closed her eyes again.

When Mr. Carl Van Doren, the last speaker, rose up to attack Humanism, and actually advocated that one should go as far as one liked in everything, our companion sat up. "He has a nice smile," she said. We told her that that meant nothing. The speaker then began to say funny things, attacking decorum in a most indecorous and unfair manner, abandoning logic and reason—to which the Humanist orators had admirably adhered. We called our companion's attention to the lamentable injustice of this method. "He has lovely hair," she said, admiringly. (Mr. Van Doren's hair is iron-gray, Mr. Babbitt's a palish white, and Mr. Canby is slightly bald.) "He's been playing tennis, too," said our lady. "See how ruddy and healthy he looks." At this, we sharply demanded, under our breath, if she thought that excess, lack of decorum, unrestraint, going too far, etc., were all right simply because a ruddy-looking man, who seems to have been playing tennis, advocates them. "Yes," she said, and we lapsed into a contemptuous silence.

When it was all over, our companion said that she was an anti-Humanist. "What, then," we demanded, coldly, "is the difference between monism and dualism?" (You have to know that in order to know whether you are a Humanist or not.) "I don't know," she said, and giggled. Later, out in the street, while we looked for a cab, she began again. "The last debate I heard here," she said, "was between Clarence Darrow and Wayne Wheeler, on prohibition. Mr. Darrow was a much older man, but he looked *years* younger, and he said he had never gotten too much to drink in his life—or enough, I guess it was. He's a very attractive man, whereas Mr. Wheeler—"

"Mr. Wheeler," we interrupted, in a stern, admonishing tone, "is dead."

"I know he is," she said.

The High Place

ONE MINUTE we are comfortably reading the "Idylls of the King" and the next thing we know we are climbing up scaffolding. Last week it was the Empire State Building, to which we were lured from our Tennyson, out of a preposterous desire to climb to a point where we could kiss the Chrysler Building good-bye and report the sensation to our earthbound readers.

It was a pleasant day and the outside of the building was shining in the sun. You've noticed that gleam. It is obtained by the use of "Allegheny metal," an alloy of iron and chrome-nickel tougher than aluminum, lighter than steel, and calculated to glitter seven years without cleaning. Just now it represents the bright face of danger. Inside the building, seven thousand workmen chevy you about. High-voltage coils have to be stepped around. Elevators take you by fits and starts as high as the seventy-eighth floor; from there you have to walk. (These elevators, by the way, will go at a speed of a thousand feet a minute in the completed building, this by special dispensation of the

313

building commission, which has never permitted elevators to go that fast before.)

If we counted right we got to the eighty-first floor, from which point the apple-vendors looked like midgets selling red peppermint hearts. Al Smith recently went that high, looked down, and decided he was high enough. He likes to have walls around him. It had been planned to have Mr. Smith go up to the tiptop of the steelwork, when it is completed around Thanksgiving Day, and put a golden bolt in the last beam, but chances are he won't. Even the steelworkers themselves felt a bit jittery when they got to the eighty-fifth floor, and asked for a bonus. They got it. There have been few accidents on the job. Steel was hoisted up on the inside, a new idea to avoid endangering passers-by. The schedule was so carefully timed that a minute or two after a steel beam arrived from Pittsburgh by way of Weehawken, it was on its way up to its appointed place. It represents the fastest job of steel construction on record. The men wanted to celebrate this and asked Al Smith, when he was there, if they could build a hundred-and-twenty-foot brown derby and stick it on top of the mooring mast for a while. He was too modest to allow this.

The mooring mast, the builders say, is no publicity stunt, no ornament to be set on top of the building for beauty's sake. So they say. It will cost a hundred and twenty thousand dollars. The topmost room in the building will be in the mooring mast and will hold fifty people easily and staunchly. The roof of it will also hold fifty people, and sometime next spring these fifty will be balloon-moorers, for plans are being made to anchor a Zeppelin to the mast next May or June—the ZRS-4, a thousand-footer, now being built by Goodyear. The dirigible will drop a grappling hook to the roof, draw up a mooring line, and then (if all goes well) the moorers will drag the ship down by a winch on the roof. Passengers will exit into the tower through a door in the airship's nose. Anyway, that's the plan. Sightseers can't use the mast; there'll be a glassed-in observation-room for them on the roof of the eighty-fifth floor. The last office floor will be the eightieth—and will be occupied by the Messrs. Smith, Raskob, Pierre du Pont, and Louis G. Kaufman.

The Empire State is sunk in solid rock; three hundred thousand tons were removed and the building will weigh only half of that. Safe, you see. As for the old Waldorf, most of it rests today at the bottom of the ocean. The building was so toughly constructed that it cost nine hundred thousand dollars to tear it down. Usually wreckers pay for the privilege and make money on what they salvage, but much of the Waldorf had to be ruined to knock it loose, and the ruins were towed to sea in barges and dumped.

Big and Costly
NOVEMBER 22, 1930

WE'VE BEEN through the Hotel St. George in Brooklyn, or as much of it as we could get through at our age. We promised to make the trip a long time ago when we hurt the St. George's feelings by saying the Hotel New Yorker was the second biggest in the world. The St. George has a hundred and twenty-nine rooms more than the New Yorker, two thousand six hundred and thirty-two in all. We were technically right, however, for at the time we wrote the St. George wasn't quite finished. The Stevens in Chicago is the largest hotel in the world: three thousand rooms.

Our guide reeled off stupendous figures, such as four hundred and eighty million (the candlepower of the largest air beacon in the world). Practically everything the St. George has is the largest in some vast area, usually the world. It has the largest ballroom in the world (capacity, three thousand persons), the largest banquet facilities in the world ("sixteen gorgeous rooms"), and the world's largest collection of sheets and pillow-cases (six hundred and ten thousand and five hundred and sixty thousand

315

respectively). The St. George has seven miles of corridors, sixty-six thousand four hundred and six light bulbs, four hundred and sixty-six private fire-alarm boxes (world's largest fire-alarm system), twenty thousand chairs, and, on the Colorama control, five hundred and forty-six levers, buttons, and toggles.

The Colorama is an electric-lighting device by means of which the largest number of shades and hues in the world are produced in the grand ballroom. Boy, when they get it going it's spectacular! The walls are covered with tier on tier of "flutes and coves" containing yellow, red, blue, and green lights. More than a million watts are used. There can't be anything in Hell like it.

Off the main lobby a wide hallway, whose walls give an effect of blue sea waves, leads to the most costly indoor swimming pool ever built (one million two hundred and sixty-three thousand dollars), "the most beautiful room in the world, the most attractive in history." It's worth seeing, even if you don't swim. White lights, in modernistic fixtures, are reflected from the world's largest areas of mirrors. They are gold mirrors; that is, they reflect the white light so that it looks golden. The illusion created by the inter-reflecting mirror areas is impressive. You seem to see for a hundred miles. It looks like the ocean. It darn near *is* the ocean. The balcony around the pool has room for two million spectators. No, no, two thousand.

The St. George is four minutes from Wall Street, fifteen from Times Square by subway. A day's registration runs from two hundred to a thousand persons. They come from Manhattan, Milwaukee, Florida, Pernambuco, London, Buenos Aires. Mickey Walker has stayed there, and Mabel W. Willebrandt, and the Brooklyn baseball team. It's a big hotel, but chummy. A social director, busy every minute, organizes hikes, reading circles, ping-pong games, bridge tournaments. The bridge winners two weeks ago were Miss Ella Bernath in Room 10009 and Miss Rose

Wormtorth in Room 20009. Sometimes thirty organizations are meeting at one time in the ballrooms, salons, and parlors. When we were there the Peck Memorial Hospital was dancing in the Italian Village, the house guests were taking French lessons in the Lorelei Room, and the National Lead Company fellows were meeting in the Vanity Fair Room.

The Egyptian Roof (turn right when you get out of the elevator or you're in the Chinese Room) has a marvellous view of the harbor and the sky line. From where we stood we could look far down on the modest little Hotel Margaret, where Joseph Pennell, the etcher, lived. He used to say that his view from the Margaret was the finest in the world. The Egyptian Roof of the St. George is fifteen stories or so higher. The view is that much better than the finest in the world.

Sapolio

OUR STORY of the lady who picked up a first edition of "Leaves of Grass" at a country auction for a dime has brought forth word from a collector about a Bret Harte item that few people of today have ever heard of. It's a paper pamphlet, an advertising throwaway, a forerunner of the kind the mailman now delivers to you. On the cover (we have seen one) are the words: " 'Excelsior,' by Bret Harte, Presented by Enoch Morgan's Sons Co." Inside, on cheap, yellowish paper, are eight stanzas parodying Longfellow. Like this:

> The shades of night were falling fast,
> As through an Eastern village passed
> A youth who bore, through dust and heat,
> A stencil-plate, that read complete—"Sapolio."

Harte wrote these jingles in 1877. He mailed them to Morgan's Sons in New York and received a cheque for fifty dollars. They were first printed on a single sheet of paper and distributed as advertising matter. None of these dodgers are known to be in existence. If your mother or grandmother put one aside and you can find it, it is probably worth two or three hundred dollars. Later the stanzas were made into the booklet. About a million of these were distributed. Only four are known to be in existence. People with old houses might profitably look through their attics, as one of the four cost two hundred and twenty-five dollars at an auction. When the present Morgan's Sons people heard that the booklets were selling for big prices they hopefully ransacked their old factory, at West and Bank Streets. They found only one copy.

You mustn't assume from the foregoing that Harte also wrote the famous Spotless Town jingles for Sapolio. The author of these was J. K. Fraser, who now, in his late fifties, is president of the Blackman Company, the advertising concern. He wrote the jingles shortly after getting out of college and was surprised when they became about as well known as " 'Twas the night before Christmas." He was a conspicuous figure for years afterward and got tired of being pointed out as the writer of the verses. He still, they say, slips out of the room if the subject is mentioned.

Last year, when an old building was torn down at Morris Street and Broadway, a huge sign on the wall of an adjoining building was revealed for the first time since 1889. It blazoned this slogan: "Man wants but little here below, but Woman wants Sapolio." Remember? If not, your mother will. About the time this was painted Sapolio was the most-exploited article in America, perhaps in the world. In 1892, for example, a Captain Andrews sailed a fourteen-foot sloop named Sapolio from Atlantic City to Spain, attracting wide attention. The soap was put on the market in 1869, and still sells well, we are told, despite the competition from soap chips and cleaning powders. Morgan's Sons, in fact, are reviving the Spotless Town characters in connection with a renewed advertising drive. They are appearing as cut-out figures in window displays, somewhat modernized: the policemen in new uniforms, the maids with up-to-date caps and aprons, and so on.

Tea Party

SIMON & SCHUSTER gave a tea last week called the "Believe-It-or-Not" party, the occasion being the publication of a new book by that name. The idea was to get up a party which would be like the book—that is: incredible but true —and it was a success. About a hundred and fifty people, mostly literary figures, moved about with teacups and fountain pens, drinking tea and autographing books. Gene Tunney was there, and he autographed a book for Sir Hubert Wilkins, who was autographing a book for Count Felix von Luckner. Tunney wore a brown suit, with soft tan shirt and dark red tie, secured by a small gold pin. Count von Luckner wore a blue suit and a hard shiny collar. Both looked debonair but unreal.

Everybody had to sign a huge book at the door. It contains the oddest collection of names in the world and is probably worth a great deal of money. Count von Luckner was the third person to arrive. His signature, "Felix Count Luckner," was fourteen inches long and two inches high. A Mr. Joe Rosenblatt signed right under him, taking up only the same amount of space as the word "Count." Ely Culbertson signed right after we did. Sidney Lenz arrived eight signatures later. The two, as you know, have for months been challenging each other to a contract-bridge game. To everybody's surprise, the game was not played at the party. Some people thought they wouldn't even speak, but they signed each other's book and the news spread quickly through the crowd. Then Eddie Cantor signed Culbertson's book and Tunney signed Lenz' and Lenz signed Major James Doolittle's. A Mr. Sam Weisenhouse signed ours and asked us if Hendrik Van Loon had arrived yet.

It was all very crowded and now and again you signed somebody's book or somebody signed yours by accident, due to jostling. Somebody said one book was signed "Count von Wilkins," due to jostling, but we didn't see it. The Count and the Sir talked together for a long time, and we edged up to hear what was being said. Count von Luckner was saying: "Our two countries should never have fought." We were introduced *to* Tunney and *as* Tunney. A strange woman in a green hat, mistaking us for somebody else, said: "Where was you?" We said: "To the taxidermist's," and she went around telling people we were Ring Lardner. Sir Hubert thereupon came over and praised us for "The Outline of Science."

Simon & Schuster's is a lot of bright, ivory-colored rooms joined together, containing pictures of John Cowper Powys and Will Durant, Simon & Schuster authors. People moved from room to room, passing sandwich tables, passing Tunney, passing a radio to which one couple was dancing, passing a ping-pong table at which two women, wearing fur coats, were playing. At the end of three hours we hadn't met Ripley, the so-called guest of honor. We hadn't met One Long Hop, the Chinaman who was named after Lindbergh's flight, either. He was there. We asked a young lady how to find Ripley. "He's got spats," she said. A man who looked like Coolidge arrived. Believe it or not, it wasn't Coolidge.

1015   DECEMBER 19, 1931

NO CROWDS bustle without the Hotel Chatham, or surge up and down in the elevators, while Lenz and Culbertson are playing bridge there. You have to go up to the tenth floor and down the hallway before you can be sure you are in the right hotel. This hallway is busy and noisy. People hurry in and out of rooms, carrying bulletins and memoranda. Typewriters and telegraph instruments rattle. Bulletins bearing the latest scores, the latest hands, the latest comment from Culbertson, are constantly being thumbtacked on the walls of the rooms. He keeps sending pencilled notes out of Room 1015, *the* room. Its door is shut and a silent man stands guard. The master's notes are hastily typewritten and posted. This one was put up as we stood by: "Rubber 24. Board 135. Contract—4 spades by Mr. Lenz. Result—4 spades. Remarks: Complete accuracy of this hasty analysis cannot be guaranteed. Furthermore, it is understood this is my personal opinion. O. Jacoby has not 1 plus quick trick to respond with 2 No Trumps according to official system, but it's very close. Very lucky hand on the play." This communiqué, which didn't seem to excite anybody, was covered up presently by a newer one.

About ten o'clock a tiptoeing man with his fingers to his lips let us into 1015 and pointed to chairs placed behind a screen. We could see the players by peeping through the cracks where the panels joined. It was like peeping through a fence at a ballpark and made us feel silly. The card table was ten feet away. Culbertson, teetering on his chair, had his back to us, and we caught only occasional glimpses of his profile. He looked gaunt and grim. Mrs. Culbertson, opposite, kept frowning and compressing her lips, which are thin and determined. Lenz thoughtfully flicked his nose with his thumb from time to time. Oswald Jacoby, curly-haired and healthy-looking, seemed the least tense of them all. Lenz looked at his cards close to the chest, poker fashion, when they were dealt to him, examining them slowly, one at a time. The others swept up theirs and met the news, good or bad, at once. The four played rapidly and at the end of each round spoke a few words, in low tones, rather strained. There were no protests, sharp words, or arguments while we were there. Nobody seemed disagreeable, but nobody seemed happy. Sitting at some distance from the table were four or five silent watchers:

scorers, the referee, etc. A tall, dark woman kept track, with sharp eyes, of each lead and jotted it down. Culbertson scribbled intermittently.

The players do not take in the tricks that they win, for that would mix up the cards. Each player keeps his cards, after they are played, in a pile in front of him, so that they can be hastily recorded and the news rushed to the world. Somebody behind the screen with us snickered. "Silence!" hissed an attendant. After ten minutes of peeping, we were told our time was up. In the rooms off the hallway, checker games and bridge games were going on. The Culbertson children sleep through it all in a room whose door says: "Children are asleep—and dreaming—here." You can't get in to see them.

Unveiling   JULY 9, 1932

THE CLASSIEST orange-drink stand in town was unveiled last week. We don't mean figuratively, either; we mean literally. It was unveiled at 6:07 P.M. one sticky afternoon by no less an unveiler than the Honorable Harvey D. Gibson, the banker. He twitched a rope and caused two big canvas curtains to fall down, revealing, behind the counter of the newest Nedick's, four or five grinning boys and girls ready to serve orange drinks. The new stand, Nedick's Mayfair, is at the northeast corner of Seventh Avenue and Forty-seventh Street, right on the sidewalk. It was for this reason an unavoidably crowded and rather awkward unveiling. Most of the people surging by—messenger-boys, missing husbands, muttering women—thought there had been a raid or that somebody was hurt. The cops on hand gave that impression, too; they told people to "keep ahn movin' nah!" That's not the way to treat people who are watching such a ceremony; something is lost if you are chivied at an unveiling.

There were several Unique Features, not the least of

which was a big Mack truck that stood at the curb, its bumper and running-boards trimmed with dainty green and yellow paper (the colors of Old Nedick's) and with a flounce, running around its chassis, stamped in an old-fashioned-flower-garden motif. Was the Mack's face red! On the truck was a small sad man and a real genuine live Florida orange tree with real genuine live Florida oranges on it, skillfully tied to the branches. Just before the unveiling a bevy of pretty girls showed up, each with a green wicker basket into which the man on the truck placed California Sunkist oranges; he got them from boxes under the Florida orange tree. The girls pushed coolly through the crowd, selling the oranges for a quarter or what had you. The money was for the benefit of the Actors' Dinner Club, which explains the hookup except for the Harvey D. Gibson angle, which is unexplained. With each orange you got a chance in a raffle.

Twelve prizes, we almost forgot to say, hung on the walls behind the orange-drink counter: Paul Whiteman's belt, Ann Pennington's tap shoes, Daniel Frohman's wallet, a hanky belonging to Beverly Bayne, a hanky belonging to Walter Hampden, the key Sam Jaffe used as Kringelein in "Grand Hotel." . . .

The dots above indicate a lapse of five hours and a half. At eleven-thirty that same night, we were back at Nedick's Mayfair for the pulling of the lucky numbers out of a fish bowl by a pretty actress. It was crowded again, and again a lot of people didn't know what was going on. One tipsy gentleman had to be removed. "I can take it," he kept saying. "I'm a man." Apparently he thought there was a fight and that they didn't deem him capable of doing his share. As the girl drew the lucky numbers, De Wolf Hopper read them off to a man with a megaphone who shouted them out. The first prize, a tablecover signed by one hundred Broadway actors, managers, and crooners, was won by a gentleman who pushed through the jam to the goldfish-bowl holder and whispered that he didn't want the prize. Another number had to be drawn. It was all over by midnight and we turned to go; a man who had been standing near us all the while said, "Hey, Buddy, what was it, d'ye know?"

The stand was designed by John Vassos, the artist. It is trimmed in aluminum, and in green and tan, and has a nice overhead-lighting effect. Artistic, modern, but not gaudy. A really nice orange-drink stand.

Names, Names, Names   NOVEMBER 12, 1932

MR. FRANK D. WATERMAN, the fountain-pen genius, a gray and twinkly gentleman carrying four pens, all told, in his vest pockets, was in his element one day last week at the Waldorf. It was a big moment for him, or, rather, a big six or seven hours. In a room on the eighteenth floor, three men and a woman sat examining hundreds of Waterman Autograph Albums to determine which relentless little child in America had successfully accosted (in person or by mail) the finest all-round set of autograph-writers. No matter where you've been in the past six months, you've probably tripped over some of the youngsters going around with albums and pens. They were at doors, under beds, behind fire screens—everywhere, it seemed. Some of the kiddies (the age limit was sixteen) spent twenty-five to forty dollars on stamps writing to celebrities who lived too far away to be called on personally, such as the Prince of Wales. The Prince heard first from an enterprising little Waterman girl in Chicago and generously wrote his name for her and a small message of hope. Later, requests began to come in upon him by the thousands and the Lord Chamberlain or somebody complained to the Waterman company.

A little Nebraska boy named Tommy Leonard won the first prize, one thousand bucks. There probably will be no living with him. We examined his neat album of a hundred and fifty assorted names, ranging from Addams, Jane, to Zimmerman, Don. In between were Jackie Coogan, Coolidge, Eddie Tolan, Lloyd George, Ellsworth Vines, O. O. McIntyre, Ed Wynn, Rabbit Maranville, Irving Berlin, Ely Culbertson, and the Crosbys, Bing and Percy. He also had the names of Josephine Schain, national director of the Girl Scouts; Mr. Waterman himself, and Mr. Alwin J. Scheuer. Miss Schain and Mr. Scheuer were two of the judges, but we are not making any insinuations— their autographs appeared in scores of albums. Tommy's collection was probably the "best and most varied," even though he ended up in a cloud of football- and baseball-players, including three of the Four Horsemen of Notre Dame. Mr. Scheuer, who is an expert on autographs, went over the autographs with a fine-tooth magnifying-glass. He found a phony James Branch Cabell and numerous rubber-stamped Mayor Cermaks and Frank Roosevelts. Mr. Chrysler, the auto man, who must have got thousands of requests for autographs, finally had a card printed reading "Below you will find the autograph which you requested," or words like that, only more elegant.

The names we got sickest of in looking over twenty or more albums were: Calvin Coolidge, who was *way* ahead of everybody else; Roosevelt, Hoover, Garner, Curtis, Dolly Gann, Rudy Vallée, Will Beebe, Captain Eddie Rickenbacker, Mary Pickford, Christopher Morley, Martin and Osa Johnson, and Gene Tunney. Nobody got Al Capone or John D., Sr., or the Pope or the Mahatma. Or, as far as we looked, Red Grange (*sic transit gloria*). There was only one Garbo and only one Lindbergh; the latter got by a Manhattan youth. The small-town youngsters far outdid our own boys and girls. Practically the only celebrities in Manhattan that the average New York child could think of were Babe Ruth, Lou Gehrig, and Joe McKee. There were a few Jimmy Walkers, two King Carols, and a rare One-Eye Connelly, the Button Gwinnett of his time. Billy

Sunday popped up every third album or so in a strong, accusing hand. After his name he always wrote either "Psalm 91" or "Psalm 34," neither of which we have looked up yet. Oddly enough, there were dozens of Frank B. Kelloggs. Remember him?

Our favorite album was by a boy who lives in Newark, N. J., and nobly tried to revolutionize the whole tiresome process by simply going up and down the streets of his town writing in his album, with his own hand, the names of dentists, butchers, haberdashers, etc., which he copied off signs and show windows. In honor of this Unknown Contestant, we suggest two minutes of silence, in which nobody in the nation writes a single word.

Field Music JULY 15, 1933

WE WENT to the first concert of that symphony orchestra in a meadow in Connecticut last week, getting our ticket at a ticket window cut into one end of a barn. A white round moon came up over the elms behind the orchestra shell and shone on fifteen hundred people sitting quietly, in spite of a zigzagging bat, on rows of wooden benches that marched up a slowly rising natural incline to a dark woods. A surprised whippoorwill, in excellent voice, provided a clear, if simple, obbligato from one of the trees during the scherzo of Beethoven's "Eroica." In the final movement, the bright rising blend of the instruments threw him badly off his rhythm, and he repeated whip and left out poor altogether, probably for the first time in his life. He disappeared during the overture to Tschaikowsky's "Romeo and Juliet" but came back with fine assurance for Debussy's "The Afternoon of a Faun." The Boston mail plane, which usually flies right over where the orchestra sits, had been spoken to, and courteously detoured half a mile or so, its muffled roaring lost in the sky. All in all, the country noises are softer, however, than the city noises at Lewisohn Stadium. The concert was a great success.

Nikolai Sokoloff, the director of the New York Orchestra—which drove up to the playing field in buses from New York—lives in a farmhouse only thirty paces from the bandstand. It's an ancient farmhouse, bought by Sokoloff three years ago, after old Lem Gould died. Lem's grandfather built the house nigh on two hundred years ago. Old Lem was ninety-three when he died, and up to the last, of quiet evenings, he used to sit out under a pear tree, a stone's toss from what is now the violin section, gassing with neighbors and chawing tobacco. Lem was a famous shot, with gun or tobacco juice.

The New York Orchestra is a cooperative orchestra, with no donors behind it, the members divvying up whatever comes in from the sale of tickets. Many of the players used to be with the old New York Symphony or the Philharmonic before the two combined. The orchestra will give three concerts a week—Tuesdays, Thursdays, and Saturdays—for a month. All of the soloists live in or around Weston, the village nearest to the concert field, which is seven miles from Westport, over country roads. Better go with somebody who knows the way.

Mr. Sokoloff was conductor of the Cleveland Symphony for many years, but most of his life in America has been lived in Connecticut. He is ashamed because the state has never heard Beethoven's Ninth Symphony, and is already getting up a chorus of Fairfield County voices in order to give it. It took him a year to make the old farm over. Dozens of huge rocks had to be dynamited out of the "auditorium," but it's smooth now. He hasn't discovered any way to get rid of whippoorwills, without hurting them. They don't bother him when he is directing, but he can't read at night when one is singing. Once he ran out of the house with a flashlight to frighten off a whippoorwill. Light at night makes whippoorwills sing.

Seventeen years ago Mr. Sokoloff conducted a symphony orchestra in San Francisco. One of his viola players was Paul Whiteman. Whiteman didn't care much for classical music—couldn't get the rhythm—and shortly left the orchestra to get up a jazz band. Five years ago, in Cleveland, he met Sokoloff for the first time since they used to work together—as well as they could. "There have been a lot of changes," said Whiteman, graciously. "I have made a lot of money, and you have become a great artist."

Rough on Rats   SEPTEMBER 2, 1933

HUEY LONG had rooms 2643-4-5-6 at the Hotel New Yorker when he was here last week. He needs a lot of space. We went down to see him one afternoon and found him sprawled on a bed in his shirtsleeves, a bit tuckered despite his famous energy. He'd just come back from a walk of a couple of miles. It wasn't his legs that were tired, though, he said; it was his eyes—not enough green grass and trees to look at along Broadway.

If you ever want to see Huey when he's in town, it's very simple. You just go down to the hotel and phone his room. He answers with a gruff "Hello!" You say you want to come up. "Come on up," he says. It doesn't make any difference who you are; he'll see anybody. The phone rang every minute or so while we talked, and he would get up and walk through a couple of rooms to answer it, and come back and fling himself heavily on the bed again, so that his shoulders and feet hit it at the same moment. He didn't relax quietly; he kept tapping the headboard with his fingers and twisting from side to side.

We tried to steer away from politics and managed it for possibly seven minutes. During that interlude, he said that he usually went to bed around midnight and got up about four-thirty in the morning to work until nine-thirty. He plays a little golf, but would rather work than anything else. He doesn't bother much about food. "I eat lightly," he said. "Greens, potlikker, and so on, not much bread." He apparently didn't really listen to what we said; he'd look at us and he wouldn't interrupt, but as soon as we finished saying something, he'd say something on a brand-new subject.

He literally leaped into politics and out of the bed, all in a moment. He started on his favorite subject of "the rats and blankety-blanks," in general and in particular. His arms waved and his eyes blazed. "I'd like to have an election down there every month," he said. "We're going to beat the blankety-blanks worse than they were ever beaten before." There was a great deal of this. We turned him to the subject of New York. He's crazy about New York. "It's the best-blankety-blank-governed city in the country," he said. "The port here is the best-managed port there is, the traffic system is wonderful, and the waterworks system is the goddam marvel of the world." He said New York people were the most courteous in the North; the only trouble is that most of 'em don't know where they are. "You go out of here into the street," he thundered, "and stop a hundred men, and ninety-five of 'em wouldn't be able to tell you where anything is."

O'Brien and LaGuardia, he said, were two rattling fine men. He thinks O'Brien will win, but he'd vote for La-Guardia, one of his favorite figures in public life. "I'd rather vote for him for President than for Mayor, though," he added. He said there were rats in New York, just as there were rats everywhere. We asked him whether he would rather be Governor of Louisiana or United States Senator; he replied that he'd rather be in the private practice of law. But in public life, he said, he had been able to do a world of good for the people. "I've saved the lives of little children, I've sent men through college, I've lifted communities from the mud, I've cured insane people with therapy,

I've—" He was making a speech again, rolling around in the bed, gesturing. Presently there was a knock on the door. "Open it, brother," he said. "Yes, sir," we said. Two men came in. We started to leave, and found a note under the door he hadn't seen. We took it back and gave it to him. "Thanks, brother," he said. It was from a couple of other men who had called while he was out. Going down the hall, we could hear his voice raised again about some horrible condition of affairs brought about by the rats. There was one last purple word as we got on the elevator.

Lenox 1734

THE MANSION where Joseph Pulitzer lived is as cold as the moon. We shivered for an hour up and down its tremendous sprawl of rooms and halls one afternoon last week; they are littered with débris and have been deserted for twenty years. The estate is turning the famous residence over to real-estate men to be made into apartments, and we wanted to see it as it was, back before the war, when the nervous genius of the *World* gloomed like a spider in his far, quiet corner of the rambling palace of sixty rooms.

Most people had forgotten the abandoned masterpiece of Stanford White on Seventy-third Street just east of Fifth Avenue until the new plans brought it into prominence again. It was completed in 1902 and for ten years vibrated to the power of the eccentric man who lived in curious soundproof rooms at one end of it. Then he died and the life went out of the place. Nobody has lived in it for two decades. None of the bells in the elaborate system of bells rings now, none of the myriad lights will light. Cold, lonely, and sad, but still magnificent, and a touch mysterious, the mansion is like a grand duchess gone blind and deaf in her old age.

Pigeons flutter disconsolately outside the windows beyond the organ loft. The organ console stands at the head of the central marble staircase, covered with dust. The gold-and-white woodwork of the impressive main salon on the second floor, fifty feet long, with a ceiling twenty feet high, is tawdry under its dust; the two large crystal chandeliers, one at each end, are gray and dismal. Dirty windows keep out the light and give the baronial dignity of the mansion a deep, melancholy gloom. Before long it will be altered, polished, and brightened up, elegant doormen and lively attendants will move about, people will live there again, but it will be a different kind of life.

Joseph Pulitzer probably was never inside of three-fourths of the rooms. He lived in a few padded rooms of his own to the west. The old doors of his hideaway, soft as leather chairs, are torn and ripped now, but the thick walls and the triple-sashed windows still shut out most of the street sounds that tore at the nerves of the publisher, whose hearing was sharpened by blindness. He had lost his sight when he moved into No. 7 and never saw the palace he had built around his isolation.

The marble façade, pierced by windows twenty feet high, is Stanford White's reworking of the front of an Italian Renaissance palace. It is still white and unmarred except for a few names scrawled by children in chalk on the entrance pillars. Graceful marble cherubs smile in languid peace above the windows, as if time and the hour had not moved in thirty years. The heavy front doors of glass and scrolled iron are locked, and propped up with strong timbers inside. We went in by a side door, whose lock protested against the unfamiliar key.

The library is filled with axes, wheelbarrows, and red lanterns belonging to the firm that will reconstruct the interior. High ceilings, wide, deep fireplaces, and elaborately carved mantels are characteristic of the house. There are many strange and unique rooms: a tall, circular breakfast room, an enormous dining room whose six pairs of windows

331

to the west are made of curved glass in panes more than four feet square, a squash court with a gallery in which we had to light matches to see anything at all. There are three floors in front and eight in back, counting mezzanines. The bathtubs are the high, clumsy monstrosities of their day, except for the master's own, which is sunk into the floor. He had a washbasin two feet higher than any we ever saw, and a specially made combined toilet seat and magazine rack.

On one faded wall a card gave the telephone number of the Pulitzer residence when it was alive: Lenox 1734. There isn't even any such exchange any more.

Excursion NOVEMBER 17, 1934

WE WENT down to see the Morro Castle last week. You come upon it suddenly, standing like a ruined merry-go-round in the midst of a carnival. Avoiding the bitter Jersey shores farther north, it drifted spang to the centre of the short stretch of fine beach upon which all the gaiety of Asbury Park converges. There is a swell view from the Berkeley-Carteret Hotel; the boardwalk is only a hundred paces away; from the second floor of the huge Convention Hall that juts out into the water, you can look right down onto the decks. They are so close that the people standing and staring and eating peanuts could almost throw the shells down on them. A small sign on the stern is clearly legible; it read "Look Out for the Propellers."

The first day the ship was there, more than ten thousand people paid a quarter each to go up to the second floor of the Hall and stare—"ten thousand eight hundred and sixty people," the proud shopkeepers and souvenir vendors in and around the Hall will tell you, brightly. Now it only costs a dime, because not so many people come down any more on the excursions the railroad runs. The Sunday we were there it was rainy and cold, and only about a thousand persons wandered around staring at the ship. Everything has conspired to put the burned-out hulk on exhibition. A spit of sand formed in the last two months by the wash of water around the bow and stern reaches to within ten feet of the blistered port side. If you don't mind getting your feet wet, you can wade out and touch the Morro Castle with your hands. Just above you hang the three twisted port-side lifeboats askew on their davits. They look small and tinny with their paint burned off, but they are capacious enough to have carried all the people who died, with room to spare.

The barking of souvenir vendors and postcard salesmen goes on all around the place. There are seven or eight souvenir stands inside the Hall itself, and twenty or thirty men outside walk around offering views of the ship (some of them colored red to show the fire at night), and pamphlets about the tragedy and poems inspired by it. One man in the Hall sits at a stamping machine and stamps copper caps on pennies for souvenirs. The caps cover one side of the pennies and show the ship, with the words "Morro Castle Fire, September, 1934, Asbury Park." On the reverse is the head of Lincoln. The salesmen and shopkeepers are bright and cheerful. One of them told us that the Hall postcard stands sold a hundred and fifty thousand cards a day during the first few days. "Of course," another vendor said (a woman), "it was a terrible tragedy, but it was a godsend to us."

The carnival spirit is a little dampened on days when a northeast wind blows, because of the rotting cargo of hides in the ship. The northeast wind blows the stench of them across the town. Sometimes men go aboard the hulk and pour chloride of lime around. "That chloride of lime is a God's blessing," said the woman we were talking with. She, and all the rest of the shopkeepers and souvenir sellers who have profited by the burning of the Morro Castle, will be saddened when the tugs and derrick barges now at work trying to shake the hulk loose finally haul it away. There was some talk of making the ship into a kind of museum and selling tickets to sightseers who wanted to go aboard, but that petered out. Coast guards stand around and prevent anybody trying to climb up the side of the ship. Everybody hopes it will take a long time to get the Morro Castle out of the sand.

The ship doesn't look as big as we thought it would. With its paint burned away, it is lumpish and unimpressive. The majesty has gone out of it, and a little of the horror, too. It is just a rusty, sulky-looking pile of junk, as cold and dead as a fallen meteor. But the souvenir sellers try to keep the horror warm and vivid. "Read about the woman passenger that's still on the ship," one man shouted, waving a pamphlet at us. We went over to the Berkeley-Carteret bar and had a drink. The bar has done a nice business since the night of September 8th.

Gtde   NOVEMBER 24, 1934

MISS STEIN was seven or eight minutes late for her autographing at Brentano's last week and about fifty people were waiting restlessly for her when she solidly arrived with Alice B. Toklas pertly in tow. On a table were arranged solid stacks of Miss Stein's books, and next to the table was a big desk at which she sat solidly down. She was calm, quick, and smiling throughout the ordeal. Of course, it wasn't as exciting as the immortal Hugh Walpole-Gene Tunney autographing, but it had its moments. As soon as she sat down, Miss Stein looked up expectantly and people began pushing toward the desk, carrying books. Clerks fluttered about, selling the pushers whatever book of Miss Stein's they might want: the books ran in price from ninety-five cents (the Modern Library edition of "Three Lives") to $3.50. At an autographing, you are supposed to write down on a card your name, or Aunt Lisbeth's name, or the name of whomever you are buying the book for, and hand the book and the card to the autographer. This speeds things up, because people standing in front of an author and meeting the author's eyes are likely to get timid and dry-throated and say "Zassfrank Dooselinch" or what sounds like "Zassfrank Dooselinch" to the author. Miss Stein doesn't like people to be incoherent about names.

She signed two hundred and seventy-five books in all, and her signing time was a little under an hour and a half. She wrote with a big pen, vigorously. We bought one of her books and got in line behind a man named Twifflefinks, Moited Twifflefinks (he hadn't written his name on a card). That was straightened out after a while—Miss Stein is always gracious and patient. We just handed our book to her, and she glanced at us with her keen, humorous eyes and, seeing that we didn't have a name, simply put her own name on the flyleaf, and the date. She signs herself always Gtde Stein. Now and again somebody (once it was a girl of twelve) would slip her an autograph book or a blank sheet of paper, but she would push these away and say "No," and these autograph-hunters would retreat in humiliation. There are ethics in autographing: you can't just walk into a bookstore out of the street and get an author to sign his name for you. You have to buy or bring one of the author's books.

One confused man somehow found himself standing in front of Miss Stein without a book, so he shouted at a clerk, " 'Three Saints'! 'Three Saints'!" he said. "Give me a 'Three Saints'!" The right title is "Four Saints," a clerk corrected the gentleman coldly. Miss Stein just laughed. She doesn't get peeved about things like that. Behind us was a lady named Mielziner. Miss Stein, hearing the name, looked up and asked about Leo Mielziner, Jr. "Leo Mielziner is Kenneth MacKenna," said the lady. Miss Stein took that in her stride. Now and again someone would ask the hovering Toklas to sign a book, and she always did.

Somebody asked Miss Stein what had been her greatest thrill in America. She said her airplane trip to Chicago.

A friend of ours who heard the great lady lecture a few days after the autographing said it was very interesting and seemed to make sense. Our friend, however, copied down a few sentences that Miss Stein said and showed them to us. Our favorite was "When the inside had become so solidly inside that all the outside could be outside and the inside inside." The lady who listened said that when you hear Gtde talk that way, you can see what she means, or think you can. People who hear her always like her as a person. After her lectures she will answer any questions—if they are sensible. Once she waved her hand and said pooh at a woman who asked her what she thought of the effect of psychology on literature. She then said that psychology hasn't any effect on literature. She told some other questioner that she doesn't believe much in the subconscious. "It's subconscious because it's inarticulate," she said.

Mighty Match   APRIL 6, 1935

WE WENT up to the Crockford Club one night last week to watch the Culbertsons play bridge with the Simses. Mr. Culbertson was twenty minutes late. Mr. Sims waited, somewhat irritably, on the second floor, sprawled in an armchair between the press-room and the playing-room. His opponent showed up finally, suavely arrogant in evening clothes. Mr. Sims wore a dark-gray coat that didn't fit too well around his bulky shoulders, brown trousers, and a soft white shirt with tan tie. The penalty for being late had been fixed at five dollars a minute, and Mr. Sims wanted a hundred dollars. "Fifty, anyway," he said. "I gave up my dessert to be here at nine." They joined the ladies at the table, still discussing the penalty. Mr. Culbertson made some notation on a piece of paper and they dropped the argument.

It was easier to watch than the Lenz-Culbertson match, which we peered at through the crack of a screen that shielded the table. This table was right out in the open, cutely surrounded by silken ropes which were supposed to give the appearance of a prize ring. Two tiers of chairs around the walls were soon filled with spectators, about seventy-five, all smoking cigarettes. The room became a misty blue before long. All the players smoked cigarettes, too; Mr. Culbertson gold-tipped ones, Mrs. Sims curious long thin ones. Mrs. Culbertson wore a smart black velvet gown with a lace jabot; she toyed now and then with a scarlet chiffon handkerchief. Mrs. Sims was in street clothes; unlike Mrs. Culbertson, her fingernails were not enamelled. Mr. Culbertson drank coffee out of a black-and-gold cup.

They had been playing all afternoon and seemed a bit tired. There was a hint of querulousness, to begin with. Mr. Sims fished some spectacles out of his pocket. When he peers over them, he looks like an owl surprised by a flash-light. Mrs. Culbertson put on her spectacles. Mrs. Sims had hers at hand but didn't wear them. Mr. Culbertson has the eyes of a hawk. From the talk during the first shuffle, we learned that Mrs. Culbertson is nearsighted, Mrs. Sims far-sighted. We are nearsighted. It wasn't too easy to follow the hands, because each player turns up in front of him the card he wants to play, and then turns it face down. This is so each hand, as dealt, may be preserved. After each game the hands are tucked separately into a special holder and handed to an official.

The games were run off quickly, and without spirit. There was none of the tensity of the Lenz match. Mr. Cul-bertson, who a few months ago deliberated forty-seven minutes over one card, never took longer than half a minute to make up his mind. There were no remarkable hands. There was a lot of underbidding. Now and again the audi-ence would rise in a body to get a better view. Nothing thrilling happened. As in a game among mere mortals, the players would say, "Is it my lead?", "What's trump?", "Who dealt this?", etc. The gentlemen called their wives "sweet," "sweetheart," "my sweet," "darling," and "my dear"—with varying inflections. Twice Mr. Sims told his wife after a hand how she could have played it better. Once Mr. Culbertson pointed out an error in his wife's play. Wisecracks between the gentlemen fell like leaden nickels all during the play. "Will you have water or Coca-Cola?" asked Mr. C. "Water," said Mr. S. "You endorse Coca-Cola," said Mr. C. There was a pause. "You endorse that pencil there, but you don't eat it," said Mr. S. The wives said little.

We left after about an hour, to get some Coca-Cola. An hour is plenty long enough to watch anybody play bridge, except possibly the four Marx brothers.

Street Scene DECEMBER 28, 1935

WE WALKED up and down Fourteenth Street a night or two before Christmas, moving slowly through a throng of shoppers, pitchmen, mendicants, policemen, picketers, and, we suppose, pickpockets (we came out even except for a toy dog we bought which plays on a toy drum when you wind him up). There's a touch of carnival and a hint of riot about Fourteenth Street on a holiday night. Somebody had told us there was a Santa Claus in one of the Woolworth stores, but we found out that he went off duty at six o'clock. We had wanted to see a ten-cent-store Santa Claus. Almost next door to Woolworth's two picketers with placards tromped up and down in front of a shoe-store, droning at the passers-by not to go inside. "We work seventy and eighty hours a week for fourteen dollars," they kept saying. "There are thirty-five other shoestores in Fourteenth Street." The cop assigned to the store paid no attention. We asked one of the men if there were any customers in the store—we couldn't see. "A few," he said, mildly. Most of the other stores, gathered about the matriarchal feet of Hearns, were squirming with people.

Between Fifth and Sixth Avenues the pitchmen stood at intervals of a few feet, fifty or more of them, their fly-by-night stands, consisting of pasteboard cartons supported by soapboxes, obstructing the sidewalk (the cops drive them off Forty-second Street, but Fourteenth Street seems to be sanctuary). They shouted their wares, stamping their feet against the cold: shoestrings, mufflers (regla dollan-a-half valyas for thirty-five cents), Mickey Mouse balloons, razor blades, neckties for ten and fifteen cents. There must have been ten thousand neckties and mufflers for sale that night between Fifth and Sixth Avenues.

When we crossed Fifth to go east on Fourteenth, a gentleman airing his brace of Scotties got into momentary trouble with a vendor who was making his small mechanical dogs scurry about on the sidewalk. The vendor didn't care—it attracted a laughing crowd; the gentleman was deeply embarrassed; the Scotties were highly indignant. East of Fifth, on such a night, you come upon the chestnut men, and the pretzel women who look exactly alike, dumpy, bell-shaped, wound about with brown sweaters and brown mufflers. This year there were more wooden stands than ever between University Place and Third Avenue, selling cheap sofa cushions, Fine Candies (five pounds for eighty-five cents, in lemon-yellow and scarlet boxes), mechanical toys, dolls, odds and ends. At one doll stand, a man in a gray felt hat, who looked remarkably like the late Jack Diamond, kept chanting, "Mamma dahs, walkin' dahs, baby dahs, mamma dahs, baby dahs, walkin' dahs." A man selling the *Daily Worker* and the Moscow *News* asked him to change a dime.

A pale old man, quite drunk, was haranguing a group of grinning idlers in front of Luchow's (which has the finest Christmas tree and the most expensive beer in the region).

339

He was almost incoherent, but we caught one sentence: "Yer payin' too much for yer integrity." Near him a small, alert man was selling harmonicas and cowboy songs. He was playing "Oh! Susanna" on a harmonica when we reached him and pointing to the name of the song in his book. To draw attention to a small night club, its doorman kept tootling on a kazoo, a little instrument that sounds like tissue paper on a comb when you blow on it. We missed this year the vendors of those old-fashioned German Christmas cards with the tinsel snow and the rich colors. There used to be several of them around, and a sad man who played "O Little Town of Bethlehem" on a flute. Nobody seemed to know what had become of them.